SECOND LANGUAGE LEARNING THEORIES

ROSAMOND MITCHELL

School of Education, University of Southampton

and

FLORENCE MYLES

School of Modern Languages, University of Southampton

A member of the Hodder Headline Group
LONDON • NEW YORK • SYDNEY • AUCKLAND

First published in Great Britain in 1998 by
Arnold, a member of the Hodder Headline Group,
338 Euston Road, London NW1 3BH

http://www.arnoldpublishers.com

Co-published in the United States of America by
Oxford University Press Inc.,
198 Madison Avenue, New York, NY 10016

British Library Cataloguing in Publication Data
A catalogue record for this book is available from the British Library

Library of Congress Cataloging-in-Publication Data
Mitchell, Rosamond.
Second Language Learning Theories / Rosamond
Mitchell and Florence Myles.
p. cm.
Includes bibliographical references and index.
ISBN 0–340–66311–1. — ISBN 0–340–66312–X (pbk.)
1. Second language acquisition. I. Myles, Florence. II. Title.
P118.2.M58 1998
418—dc21 98–20001
CIP

ISBN 0 340 66311 1 (hb)
0 340 66312 X (pb)

3 4 5 6 7 8 9 10

Production Editor: Julie Delf
Production Controller: Priya Gohil
Cover Design: Juan Hayward

Typeset in 10/12pt Sabon by J&L Composition Ltd, Filey, North Yorkshire
Printed and bound in Great Britain by MPG Books Ltd, Bodmin, Cornwall

What do you think about this book? Or any other Arnold title?
Please send your comments to feedback.arnold@hodder.co.uk

To Paul, Francis and David

Contents

Acknowledgements

The authors and publishers wish to thank the following for permission to use copyright material:

Ablex Publishing Corporation: extract from 'Collective scaffolding in second language learning', by R. Donato, in *Vygotskian approaches to second language research,* edited by J. P. Lantolf and G. Appel, 1994.

Academic Press: figure from 'From discourse to syntax: grammar as a processing strategy', by T. Givón, in *Syntax and Semantics* 12, 1979. Academic Press and the authors: table from 'Information-processing approaches to research on second language acquisition and use', by B. McLaughlin and R. Heredia, in *Handbook of second language acquisition*, edited by W. C. Ritchie and T. K. Bhatia, 1996.

Addison Wesley Longman: extracts from *Achieving understanding: discourse in intercultural encounters,* by K. Bremer, C. Roberts, M.-T. Vasseur, M. Simonot and P. Broeder, 1996. Material adapted from 'You can't learn without goofing: an analysis of children's second language errors' by H. Dulay and M. Burt, in *Error analysis*, edited by J. Richards, 1974. Figure from 'Investigating communication strategies in L2 reference: pros and cons', by G. Yule and E. Tarone, in *Communication strategies: psycholinguistic and sociolinguistic perspectives*, edited by G. Kasper and E. Kellerman 1997. All reprinted by permission of Addison Wesley Longman Ltd.

Blackwell Publishers: material adapted from 'Is there a "natural sequence" in adult second language learning?', by N. Bailey, C. Madden and S. Krashen, *Language Learning* 24, 1974. Extract from 'Research on negotiation: what does it reveal about second language learning conditions, processes and outcomes?', by T. Pica, *Language Learning* 44, 1994.

Cambridge University Press: figure and extract from 'Input, interaction and second language production', by S. Gass and E. M. Varonis, *Studies in Second Language Acquisition* 16, 1994. Table and extract from 'negative feedback in child NS-NNS conversation', by R. Oliver, *Studies in Second Language Acquisition* 17, 1995. Table from *Learning strategies in second language acquisition*, by J. O'Malley and A. Chamot, 1990.

Georgetown University Press: material adapted from 'A new approach to discovering universals of child second language acquisition', by H. Dulay and M. Burt, in *Developmental psycholinguistics* (Monograph Series on Languages and Linguistics), edited by D. Dato, 1975.

Gunter Narr Verlag: extracts from *The syntax of conversation in interlanguage development*, by C. Sato, 1990.

John Benjamins B V: extracts from *Utterance structure: developing grammars again*, by W. Klein and C. Perdue, 1992. Tables from 'Variationist perspectives on second language acquisition', by D. R. Preston, in *Second language acquisition and linguistic variation*, edited by R. Bayley and D. R. Preston, 1996.

Macmillan Press: figure from *Contact languages: pidgins and creoles*, by M. Sebba, 1997.

MIT Press: figure adapted from *Rethinking innateness: a connectionist perspective on development*, by J. Elman, E. Bates, M. Johnson, A. Karmiloff-Smith, D. Parisi and K. Plunkett, 1996.

Multilingual Matters Ltd. and the authors: extract from 'Language and the guided construction of knowledge', by N. Mercer, in *Language and education*, edited by G. Blue and R. F. Mitchell, 1996. Figure from *Approaches to second language acquisition*, by R. Towell and R. Hawkins, 1994.

Oxford University Press: figures from *Language two* by M. Burt, H. Dulay and S. Krashen, reproduced by permission of Oxford University Press. Copyright © 1982 Oxford University Press, Inc. Figure from *The study of second language acquisition*, by R. Ellis, reproduced by permission of Oxford University Press. Copyright © Rod Ellis 1994. Figure from *Conditions for second language learning*, by B. Spolsky, reproduced by permission of Oxford University Press. Copyright © Bernard Spolsky 1989. Extract from 'The role of consciousness in language learning' by R. Schmidt, *Applied Linguistics* 11, 1990, reproduced by permission of Oxford University Press and the author.

Teachers of English to Speakers of Other Languages Inc. (TESOL) and the authors: table from 'The impact of interaction on comprehension', by T. Pica, R. Young and C. Doughty, *TESOL Quarterly* 21. Copyright © 1987 Teachers of English to Speakers of Other Languages Inc.; excerpt from p 740 used with permission. Extracts from 'Becoming first graders in an L2: an ethnographic study of L2 socialization', by J. Willett, *TESOL Quarterly* 29. Copyright © 1995 Teachers of English to Speakers of Other Languages Inc.; excerpts from pp 489–90 and 493–4 used with permission.

University of Wisconsin Press: excerpt from 'Negative feedback as regulation and second language learning in the Zone of Proximal Development', by A. Aljaafreh and J. P. Lantolf, *Modern Language Journal* 78. Copyright © 1994, reprinted by permission. Excerpt from 'A sociocultural perspective on language learning strategies: the role of mediation', by R. Donato and D. McCormick, *Modern Language Journal* 78. Copyright © 1994, reprinted by permission. Excerpt from 'Adult second language learners' use of private speech: a review of studies', by S. G. McCafferty, *Modern Language Journal* 78. Copyright © 1994, reprinted by permission.

Introduction

Aims of this book

This book is the result of a collaboration between a linguist with research interests in second language (L2) acquisition (Myles), and an educationist with research interests in second language teaching and learning in the classroom (Mitchell). Our general aim is to provide an up-to-date, introductory overview of the current state of second language learning studies. Our intended audience is wide: undergraduates following first degrees in language/linguistics, graduate students embarking on courses in foreign language education/EFL/applied linguistics, and a wider audience of teachers and other professionals concerned with L2 education and development. Second language learning is a field of research with potential to make its own distinctive contribution to fundamental understandings, e.g. of the workings of the human mind or the nature of language. It also has the potential to inform the improvement of social practice in a range of fields, most obviously in language education. We ourselves are interested in second language learning (SLL) from both perspectives, and are concerned to make it intelligible to the widest possible audience.

The book is intended in part as a successor to McLaughlin's 1987 book *Theories of Second Language Learning.* This highly successful and authoritative volume provided readers with a selective introduction to key L2 learning theories of the day. We aim to do a similar job, but concentrating on theoretical orientations on language learning which seem most productive and significant from the perspective of the late 1990s.

All commentators recognize that while the field of second language learning research has been extremely active and productive in recent decades, we have not yet arrived at a unified or comprehensive view of how second languages are learned. McLaughlin organized his book as a critical review of a number of different theories of SLL, which can broadly be viewed as linguistic, psycholinguistic and sociolinguistic, and we intend to adopt a similar approach.

While the field of second language learning research has been immensely active and productive subsequently, in many respects the 'map' proposed by McLaughlin survives today. Some strands of research already active ten years ago have continued to flourish, the most obvious example being the linguistic research inspired by the Universal Grammar theory of Noam Chomsky. However, strong and productive though this vein of theorising and empirical investigation remains, it has not succeeded in capturing the whole field, nor indeed attempted to do so. No single theoretical position has achieved dominance, and new theoretical orientations continue to appear. Whether this is a desirable state of affairs or not, has been an issue of some controversy for SLL researchers (Beretta 1993; Lantolf 1996; van Lier 1994). On the whole, though we accept fully the arguments for the need for cumulative programmes of research within the framework of a particular theory, we incline towards a pluralist view of SLL theorising. In any case, it is obvious that students entering the field today need a broad introduction to a range of theoretical positions, with the tools to evaluate their goals, strengths and limitations, and this is what we aim to offer.

Distinctive features of this book

As one sign of the vigour and dynamism of second language learning research, a good number of surveys and reviews are already on the market. Reflecting the variety of the field, these books vary in their focus and aims. Some are written to argue the case for a single theoretical position (e.g. Sharwood Smith 1994); some are encyclopaedic in scope and ambition (e.g. Ellis 1994); some pay detailed attention to research methods and data analysis (e.g. Larsen-Freeman and Long 1991).

This book is intended as an introduction to the field, for students without a substantial prior background in linguistics. We have adopted a 'pluralist' approach, and taken a selection from across the range of second language learning studies, offering theoretical positions which we believe are most active and significant in the 1990s. Some of the theories we review are well established in SLL research, but evolving in the light of new evidence (e.g. Universal Grammar theory, reviewed in Chapter 3); others are relative newcomers to SLL studies, but offer a productive challenge to established thinking (e.g. connectionism, discussed in Chapter 4, or sociocultural theory, discussed in Chapter 7).

From its early days, second language learning research has been a varied field, involving a variety of disciplinary perspectives. However, it is fair to say that the dominant theoretical influences have been linguistic and psycholinguistic, and this continues to be true of many contemporary reviews of the subject (e.g. Gass and Selinker 1994; Ritchie and Bhatia 1996b; Sharwood

Smith 1994). That is, on the whole, SLL theorists have concentrated on trying to elucidate the linguistic 'route' of development followed by the learner,
and to account for it in terms of the workings of internal psychological mechanisms, whether language specific or more general. They have commonly
viewed the learner as an individual, with a range of relatively fixed characteristics − age, intelligence, personality, language aptitude, motivation −
which may promote or inhibit the 'rate' of L2 learning, and impact on the
eventual degree of success which the learner attains. While more socially oriented views of learning and the learner have been proposed from time to
time, they have remained relatively marginal in the field overall. This has
remained generally true despite widespread acceptance of the sociolinguistic
construct of 'communicative competence' as the goal of second language
learning and teaching (Brumfit and Johnson 1979).

We have made a special effort to include in this volume discussion of some
theoretical positions which view the language learning process as essentially
social, and which also view the learner as essentially a social being, whose
identity is continually reconstructed through the processes of engagement
with the L2 and its speech community. To illustrate the first of these positions
we have concentrated on Vygotskian sociocultural theory, now making an
appearance in the SLL field as part of its growing influence on educational
thinking and learning theory more generally (discussed in Chapter 7). To
illustrate the second, we look at recent work in the ethnography of L2 communication (e.g. Bremer *et al.* 1996), and in second language socialization
(Willett 1995): see discussion in Chapter 8.

Just as we have been selective in choosing the theories we wish to discuss,
we have also been selective in reviewing the empirical evidence which under-
pins these theories. On the whole, our approach has been to illustrate a particular theoretical position by discussion of a small number of key studies
which have been inspired by that approach. We use these studies to illustrate:
the kind of research approach which is characteristic of the different traditions in SLL research (from controlled laboratory-based studies of people
learning artificial languages to naturalistic observation of informal learning
in the community); the scope and nature of the language 'facts' which are felt
to be important; and the kinds of generalizations which are drawn. Where
appropriate, we refer our readers to more comprehensive treatments of the
research evidence relevant to different theoretical positions (e.g. Ellis 1994;
Larsen-Freeman and Long 1991).

Finally, the field of SLL research and theorising has historically depended
heavily on theories of first language learning, as well as on theoretical and
descriptive linguistics. We think that students entering the field need to understand something about these origins, and have therefore included brief
overviews of relevant thinking in L1 acquisition research, at several points in
the book (most prominently in Chapters 2, 3, 5 and 8).

Ways of comparing SLL perspectives

We want to encourage our readers to compare and contrast the various theoretical perspectives we discuss in the book, so that they can get a better sense of the kinds of issues different theories are trying to explain, and the extent to which they are supported to date with empirical evidence. In reviewing our chosen perspectives, therefore, we evaluate each individual theory systematically, paying attention to the following factors:

- the claims and scope of the theory;
- the view of language involved in the theory;
- the view of the language learning process;
- the view of the learner;
- the nature and extent of empirical support.

In Chapter 1 we discuss each of these factors briefly, introducing key terminology and critical issues which have proved important in distinguishing one theory from another.

1

Second language learning

Key concepts and issues

1.1 Introduction

This preparatory chapter provides an overview of key concepts and issues that will recur throughout the book in our discussions of individual perspectives on second language learning. We offer introductory definitions of a range of key terms, and try to equip the reader with the means to compare the goals and claims of particular theories with one another. We also summarize key issues, and indicate where they will be explored in more detail later in the book.

The main themes to be dealt with in following sections are:

1.2 What makes for a 'good' explanation or theory
1.3 Views on the nature of language
1.4 Views of the language learning process
1.5 Views of the language learner
1.6 Links between language learning theory and social practice.

First, however, we must offer a preliminary definition of our most basic concept, 'second language learning'. We define this broadly to include the learning of any language to any level, provided only that the learning of the 'second' language takes place sometime later than the acquisition of the first language. (Simultaneous infant bilingualism is a specialist topic, with its own literature, which we do not try to address in this book. See for example relevant sections in Hamers and Blanc 1989; Romaine 1995.)

For us, therefore, 'second languages' are any languages other than the learner's 'native language' or 'mother tongue'. They encompass both languages of wider communication encountered within the local region or community (e.g. at the workplace, or in the media), and truly foreign languages, which have no immediately local uses or speakers. They may indeed be the second language the learner is working with, in a literal sense, or they may be their third, fourth, fifth language ... We believe it is sensible to include 'foreign' languages under our more general term of 'second' languages, because we believe that the underlying learning processes are essentially the same for more local and for more remote target languages, despite differing learning purposes and circumstances.

We are also interested in all kinds of learning, whether formal, planned and systematic (as in classroom-based learning), or informal and unstructured (as when a new language is 'picked up' in the community). Some second language researchers have proposed a principled distinction between formal, conscious *learning* and informal, unconscious *acquisition*. This distinction attracted much criticism when argued in a strong form by Stephen Krashen 1981; it still has both its active supporters and its critics (e.g. Zobl 1995; Robinson 1997). We think it is difficult to sustain systematically when surveying SLL research in the broad way proposed here, and unless specially indicated we will be using both terms interchangeably.

1.2   What makes for a good theory?

Second language learning is an immensely complex phenomenon. Millions of human beings have experience of second language learning, and may have a good practical understanding of the activities which helped them to learn (or perhaps blocked them from learning). But this practical experience, and the common-sense knowledge which it leads to, are clearly not enough to help us understand fully how the process happens. We know, for a start, that people cannot reliably describe the language rules which they have somehow internalized, nor the inner mechanisms which process, store and retrieve many aspects of that new language.

We need to understand second language learning better than we do, for two basic reasons.

1 Improved knowledge in this particular domain is interesting in itself, and can also contribute to more general understanding about the nature of language, of human learning, and of intercultural communication, and thus about the human mind itself, as well as how all these are interrelated and affect each other.
2 The knowledge will be useful. If we become better at explaining the learning process, and are better able to account for both success and failure in L2 learning, there will be a pay-off for millions of teachers, and tens of millions of students and other learners, who are struggling with the task.

We can only pursue a better understanding of L2 learning in an organized and productive way if our efforts are guided by some form of theory. (The 'perspectives' of our book title are best understood as clusters or families of related L2 learning theories.) For our purposes, a *theory* is a more or less abstract set of claims about the units that are significant within the phenomenon under study, the relationships that exist between them, and the processes that bring about change. Thus a theory aims not just at description, but at explanation. Theories may be embryonic and restricted in scope, or more elaborate, explicit and comprehensive. (A theory of L2 learning may deal only with a particular stage or phase of learning, or with the learning of some particular sub-aspect of language; or it may propose learning mechanisms which are much more general in scope.) Worthwhile theories are collaborative affairs, which evolve through a process of *systematic enquiry*, in which the claims of the theory are assessed against some kind of evidence or data. This may take place through a process of *hypothesis testing* through formal experiment, or through more ecological procedures, where naturally occurring data is analysed and interpreted. (See Brumfit and Mitchell 1990 for fuller discussion and exemplification of methods.) Finally, the process of theory building is a reflexive one; new developments in the theory lead to the need to collect new information and explore different phenomena and different patterns in the potentially infinite world of 'facts' and data. Puzzling 'facts', and patterns which fail to fit in, lead to new theoretical insights.

To make these ideas more concrete, an example of a particular theory or 'model' of second language learning is shown in Figure 1.1, taken from Spolsky 1989, p. 28. This represents a 'general model of second language learning', as the proposer describes it (Spolsky 1989, p. 14). The model encapsulates this researcher's theoretical views on the overall relationship between contextual factors, individual learner differences, learning opportunities, and learning outcomes. It is thus an ambitious model, in the breadth of phenomena it is trying to explain. The rectangular boxes show the factors (or variables) which the researcher believes are most significant for learning, i.e. where variation can lead to differences in success or failure. The arrows connecting the various boxes show directions of influence. The contents of the various boxes are defined at great length, as consisting of clusters of interacting 'Conditions' (74 in all: 1989, pp. 16–25), which make language learning success more or less likely. These summarize the results of a great variety of empirical language learning research, as Spolsky interprets them.

How would we begin to 'evaluate' this or any other model, or even more modestly, to decide that this was a view of the language learning process with which we felt comfortable and within which we wanted to work? This would depend partly on broader philosophical positions: e.g. are we satisfied with an account of human learning which sees individual differences as both relatively fixed, and also highly influential for learning? It would also depend on the particular focus of our own interests, within second language learning; this particular model seems well adapted for the study of the individual learner, but has relatively little to say about the social relationships in which they engage, for example.

But whatever the particular focus of a given theory, we would expect to find the following:

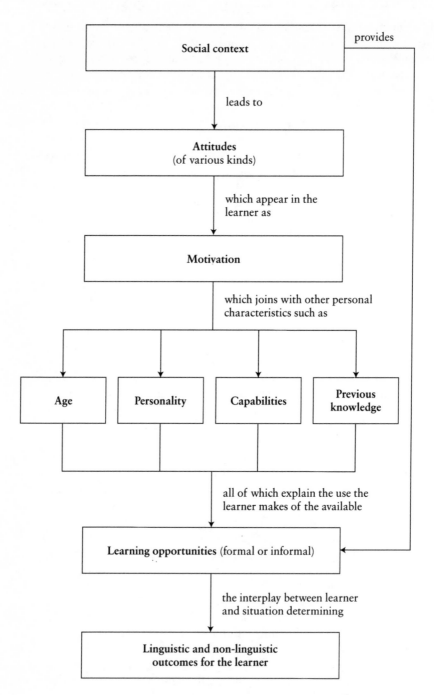

Fig. 1.1 Spolsky's general model of second language learning

1 clear and explicit statements of the ground the theory is supposed to cover, and the claims which it is making;
2 systematic procedures for confirming/disconfirming the theory, through data gathering and interpretation;
3 not only descriptions of L2 phenomena, but attempts to explain why they are so, and to propose mechanisms for change;
4 last but not least, engagement with other theories in the field, and serious attempts to account for at least some of the phenomena which are 'common ground' in ongoing public discussion (Long 1990a). Remaining sections of this chapter offer a preliminary overview of numbers of these.

For fuller discussion of evaluation criteria, see e.g. McLaughlin 1987, pp. 12–18; Long 1993.

1.3   Views on the nature of language

1.3.1   Levels of language

Linguists have traditionally viewed language as a complex communication system, which must be analysed on a number of levels: *phonology, syntax, morphology, semantics* and *lexis, pragmatics, discourse*. (Readers unsure about this basic descriptive terminology will find help in a range of introductory linguistics texts, such as Cook 1997.) They have differed about the degree of separateness/integration of these levels; e.g. while Chomsky argued at one time that 'grammar is autonomous and independent of meaning' (1957, p. 17), another tradition initiated by the British linguist Firth claims that 'there is no boundary between lexis and grammar: lexis and grammar are interdependent' (Stubbs 1996, p. 36). In examining different perspectives on second language learning, we will first of all be looking at the levels of language which they attempt to take into account, and the relative degree of priority they attribute to the different levels. (Does language learning start with words, or with discourse?) We will also examine the degree of integration/separation that they assume, across the various levels. We will find that the control of syntax is commonly seen as somehow 'central' to language learning, and that most general SLL theories try to account for development in this area. Other levels of language receive much more variable attention, and some areas are commonly treated in a semi-autonomous way, as specialist fields; this is often true for SLL-oriented studies of pragmatics and of lexical development (see e.g. Kasper 1996 on pragmatics; Meara 1996a, 1996b on vocabulary).

1.3.2 Competence and performance

Throughout the twentieth century, linguists have also disagreed in other ways over their main focus of interest and of study. Should this be the collection and analysis of actual attested samples of language in use, for example by recording and analysing people's speech? Or should it be to theorise underlying principles and rules which govern language behaviour, in its potentially infinite variety? The linguist Noam Chomsky has famously argued that it is the business of theoretical linguistics to study and model underlying language *competence*, rather than the *performance* data of actual utterances which people have produced (Chomsky 1965). By competence, Chomsky is referring to the abstract and hidden representation of language knowledge held inside our heads, with its potential to create and understand original utterances in a given language. As we shall see, this view has been influential in much second language learning research.

However, for linguists committed to this dualist position, there are difficulties in studying competence. Language performance data are believed to be an imperfect reflection of competence, partly because of the processing complications which are involved in speaking or other forms of language production, and which lead to errors and slips. More importantly, it is believed that, in principle, the infinite creativity of the underlying system can never adequately be reflected in a finite data sample (see e.g. Chomsky 1965, p. 18). Strictly speaking, many students of language competence believe it can be accessed only indirectly, and under controlled conditions, e.g. through *grammaticality judgement tests* (roughly, when people are offered sample sentences, which are in (dis)agreement with the rules proposed for the underlying competence, and invited to say whether they think they are grammatical or not: Sorace 1996).

This split between competence and performance has never been accepted by all linguists, however, with linguists in the British tradition of Firth and Halliday arguing for radically different models in which this distinction between competence and performance does not appear. In a recent review of this tradition, Stubbs quotes Firth as describing such dualisms as 'a quite unnecessary nuisance' (Firth 1957, p. 2n, quoted in Stubbs 1996, p. 44). In the Firthian view, the only option for linguists is to study language in use, and there is no opposition between language as system, and observed instances of language behaviour; the only difference is one of perspective.

Of course, the abstract language system cannot be 'read' directly off small samples of actual text, any more than the underlying climate of some geographical region of the world can be modelled from today's weather (a metaphor of Halliday's: Stubbs 1996, pp. 44–5). The arrival of *corpus linguistics*, in which very large corpora comprising millions of words of running text can be stored electronically and analysed with a growing range of software tools, has revitalized the writing of 'observation-based grammars' (Aarts 1991), of the integrated kind favoured by Firthian linguistics. 'Work with corpora provides new ways of considering the relation between data and theory, by showing how theory can be grounded in publicly accessible corpus data' (Stubbs 1996, p. 46). For example, the English corpus-based work of the COBUILD team directed by John Sinclair has claimed to reveal 'quite unsuspected patterns of language' (Sinclair 1991, p. xvii), offering new insights into the interconnectedness of lexis and grammar.

In making sense of contemporary perspectives on SLL, then, we will also need to take account of the extent to which a competence/performance distinction is assumed. This will have significant consequences for the research methodologies associated with various positions, e.g. the extent to which these pay attention to naturalistic corpora of learner language samples, or rely on more controlled and focused – but more indirect – testing of learners' underlying knowledge. For obvious reasons, theorists' views on the relationship between competence and performance are also closely linked to their view of the language learning process itself, and in particular, to their view of the way in which *language use* (i.e. speaking or writing a language) can contribute to *language learning* (i.e. developing grammatical or lexical competence in the language).

1.4 The language learning process

1.4.1 *Nature and nurture*

Discussions about processes of second language learning have always been coloured by debates on fundamental issues in human learning more generally. One of these is the *nature–nurture* debate. How much of human learning derives from innate predispositions, i.e. some form of genetic pre-programming, and how much of it derives from social and cultural experiences which influence us as we grow up? In the twentieth century, the best-known controversy on this issue as far as first language learning was concerned involved the behaviourist psychologist B. F. Skinner and the linguist Noam Chomsky. Skinner attempted to argue that language in all its essentials could be and was taught to the young child by the same mechanisms which he believed accounted for other types of learning. (In Skinner's case, the mechanisms were those envisaged by general behaviourist learning theory – essentially, copying and memorizing behaviours encountered in the surrounding environment. From this point of view, language could be learned primarily by imitating caretakers' speech. The details of the argument are discussed further in Chapter 2.)

Chomsky, on the other hand, has argued consistently for the view that human language is too complex to be learned, in its entirety, from the performance data actually available to the child; we must therefore have some innate predisposition to expect natural languages to be organized in particular ways and not others. For example, all natural languages have word classes such as Noun and Verb, and grammar rules which apply to these word classes. It is this type of information which Chomsky doubts children could discover from scratch, in the speech they hear around them. Instead, he argues that there must be some innate core of abstract knowledge about language form, which pre-specifies a framework for all natural human languages. This core of knowledge is currently known as *Universal Grammar* (see Chapter 3 for detailed discussion).

For our purposes, it is enough to note that child language specialists now generally accept the basic notion of an innate predisposition to language, though this cannot account for all aspects of language development, which results from an interaction between innate and environmental factors. That is, complementary mechanisms, including active involvement in language use, are equally essential for the development of communicative competence (see e.g. Foster 1990).

How does the nature–nurture debate impact on theories of second language learning? If humans are endowed with an innate predisposition for language, then perhaps they should be able to learn as many languages as they need or want to, provided (important provisos!) that the time, circumstances, and motivation are available. On the other hand, the environmental circumstances for L2 learning differ systematically from L1 learning, except where infants are reared in multilingual surroundings. Should we be aiming to reproduce the 'natural' circumstances of L1 learning as far as possible for the L2 student? This was a fashionable view in the 1970s, but one which downplayed some very real social and psychological obstacles. In the last twenty years there has been a closer and more critical examination of 'environmental' factors which seem to influence L2 learning; some of these are detailed briefly below, in Section 1.4.8, and will be elaborated on in a number of following chapters (especially Chapters 6, 7 and 8).

1.4.2   Modularity

A further issue of controversy for students of the human brain has been the extent to which the brain should be viewed as *modular* or unitary. That is, should we see the brain as a single, flexible organism, with one general set of procedures for learning and storing different kinds of knowledge and skills? Or, is it more helpfully understood as a bundle of *modules*, with distinctive mechanisms relevant to different types of knowledge (e.g. Fodor 1983)?

The modular view has consistently found support from within linguistics, most famously in the further debate between Chomsky and the child development psychologist, Jean Piaget. This debate is reported in Piatelli-Palmarini (1980), and has been re-examined many times; a helpful recent summary is offered by Johnson (1996, pp. 6–30). Briefly, Piaget argued that language was simply one manifestation of the more general skill of symbolic representation, acquired as a stage in general cognitive development; no special mechanism was therefore required to account for first language acquisition. Chomsky's general view is that not only is language too complex to be learned from environmental exposure (his criticism of Skinner), it is also too distinctive in its structure to be learnable by general cognitive means. Universal Grammar is thus endowed with its own distinctive mechanisms for learning (so-called *parameter-setting*: see Chapter 3).

There are many linguists today who support the concept of a distinctive language module in the mind. As we shall see later in the book, there are also those who argue that language competence itself is modular, with different aspects of language knowledge being stored and accessed in distinctive ways. However, there is no general agreement on the number and nature of such modules, nor on how they relate to other aspects of cognition.

1.4.3   Modularity and second language learning

The possible role of an innate, specialist language module in second language learning has been much discussed in recent years. If such innate mechanisms indeed exist, there are four logical possibilities:

1 that they continue to operate during second language learning, and make key aspects of second language learning possible, in the same way that they make first language learning possible;
2 that after the acquisition of the first language in early childhood, these mechanisms cease to be operable, and second languages must be learned by other means;
3 that the mechanisms themselves are no longer operable, but that the first language provides a model of a natural language and how it works, which can be 'copied' in some way when learning a second language;
4 that distinctive learning mechanisms for language remain available, but only in part, and must be supplemented by other means. (From a Universal Grammar point of view, this would mean that UG was itself modular, with some modules still available and others not.)

The first position was popularized in the second language learning field by Stephen Krashen in the 1970s, in a basic form (see Chapter 2). While Krashen's theoretical views have been criticized, this has by no means led to the disappearance of modular proposals to account for SLL. Instead, this particular perspective has been revitalized by the continuing development of Chomsky's Universal Grammar proposals (Cook and Newson 1996). A current example is Sharwood Smith (1994), who argues not only for the continuing contribution of a UG 'module' to SLL, but for a view of SLL which is itself modular, i.e. where a range of distinct learning mechanisms contribute to the learning of different aspects of language. (So that vocabulary and pragmatics, for example, would be learned by mechanisms quite different from those which account for grammar learning; 1994, p. 171.) Such UG-based views are discussed more fully below, in Chapter 3.

On the other hand, thinking about those general learning mechanisms which may be operating at least for adult learners of second languages has also developed further, since e.g. the original proposals of McLaughlin (1987, pp. 133–53). Most obviously, the work of the cognitive psychologist J. R. Anderson on human learning, from an information processing perspective, has been applied to various aspects of second language learning by different researchers (Johnson 1996; O'Malley and Chamot 1990; Towell and Hawkins 1994). This work is reviewed in detail in Chapter 4 below; here it is worth pointing out the attempt of Towell and Hawkins in particular to integrate information processing with Universal Grammar, as two complementary mechanisms which together develop L2 fluency as well as L2 knowledge.

1.4.4 *Systematicity and variability in L2 learning*

When the utterances produced by L2 learners are examined and compared with target language norms, they are often condemned as full of errors or mistakes. Traditionally, language teachers have often viewed these errors as the result of carelessness or lack of concentration on the part of learners. If only learners would try harder, surely their productions could accurately reflect the TL rules which they had been taught! In the mid-twentieth century, under the influence of behaviourist learning theory, errors were often viewed as the result of 'bad habits', which could be eradicated if only learners did enough rote learning and pattern drilling using target language models.

As will be shown in more detail in Chapter 2, one of the big lessons which has been learned from the research of recent decades is that though learners' L2 utterances may be deviant by comparison with target language norms, they are by no means lacking in *system*. Errors and mistakes are patterned, and though some regular errors are due to the influence of the first language, this is by no means true of all of them, or even of a majority of them. Instead, there is a good deal of evidence that learners work their way through a number of *developmental stages*, from very primitive and deviant versions of the L2, to progressively more elaborate and target-like versions. Just like fully proficient users of a language, their language productions can be described by a set of underlying rules; these interim rules have their own integrity and are not just inadequately applied versions of the TL rules.

A clear example, which has been studied for a range of target languages, has to do with the formation of negative sentences. It has commonly been found that learners start off by tacking a negative particle of some kind on to the end of an utterance (*no you are playing here*); next, they learn to insert a basic negative particle into the verb phrase (*Mariana not coming today*); and finally, they learn to manipulate modifications to auxiliaries and other details of negation morphology, in line with the full TL rules for negation (*I can't play that one*) (examples from Ellis 1994, p. 100). This kind of data has commonly been interpreted to show that, at least as far as key parts of the L2 grammar are concerned, learners' development follows a common *route*, even if the *rate* at which learners actually travel along this common route may be very different.

This *systematicity* in the language produced by L2 learners is of course paralleled in the early stages through which first language learners also pass in a highly regular manner, described more fully in Chapter 2. Towell and Hawkins identify it as one of the key features which L2 learning theories are required to explain (1994, p. 5), and throughout the book we will be examining how current explanations handle this feature.

However, learner language (or *interlanguage*, as it is commonly called) is not only characterized by systematicity. Learner language systems are presumably – indeed, hopefully – unstable and in course of change; certainly, they are characterized also by high degrees of *variability* (Towell and Hawkins 1994, p. 5). Most obviously, learners' utterances seem to vary from moment to moment, in the types of 'errors' which are made, and learners seem liable to switch between a range of correct and incorrect forms over lengthy periods of time. A well-known example offered by Ellis involves a child learner of English as L2 who seemed to produce the utterances *no look my card, don't look my card* interchangeably over an extended period (1985a). Myles *et al.* (forthcoming 1998) have produced similar data from a classroom learner's French as L2, who variably produced forms such as *non animal, je n'ai pas de animal* within the same 20 minutes or so (to say that he did not have a pet; the correct TL form should be *je n'ai pas d'animal*). Here, in contrast to the underlying systematicity earlier claimed for the development of rules of negation, we see performance varying quite substantially from moment to moment.

Like systematicity, variability is also found in child language development. However, the variability found among L2 learners is undoubtedly more 'extreme' than that found for children; again, variability is described by Towell *et al.* (1996) as a central feature of learner interlanguage which L2 theories will have to explain, and we will see various attempts to do this in later chapters (especially Chapters 4 and 8).

1.4.5   *Creativity and routines in L2 learning*

In the last section, we referred to evidence which shows that learners' interlanguage productions can be described as systematic, at least in part. This systematicity is linked to another key concept, that of *creativity*. Learners' surface utterances can be linked to underlying rule systems, even if these seem primitive and deviant compared with the target language system. It logically follows that learners can produce original utterances, i.e. that their rule system can generate utterances appropriate to a given context, which the learner has never heard before.

There is of course plenty of common-sense evidence that learners can put their L2 knowledge to creative use, even at the very earliest stages of L2 learning. It becomes most obvious that this is happening, when learners produce utterances like the highly deviant *non animal* (no animal = 'I haven't got any pet'), which we cited before. This is not an utterance which any native speaker of French would produce (other than, perhaps, a very young child); much the most likely way that the learner has produced it is through applying an extremely primitive interlanguage rule for negation, in combination with some basic vocabulary.

But how did this same learner manage to produce the near-target *je n'ai pas de animal*, with its negative particles correctly inserted within the verb phrase, and corresponding almost-perfect modification to the morphology of the noun phrase, within a few minutes of the other form? For us, the most likely explanation is that at this point he was reproducing an utterance which he has indeed heard before (and probably rehearsed), which has been memorized as an unanalysed whole, a formula or a *prefabricated chunk*.

Work in corpus linguistics has led us to the increasing recognition that formulas and routines play an important part in everyday language use by native speakers; when we talk, our everyday L1 utterances are a complex mix of creativity and prefabrication (Sinclair 1991). In L1 acquisition research also, the use of unanalysed chunks by young children has been commonly observed. For L1 learners, the contribution of chunks seems limited by processing constraints; for older L2 learners, however, memorization of lengthy, unanalysed language routines is much more possible. (Think of those opera singers who successfully memorize and deliver entire parts, in languages they do not otherwise control!)

Analysis of L2 data produced by classroom learners in particular, seems to show extensive and systematic use of chunks to fulfil communicative needs in the early stages (Myles *et al.* forthcoming 1998, 1999). Studies of informal learners also provide some evidence of chunk use. This phenomenon has attracted relatively little attention in recent times, compared with that given to learner creativity and systematicity (Weinert 1995). However, we believe it is common enough in L2 spontaneous production (and not only in the opera house), to need some more sustained attention from L2 learning theory.

1.4.6   *Incomplete success and fossilization*

Young children learning their first language embark on the enterprise in widely varying situations around the world, sometimes in conditions of extreme poverty and deprivation, whether physical or social. Yet with remarkable uniformity, at the end of five years or so, they have achieved a very substantial measure of success. Teachers and students know to their cost that this is by no means the case with second languages, embarked on after these critical early years. Few, if any, adult learners ever come to blend indistinguishably with the community of target language 'native speakers'; most remain noticeably deviant in their pronunciation, and many continue to make grammar mistakes and to search for words, even when well motivated to learn, after years of study, residence and/or work in contact with the target language.

Second language learning, then, is typified by *incomplete success*; the claimed systematic evolution of our underlying interlanguage rules towards the target language system seems doomed, most often, never to integrate completely with its goal. Indeed, while some learners go on learning, others seem to cease to make any visible progress, no matter how many language classes they attend, or how actively they continue to use their second language for communicative purposes. The term *fossilization* is commonly used to describe this phenomenon, when a learner's L2 system seems to 'freeze', or become stuck, at some more or less deviant stage.

These phenomena of incomplete success and fossilization are also significant 'facts' about the process of L2 learning, which any serious theory must eventually explain. As we will see, explanations of two basic types have in fact been offered. The first group of explanations are *psycholinguistic*: the language-specific learning mechanisms available to the young child simply cease to work for older learners, at least partly, and no amount of study and effort can recreate them. The second group of explanations are *sociolinguistic*: older L2 learners do not have the social opportunities, or the motivation, to identify completely with the native speaker community, but may instead value their distinctive identity as learners or as foreigners. These are discussed in more detail in the relevant chapters which follow.

1.4.7   Cross-linguistic influences in L2 learning

Everyday observation tells us that learners' performance in a second language is influenced by the language, or languages, that they already know. This is routinely obvious from learners' 'foreign accent', i.e. pronunciation which bears traces of the phonology of their first language. It is also obvious when learners make certain characteristic mistakes, e.g. when a native speaker of English says something in French like *je suis douze*, an utterance parallel to the English 'I am twelve'. (The correct French expression would of course be *j'ai douze ans* = I have twelve years.)

This kind of phenomenon in learner productions is often called by the term *language transfer*. But how important is the phenomenon, and what exactly is being transferred? Second language researchers have been through several 'swings of the pendulum' on this question, as Gass puts it (1996), and as we shall see in a little more detail in Chapter 2. Behaviourist theorists viewed language transfer as an important source of error and interference in L2 learning, because L1 'habits' were so tenacious and deeply rooted. The interlanguage theorists who followed downplayed the influence of the L1 in

L2 learning, however, because of their preoccupation with identifying creative processes at work in L2 development; they pointed out that many L2 errors could not be traced to L1 influence, and were primarily concerned with discovering patterns and developmental sequences on this creative front.

Theorists today, as we shall see, would generally accept once more that cross-linguistic influences play an important role in L2 learning. However, we will still find widely differing views on the extent and nature of these influences. In Chapter 5 we discuss multilingual research on the acquisition of a range of L2s by adult migrants in Europe, conducted by a team sponsored by the European Science Foundation (ESF). These ESF researchers argue that the early grammars produced by learners in their multilingual study show little trace of L1 influence, though they do not discount the likelihood of increasing variation due to L1 influence as L2 grammars become more complex. Some researchers have in fact claimed that learners with different L1s progress at somewhat different rates, and even follow different acquisitional routes, at least in some areas of the target grammar (e.g. Keller-Cohen 1979, Zobl 1982, quoted in Gass 1996, pp. 322–3).

From a Universal Grammar perspective, the language transfer problem is looked at somewhat differently. If second language learners have continuing *direct* access to their underlying Universal Grammar, L1 influence will affect only the more peripheral areas of L2 development. If, on the other hand, learners' only access to UG is *indirect*, via the working example of a natural language which the L1 provides, then L1 influence lies at the heart of L2 learning. In Chapter 3 we will review some of the evidence for these different views current among different UG-inspired researchers.

1.4.8   The relationship between second language use and second language learning

In Section 1.3.2, we considered the distinction between language *competence* and *performance*, which many linguists have found useful. Here, we look more closely at the concept of performance, and in particular, look at the possible relationship between using (i.e. performing in) an L2, and learning (i.e. developing one's competence in) that same language.

We should note first of all, of course, that 'performing' in a language not only involves speaking it. Making sense of the language data that we hear around us is an equally essential aspect of performance. Indeed, it is basic common ground among all theorists of language learning, of whatever description, that it is necessary to interpret and to process incoming language data in some form, for normal language development to take place. There is thus a consensus that language *input* of some kind is essential for normal language learning. In fact, during the late 1970s and early 1980s, the view was argued by Stephen Krashen and others that input (at the right level of difficulty) was all that was necessary for L2 acquisition to take place (Krashen

1982, 1985: see fuller discussion of the *comprehensible input hypothesis* in Chapter 2). This position has been viewed by more recent theorists as inadequate, but a modified and refined version has been developed, as we shall see most obviously in Chapter 6.

Krashen was unusual in not seeing any central role for language production in his theory of second language acquisition. Most other theoretical viewpoints support in some form the common-sense view that speaking a language is helpful for learning it, though they offer a wide variety of explanations as to why this should be the case. For example, behaviourist learning theory saw regular (oral) practice as helpful in forming correct language 'habits'. This view has become less popular in recent decades, as part of linguists' general loss of interest in behaviourist thinking (though arguably it is enjoying something of a revival through the neo-behaviourist advocates of *connectionism*: see Chapter 4).

However, various contemporary theorists still lay stress on the 'practice' function of language production, especially in building up fluency and control of an emergent L2 system. For example, information processing theorists commonly argue that language competence consists of both a *knowledge* component ('knowing that') and a *skill* component ('knowing how'). While they may accept a variety of possible sources for the first component, ranging from parameter-setting in a Universal Grammar framework (e.g. Towell and Hawkins 1994), to systematic classroom instruction (Johnson 1996), researchers in this perspective agree in seeing a vital role for L2 use/L2 performance in developing the second, skill component. (See Chapter 4 for a fuller discussion.)

An even more strongly contrasting view to Krashen's is the so-called *comprehensible output* hypothesis, argued for by Merrill Swain and colleagues (e.g. Swain 1985; Swain and Lapkin 1995). Swain points out that much incoming L2 input is comprehensible, without any need for a full grammatical analysis. If we don't need to pay attention to the grammar, in order to understand the message, why should we be compelled to learn it? On the other hand, when we try to say something in our chosen second language, we are forced to make grammatical choices and hypotheses, in order to put our utterances together. The act of speaking forces us to try out our ideas about how the target grammar actually works, and of course gives us the chance of getting some feedback from interlocutors who may fail to understand our efforts.

So far in this section, we have seen that theorists can hold different views on the contribution both of language input and language output to language learning. However, another way of distinguishing among current theories of L2 learning from a 'performance' perspective has to do with their view of L2 *interaction* – when the speaking and listening in which the learner is engaged are viewed as an integral and mutually influential whole, e.g. in everyday conversation. Two major perspectives on interaction are apparent, one psycholinguistic, one sociolinguistic.

From a psycholinguistic point of view, L2 interaction is mainly interesting because of the opportunities it offers to individual L2 learners to fine-tune the language input they are receiving. This ensures that the input is well adapted to their own internal needs (i.e. to the present state of development of their L2 knowledge). What this means is that learners need the chance to talk with native speakers in a fairly open-ended way, to ask questions, and to clarify meanings when they do not immediately understand. Under these conditions, it is believed that the utterances that result will be at the right level of difficulty to promote learning; in Krashen's terms, they will provide true 'comprehensible input'. Conversational episodes involving the regular *negotiation of meaning* have been intensively studied by many of the Krashen-influenced researchers whose work is discussed in Chapter 6.

Interaction is also interesting to linguistic theorists, because of recent controversies over whether the provision of *negative evidence* is necessary or helpful for L2 development. By 'negative evidence' is meant some kind of input which lets the learner know that a particular form is *not* acceptable according to target language norms. In L2 interaction this might take the shape of a formal correction offered by a teacher, say, or a more informal rephrasing of a learner's L2 utterance, offered by a native-speaking conversational partner.

Why is there a controversy about negative evidence in L2 learning? The problem is that correction often seems ineffective – and not only because L2 learners are lazy. It seems that learners often cannot benefit from correction, but continue to make the same mistakes however much feedback is offered. For some current theorists, any natural language must be learnable from *positive* evidence alone, and corrective feedback is largely irrelevant. Others continue to see value in corrections and negative evidence, though it is generally accepted that these will be useful only when they relate to 'hot spots' currently being restructured in the learner's emerging L2 system.

These different (psycho)linguistic views have one thing in common, however; they view the learner as operating and developing a relatively autonomous L2 system, and see interaction as a way of feeding that system with more or less fine-tuned input data, whether positive or negative. *Sociolinguistic* views of interaction are very different. Here, the language learning process is viewed as essentially social; both the identity of the learner, and their language knowledge, are collaboratively constructed and reconstructed in the course of interaction. The details of how this is supposed to work vary from one theory to another, as we shall see. Some theorists stress a broad view of the second language learning process as an apprenticeship into a range of new discourse practices (e.g. Hall 1995); others are more concerned with analysing the detail of interaction between more expert and less expert speakers, to determine how the learner is *scaffolded* into using (and presumably learning) new L2 forms. These more social interpretations of L2 interaction and its consequences for L2 learning are examined in some detail in Chapters 7 and 8.

1.5   Views of the language learner

Who is the second language learner, and how are they introduced to us, in current SLL research? We have already made it clear that the infant bilingual (i.e. a child who is exposed to more than one language from birth, and acquires them more or less simultaneously in the first few years of life), is not the subject of this book. Instead, 'second language' research generally deals with learners who embark on the learning of an additional language, at least some years after they have started to acquire their first language. This learning may take place formally and systematically, in a classroom setting; or it may take place through informal social contact, through work, through migration, or other social forces which bring speakers of different languages into contact, and make communication a necessity.

So, second language learners may be children, or they may be adults; they may be learning the target language formally in school or college, or 'picking it up' in the playground or the workplace. They may be learning a highly localized language, which will help them to become insiders in a local speech community; or the target language may be a language of wider communication relevant to their region, which gives access to economic development and public life.

Indeed, in the late twentieth century, the target language is highly likely to be English; a recent estimate suggests that while around 300 million people speak English as their first language, another 700 million or so are using it as a second language, or learning to do so (Crystal 1987, p. 358). Certainly it is true that much research on second language learning, whether with children or adults, is concerned with the learning of English, or with a very small number of other languages, mostly European ones (French, German, Spanish). There are many multilingual communities today (e.g. townships around many fast-growing cities) where L2 learning involves a much wider range of languages. However, these have been comparatively little studied.

1.5.1   The learner as language processor

It is possible to distinguish three main points of view, or sets of priorities, among SLL researchers as far as the learner is concerned. Linguists and psycholinguists have typically been concerned primarily with analysing and modelling the *inner mental mechanisms* available to the individual learner, for processing, learning, and storing new language knowledge. As far as language learning in particular is concerned, their aim is to document and explain the developmental route along which learners travel. (We have already seen that the *route* of development is the sequence of linguistic stages through which learners seem to pass.) Researchers for whom this is the prime goal are less concerned with the speed or rate of development, or indeed with the degree of ultimate L2 success. Thus they tend to minimize or disregard social and contextual differences among learners; their aim is to document universal mental processes available to all normal human beings.

As we shall see, however, there is some controversy among researchers in this psycholinguistic tradition on the question of *age*. Do child and adult L2 learners learn in essentially similar ways? Or, is there a *critical age* which divides younger and older learners, a moment when early learning mechanisms atrophy and are replaced or at least supplemented by other compensatory ways of learning? The balance of evidence has been interpreted by Long (1990b) in favour of the existence of such a cut-off point, and many other researchers agree with some version of a view that 'younger = better in the long run' (Singleton 1995, p. 3). However, explanations of why this should be are still provisional: see Chapter 3.

1.5.2   *Differences between individual learners*

Real-life observation quickly tells us, however, that even if L2 learners can be shown to be following a common developmental route, they differ greatly in the degree of ultimate success which they achieve. Social psychologists have argued consistently that these differences in learning outcomes must be due to *individual differences* between learners, and many proposals have been made concerning the characteristics which supposedly cause these differences.

In a recent two-part review (1992, 1993), Gardner and MacIntyre divide what they see as the most important learner traits into two groups, the *cognitive* and the *affective* (emotional). Here we follow their account, and summarize very briefly the factors claimed to have the most significant influence on L2 learning success. For fuller treatment of this social psychological perspective on learner difference, we would refer the reader to sources such as Gardner (1985), Skehan (1989), and Ellis (1994, pp. 467–560).

1.5.2.1   COGNITIVE FACTORS

Intelligence: Not very surprisingly perhaps, there is clear evidence that L2 students who are above average on formal measures of intelligence and/or general academic attainment tend to do well in L2 learning, at least in formal classroom settings.

Language aptitude: Is there really such a thing as a 'gift' for language learning, distinct from general intelligence, as folk wisdom often holds? The most famous formal test of language aptitude was designed in the 1950s, by Carroll and Sapon (1959, in Gardner and MacIntyre 1992, p. 214). This 'Modern Language Aptitude Test' assesses a number of subskills believed to be predictive of L2 learning success: (a) phonetic coding ability, (b) grammatical sensitivity, (c) memory abilities, and (d) inductive language learning ability. In general, learners' scores on this and other similar tests do indeed 'correlate with ... achievement in a second language' (Gardner and

MacIntyre 1992, p. 215), and in a range of contexts measures of aptitude have been shown to be one of the strongest available predictors of success (Harley and Hart 1997).

Language learning strategies: Do more successful language learners set about the task in some distinctive way? Do they have at their disposal some special repertoire of ways of learning, or *strategies*? If this were true, could these even be taught to other, hitherto less successful learners? Much research has been done to describe and categorize the strategies used by learners at different levels, and to link strategy use to learning outcomes; it is clear that more proficient learners do indeed employ strategies that are different from those used by the less proficient (Oxford and Crookall 1989, quoted in Gardner and MacIntyre 1992, p. 217). Whether the strategies cause the learning, or the learning itself enables different strategies to be used, has not been fully clarified, however. We look more closely at learning strategies and their role in acquisition in Chapter 4.

1.5.2.2   AFFECTIVE FACTORS

Language attitudes: Social psychologists have long been interested in the idea that the attitudes of the learner towards the target language, its speakers, and the learning context, may all play some part in explaining success or lack of it. Research on L2 language attitudes has largely been conducted within the framework of broader research on motivation, of which attitudes form one part.

Motivation: For Gardner and MacIntyre, the motivated individual 'is one who wants to achieve a particular goal, devotes considerable effort to achieve this goal, and experiences satisfaction in the activities associated with achieving this goal' (1993, p. 2). So, motivation is a complex construct, defined by three main components: 'desire to achieve a goal, effort extended in this direction, and satisfaction with the task' (p. 2). Gardner and his Canadian colleagues have carried out a long programme of work on motivation with English Canadian school students learning French as a second language, and have developed a range of formal instruments to measure motivation. Over the years consistent relationships have been demonstrated between language attitudes, motivation, and L2 achievement; Gardner accepts that these relationships are complex, however, as the factors interact, and influence each other (1985, cited in Gardner and MacIntyre 1993, p. 2).

Language anxiety: The final learner characteristic which Gardner and MacIntyre consider has clearly been shown to have a relationship with learning success is language anxiety (and its obverse, self-confidence). For these authors, language anxiety 'is seen as a stable personality trait referring to the propensity for an individual to react in a nervous manner when speaking ... in the second language' (1993, p. 5). It is typified by self-belittling, feelings of apprehension, and even bodily responses such as a faster heartbeat! The anxious learner is also less willing to speak in class, or to engage target language speakers in informal interaction. Gardner and MacIntyre cite many studies which suggest that language anxiety has a negative relationship with learning success, and some others which suggest the opposite, for learner self-confidence.

1.5.3   The learner as social being

The two perspectives on the learner which we have highlighted so far have concentrated first, on universal characteristics, and second, on individual characteristics. But it is also possible to view the L2 learner as essentially a social being, and we will encounter later in this book some of the researchers who do just that.

Interest in the learner as a social being will lead to concern with their relationship with the social context, and the structuring of the learning opportunities which it makes available. The learning process itself may be viewed as essentially social, and inextricably entangled in L2 use and L2 interaction. Two major differences appear, which distinguish this view of the learner from the last (for the social psychological view of the learner which we have just dipped into is also clearly concerned with the individual learners' relationship with the 'socio-cultural milieu' in which learning is taking place).

First, interest in the learner as a social being leads to concern with a range of socially constructed elements in the learner's identity, and their relationship with learning – so *class*, *ethnicity*, and *gender* make their appearance as potentially significant for L2 learning research. Second, the relationship between the individual learner and the social context of learning is viewed as *dynamic*, reflexive and constantly changing. The 'individual differences' tradition saw that relationship as being governed by a bundle of learner traits or characteristics (such as aptitude, anxiety, etc.), which were relatively fixed and slow to change. More socially oriented researchers view motivation, learner anxiety, etc. as being constantly reconstructed through ongoing L2 experience and L2 interaction.

1.6   Links with social practice

Is second language learning theory 'useful'? Does it have any immediate practical applications in the real world, most obviously in the L2 classroom? In our field, theorists have been and remain divided on this point. Beretta and his colleagues have argued for 'pure' theory-building in SLL, uncluttered by requirements for practical application (1993). Van Lier (1994), Rampton (1995b) and others have argued for a socially engaged perspective, where theoretical development is rooted in, and responsive to, social practice, and language education in particular. Yet others have argued that L2 teaching in particular should be guided systematically by SLL research findings (e.g. Krashen 1985).

This tension has partly been addressed by the emergence of 'instructed language learning' as a distinct sub-area of research (see recent reviews by Ellis 1994, pp. 561–663; Spada 1997). However, much of the theorising and empirical evidence reviewed in this book cannot be captured within this particular sub-field. We think that language teachers, who will form an important segment of our readership, will themselves want to take stock of the relations between the theories we survey, and their own beliefs and experiences in the classroom. They will, in other words, want to make some judgement on the 'usefulness' of theorising in making sense of their own experience and their practice, while not necessarily changing it. In our general conclusions to this book, therefore, we end by some brief consideration of the connections we ourselves perceive between learning theory and classroom practice.

1.7   Conclusion

This chapter has attempted to introduce a range of recurrent concepts and issues which most theorists agree will have to be taken into account if we are to arrive eventually at any complete account of second language learning. In Chapter 2 we provide a brief narrative account of the recent history of second language learning research, plus summary descriptions of some of the more specific language learning phenomena which any theory must explain. We then move in remaining chapters of the book to a closer examination of a number of broad perspectives, or families of theories, with their distinctive views of the key questions which must be answered and the key phenomena which need to be explained.

|2|

The recent history of second language learning research

2.1   Introduction

In order to understand current developments in second language learning research, it is helpful to retrace its recent history. We will see throughout this chapter that the kind of questions researchers are asking today are for the most part firmly rooted in earlier developments in the fields of linguistics, psychology, sociology and pedagogy.

The aim of this chapter is not to provide the reader with an exhaustive description of early approaches, but rather to explore the theoretical foundations of today's thinking. More detailed reviews can be found in other sources, e.g. Dulay *et al.* (1982), Selinker (1992). We will limit ourselves to the post-war period, which has seen the development of theorising about second language learning from an adjunct to language pedagogy, to an autonomous field of research. The period since the 1950s can itself be divided into three main phases.

We will start with the 1950s and 1960s and a short description of how second languages were believed to be learnt at the time. We will then describe the impact of the 'Chomskyan revolution' in linguistics on the field of language acquisition, initially on the study of first language acquisition, and subsequently that of second language acquisition. It had a huge impact on psycholinguistics in the 1970s, and we will see that its influence is still very much felt today.

We will then briefly consider the period from the 1980s onwards, which has witnessed the development of second language acquisition theorising as a relatively autonomous field of enquiry (a 'coming of age', as Sharwood Smith put it: 1994, p. ix). During this period, the impact of Chomskyan linguistics has continued to be profound, but ideas coming from a range of other fields have also become increasingly significant. Research strands initiated in the 1980s will then systematically be reviewed and evaluated in the rest of the book, as well as some newer trends which have made their appearance in the 1990s, such as connectionism or sociocultural theory.

2.2 The 1950s and 1960s

In the 1950s and early 1960s, theorising about second language learning was still very much an adjunct to the practical business of language teaching. However, the idea that language teaching methods had to be justified in terms of an underlying learning theory was well established, since the pedagogic reform movements of the late nineteenth century at least (see Howatt 1984, pp. 169–208 for an account of these). The writings of language teaching experts in the 1950s and 1960s include serious considerations of learning theory, as preliminaries to their practical recommendations (e.g. Lado 1964; Rivers 1964, 1968).

As far as its linguistic content was concerned, 'progressive' 1950s' language pedagogy drew on a version of structuralism developed by the British linguist Palmer in the 1920s, and subsequently by Fries and his Michigan colleagues in the 1940s. Howatt sums up this approach as follows.

1 The conviction that language systems consisted of a finite set of 'patterns' or 'structures' which acted as models ... for the production of an infinite number of similarly constructed sentences.
2 The belief that repetition and practice resulted in the formation of accurate and fluent foreign language habits.
3 A methodology which set out to teach 'the basics' before encouraging learners to communicate their own thoughts and ideas.

(Howatt 1988, pp. 14–15)

Howatt's summary makes it clear that the learning theory to which language teaching experts and reformers were appealing at this time was the general learning theory then dominant in mainstream psychology, *behaviourism*, which we explain more fully in the next section.

2.2.1 Behaviourism

In the behaviourist view (Bloomfield 1933; Skinner 1957; Thorndike 1932; Watson 1924), language learning is seen like any other kind of learning, as the formation of *habits*. It stems from work in psychology which saw the learning of any kind of behaviour as being based on the notions of *stimulus* and *response*. This view sees human beings as being exposed to numerous stimuli in their environment. The response they give to such stimuli will be reinforced if successful, that is if some desired outcome is obtained. Through repeated *reinforcement*, a certain stimulus will elicit the same response time and again, which will then become a habit. The learning of any skill is seen as the formation of habits, that is the creation of stimulus-response pairings which become stronger with reinforcement. Applied to language learning, a certain situation will call for a certain response, for example meeting someone will call for some kind of greeting, and the response will be reinforced if the desired outcome is obtained, that is if the greeting is understood; in the case of communication breakdown, the particular response will not be reinforced and the learner will abandon it in favour of a response which will hopefully be successful, and therefore reinforced.

When learning a first language, the process is simple: all we have to do is learn a set of new habits as we learn to respond to stimuli in our environment. When learning a second language, however, we run into problems: we already have a set of well-established responses in our mother tongue. The second language learning process therefore involves replacing those habits by a set of new ones. The complication is that the old L1 habits interfere with this process, either helping or inhibiting it. If structures in the L2 are similar to those of the L1, then learning will take place easily. If, however, structures are realized differently in the L1 and the L2, then learning will be difficult. As Lado put it at the time:

> We know from the observation of many cases that the grammatical structure of the native language tends to be transferred to the foreign language ... we have here the major source of difficulty or ease in learning the foreign language ... Those structures that are different will be difficult.
>
> (Lado 1957, pp. 58–9, cited in Dulay *et al.* 1982, p. 99)

Take the example of an English learner learning French as a second language and wanting to say *I am twelve years old*, which in French is realized as *J'ai douze ans* (= I have twelve years), and now consider the same learner learning the same structure in German, which is realized as *Ich bin zwölf Jahre alt* (= I am twelve years old). According to a behaviourist view of learning, the German structure would be much easier and quicker to learn, and the French one more difficult, the English structure acting as a facilitator in one instance, and an inhibitor in the other. Indeed, it may well be the case that English learners have more difficulty with the French structure than the German one, as many French teachers would testify after hearing their pupils repeatedly saying **Je suis douze*[1] (I am twelve), but more about that later.

From a teaching point of view, the implications of this approach were twofold. First, it was strongly believed that practice makes perfect; in other words, learning would take place by imitating and repeating the same structures time after time.

Second, teachers needed to focus their teaching on structures which were believed to be difficult, and as we saw above, difficult structures would be those that were different in the L1 and the L2, as was the case for the English/French pair cited above. The teacher of French, in our example, would need to engage the pupils in many drilling exercises in order for them to produce the French structure correctly.

The logical outcome of such beliefs about the learning process was that effective teaching would concentrate on areas of difference, and that the best pedagogical tool for foreign language teachers was therefore a sound knowledge of those areas. Researchers embarked on the huge task of comparing pairs of languages in order to pinpoint areas of difference, therefore of difficulty. This was termed *Contrastive Analysis* (or CA for short) and can be traced back to Fries, who wrote in the introduction to his book *Teaching and Learning English as a Foreign Language*: 'The most effective materials are those that are based upon a scientific description of the language to be learned, carefully compared with a parallel description of the native language of the learner' (Fries 1945, p. 9, cited in Dulay *et al.* 1982, p. 98). Work in this tradition has some continuing influence on second/foreign language pedagogy (Howatt 1988, p. 25), in spite of the many criticisms it has suffered which we will now discuss.

2.2.2 Behaviourism under attack

Starting in the 1950s and continuing in the 1960s, both the fields of linguistics and of psychology witnessed major developments. Linguistics saw a shift from structural linguistics, which was based on the description of the surface structure of a large corpus of language, to generative linguistics which emphasized the rule-governed and creative nature of human language. This shift had been initiated by the publication in 1957 of *Syntactic Structures*, the first of many influential books by Noam Chomsky.

In the field of psychology, the pre-eminent role for the environment which was argued by Skinner in shaping the child's learning and behaviour was losing ground in favour of more developmentalist views of learning, such as Piaget's cognitive developmental theory, in which inner forces drive the child, in interaction with the environment (Piaget 1970; Piaget and Inhelder 1966; Piatelli-Palmarini 1980).

The clash of views about the way in which we learn language came to a head at the end of the 1950s with two publications. These were Skinner's *Verbal Behavior* in 1957 which outlined in detail his behaviourist view of learning as applied to language, and Chomsky's review of Skinner's book, published in 1959, which was a fierce critique of Skinner's views.

Chomsky's criticisms centred on a number of issues.

1 The creativity of language: children do not learn and reproduce a large set of sentences, but they routinely create new sentences that they have never learnt before. This is only possible because they internalize rules rather than strings of words; extremely common examples of utterances such as *it breaked* or *Mummy goed* show clearly that children are not copying the language around them but applying rules. Chomsky was incensed by the idea that you could compare the behaviour of rats in a laboratory, learning to perform simple tasks, to the behaviour of children learning language

without direct teaching, a fundamentally different task because of its sheer complexity and abstractness.

2 Given the complexity and abstractness of linguistic rules (for example, the rules underlying the formation of questions in many languages, or the rules underlying the use of reflexive pronouns in English, discussed in Chapter 3), it is amazing that children are able to master them so quickly and efficiently, especially given the limited input they receive. This has been termed 'Plato's problem' (Chomsky 1987), and refers specifically to the fact that some of the structural properties of language, given their complexity, could not possibly be expected to be learned on the basis of the samples of language around them. Furthermore, children have been shown not to be usually corrected on the form of their utterances but rather on their truth values. When correction does take place, it seems to have very little effect on the development of language structure.

For the above reasons, Chomsky claimed that children have an innate faculty which guides them in their learning of language. Given a body of speech, children are programmed to discover its rules, and are guided in doing that by an innate knowledge of what the rules should look like. We will leave fuller discussion of Chomsky's ideas until Chapter 3. Suffice to say for now that this revolutionary approach to the study of language gave a great stimulus to the field of psycholinguistics, and especially to the study of language acquisition. The next section reviews work that took place in the 1970s, which was heavily influenced by these new ideas.

2.3   The 1970s

2.3.1   *First language acquisition*

The work outlined above was a great stimulus to investigations of the acquisition of language in young children, by researchers such as Klima and Bellugi (1966), Dan Slobin (1970) or Roger Brown (1973). They found striking similarities in the language learning behaviour of young children, whatever the language they were learning. It seems that children all over the world go through similar *stages*, use similar constructions in order to express similar meanings, and make the same kinds of errors. The stages can be summarized as follows (Aitchison 1989, p. 75).

Language stage	Beginning age[2]
Crying	Birth
Cooing	6 weeks
Babbling	6 months
Intonation patterns	8 months
One-word utterances	1 year
Two-word utterances	18 months
Word inflections	2 years

Questions, negatives	2 years 3 months
Rare or complex constructions	5 years
Mature speech	10 years

These stages are not language-specific, although their actual realization obviously is.

Similarly, when studying the emergence of a number of structures in English, a consistent *order of acquisition* was found. Roger Brown's so-called 'morpheme study' is probably the best-known L1 study of that time, and was to be very influential for second language acquisition research. In an in-depth study of three children of different backgrounds, he compared the development of fourteen grammatical morphemes in English. He found that although the rate at which children learnt these morphemes varied, the order in which they acquired them remained the same for all children, as listed below in a simplified form.

Present progressive	*boy sing***ing**
Prepositions	*dolly* **in** *car*
Plural	*sweet***ies**
Past irregular	**broke**
Possessive	*baby'***s** *biscuit*
Articles	**a** *car*
Past regular	*want***ed**
3rd person singular	*eat***s**
Auxiliary *be*	*he* **is** *running.*

What is striking is that, not only do children acquire a number of grammatical morphemes in a fixed order, but they also follow fairly rigid stages during the acquisition of a given area of grammar. For example, children all over the world not only acquire negatives around the same age, but they also mark the negative in similar ways in all languages, by initially attaching some negative marker to the outside of the sentence: *no go to bed, pas faut boire* (= not need drinking) etc., and gradually moving the negative marker inside the sentence, following the stages exemplified below for English (Ellis 1994, p. 78, based on Klima and Bellugi 1966 and Cazden 1972).

Stage 1: Negative utterances consist of a 'nucleus' (i.e. the positive proposition) either preceded or followed by a negator.
   wear mitten no
   not a teddy bear

Stage 2: Negators are now incorporated into affirmative clauses. Negators at this stage include *don't* and *can't*, used as unitary items. Negative commands appear.
   there no squirrels
   you can't dance
   don't bite me yet

Stage 3: Negators are now always incorporated into affirmative clauses. The 'Auxiliary + not' rule has been acquired, as *don't, can't,* etc. are now analysed. But some mistakes still occur (e.g. copula *be* is omitted from negative utterances and double negatives occur).

I don't have a book
Paul can't have one
I not crying
no one didn't come

These stages are not unlike the stages followed by second language learners as outlined in Chapter 1 (1.4.4). Similar phenomena can be observed for the acquisition of interrogatives and other structures.

Another important characteristic of child language which started to receive attention is that it is rule-governed, even if initially the rules children create do not correspond to adult ones. As early as the two-word stage, children express relationships between elements in a sentence, such as possession, negation or location, in a consistent way. Also, it has been demonstrated convincingly that when children produce an adult-like form which is the result of the application of a rule, such as for example adding -s to *dog* in order to produce the plural form *dogs*, they are not merely imitating and repeating parrot-fashion the adult language around them. Two kinds of evidence prove that very clearly. First, children commonly produce forms such as *sheeps* or *breads*, which they have never heard before and are therefore not imitating. Second, some ingenious and now famous experiments were carried out with very young children back in the 1950s (Berko 1958) in which children were shown a picture of a strange bird-like creature and told e.g. *this is a wug*; they were then shown a picture of two of those creatures and told *Now there's another one. There are two of them. There are two ...?* Children invariably replied *wugs* (91 per cent of them), showing that they do not merely learn plurals by remembering each plural form they hear, but that they extract a plural rule from the language they hear, and then apply that rule to their own productions. This experiment did not only contain a series of nonsense nouns, but also nonsense verbs; for example, children were shown a picture of a person doing some strange action and told *This person knows how to gling. He is glinging. Yesterday, he did the same thing. Yesterday, he ...?* Children consistently answered *glinged* (77 per cent of them), again showing that they had created a rule for forming the past tense. In fact, children go through a stage initially of correctly supplying irregular past tense forms such as *took* or *went*, on the basis of having learnt these forms individually,[3] before having created the past tense rule. When they do so, they start producing forms such as *taked* and *goed* which can persist a very long time in spite of any attempts at correction by worried parents who might think their child is regressing. It is only much later that children will be able to take on board exceptions to rules.

The fact that children do not seem to correct their 'errors' on the basis of adult overt or implied correction of children's utterances is well documented in the first language acquisition literature. The following dialogue is typical of the uselessness of such attempts (quoted in Pinker 1994, p. 281). The psycholinguist Martin Braine once tried for several weeks to stamp out one of his daughter's grammatical errors. Here is the result:

CHILD:	Want other one spoon, Daddy
FATHER:	You mean, you want THE OTHER SPOON
CHILD:	Yes, I want other one spoon, please, Daddy
FATHER:	Can you say 'the other spoon'?
CHILD:	Other ... one ... spoon
FATHER:	Say ... 'other'
CHILD:	Other
FATHER:	'Spoon'
CHILD:	Spoon
FATHER:	'Other ... spoon'
CHILD:	Other ... spoon. Now give me other one spoon?

This famous example is typical of such attempts, and this child is neither slow in her development, nor particularly stubborn; it is as if she cannot make the alternative proposed by her father fit within her current grammar.

From this necessarily brief and oversimplified account of 1970s' first language acquisition research, the following characteristics emerge.

1 Children go through stages.
2 These stages are very similar across children for a given language, although the rate at which individual children progress through them is highly variable.
3 These stages are similar across languages.
4 Child language is rule-governed and systematic, and the rules created by the child do not necessarily correspond to adult ones.
5 Children are resistant to correction.
6 Children's processing capacity limits the number of rules they can apply at any one time, and they will revert to earlier hypotheses when two or more rules compete.

These findings seemed to support Chomsky's claims that children followed some kind of pre-programmed, internal route in acquiring language.

2.3.2 Second language learning: the birth of Error Analysis

The findings reported above soon came to the attention of researchers and teachers interested in second language acquisition. This was the case, not only because of their intrinsic interest, but also because the predictions made by Contrastive Analysis did not seem to be borne out in practice. Teachers were finding out in the classroom that constructions that were different in pairs of languages were not necessarily difficult, and that constructions that were similar in two languages were not necessarily easy either. Moreover, difficulty sometimes occurred in one direction but not the other. For example, the placement of unstressed object pronouns in English and French differs: whereas English says *I like* **them**, French says *Je* **les** *aime (I* **them** *like)*. Contrastive Analysis would therefore predict that object pronoun placement would be difficult for both English learners of French and French learners of English. This is not the case, however; whereas English learners of French do have problems with this construction and produce errors such as **J'aime* **les** in initial stages, French learners of English do not produce errors of the type *I* **them** *like*, as would be predicted by CA. The task of comparing pairs of languages in order to design efficient language teaching programmes now seemed to be disproportionately huge in relation to its predictive powers: if it could not adequately predict areas of difficulty, then the whole enterprise seemed to be pointless.

These two factors combined – developments in first language acquisition and disillusionment with CA – meant that researchers and teachers became increasingly interested in the language produced by learners, rather than the target language or the mother tongue. This was the origin of *Error Analysis*, the systematic investigation of second language learners' errors. The language produced by learners began to be seen as a linguistic system in its own right, worthy of description. Corder (1967) was the first to focus attention on the importance of studying learners' errors, as it became evident that they did not all originate in the first language by any means. The predictions of Contrastive Analysis, that all errors would be due to interference from the L1, were shown to be unfounded, as many studies showed convincingly that the majority of errors could not be traced to the L1, and also that areas where the L1 should have prevented errors were not always error-free. For example, Hernández-Chávez (1972) showed that, although the plural is realized in almost exactly the same way in Spanish and in English, Spanish children learning English still went through a phase of omitting plural marking. Such studies became commonplace, and a book-length treatment of the topic appeared in 1974 (Richards' *Error Analysis: Perspectives on Second Language Learning*).

In a review of studies looking at the proportion of errors that can be traced back to the first language, Ellis (1985) found that there was considerable variation in the findings, with results ranging from 3 per cent of errors attributed to the L1 (Dulay and Burt 1973), to 51 per cent (Tran-Chi-Chau 1975), with a majority of studies finding around a third of all errors traceable to the L1. Error Analysis thus showed clearly that the majority of the errors made by second language learners do not come from their first language.

The next question therefore was: where do such errors come from? They are not target-like, and they are not L1-like; they must be learner-internal in origin. Researchers started trying to classify these errors in order to understand them, and to compare them with errors made by children learning their mother tongue. This was happening at the same time as the developments in first language acquisition which we mentioned above, whereby child language was now seen as an object of study in its own right, rather than as an approximation of adult language. In second language learning research, coupled with the interest in understanding learner-internal errors, interest in the overall character of the L2 system was also growing.

The term *interlanguage* was coined in 1972 by Selinker to refer to the language produced by learners, both as a system which can be described at any one point in time as resulting from systematic rules, and as the series of interlocking systems that characterize learner progression. In other words, the notion of interlanguage puts the emphasis on two fundamental notions: the language produced by the learner is a *system* in its own right, obeying its own rules, and it is a *dynamic* system, evolving over time. Interlanguage studies thus moved one step beyond Error Analysis, by focusing on the learner system as a whole, rather than only on what can go wrong with it.

2.3.3 Morpheme studies and second language learning

As far as second language acquisition research is concerned, the most important empirical findings of this period were probably the results of the so-called *morpheme studies*, and at a conceptual level, Krashen's *Monitor Model*, which was a logical theoretical development arising from such studies.

The L2 morpheme studies were inspired by the work of Roger Brown (1973) in L1 acquisition which we briefly mentioned above. Brown had found a consistent order of emergence of 14 grammatical morphemes in English in his longitudinal study. The same order was confirmed by other researchers, e.g. by de Villiers and de Villiers (1973) in their cross-sectional[4] study of 20 children acquiring English as a first language.

Researchers in second language acquisition set about investigating the acquisition of the same grammatical morphemes in L2 learners. Dulay and Burt (1973, 1974c, 1975) were the first to undertake such studies, reporting first of all on the accuracy of production of eight of Brown's morphemes in Spanish-speaking children acquiring English as an L2 (1973). Their study was cross-sectional, and was based on the speech of three groups of Spanish-speaking children of different abilities (in terms of their length of exposure to English as immigrants in the United States).

There were 151 children in the study, and the method used for eliciting speech was the Bilingual Syntax Measure, a structured conversation elicitation technique based on cartoons and designed to elicit certain grammatical constructions. They found that 'the acquisition sequences obtained from the three groups of children were strikingly similar. This was so even though each group on the whole was at a different level of English proficiency' (Dulay *et al.* 1982, p. 204). Dulay and Burt (1974c) then carried out a similar study, but this time using children from different L1s, namely Chinese and Spanish. They found very similar acquisition orders for these structures for both Spanish and Chinese children for 11 of Brown's grammatical morphemes. Encouraged by these results, Dulay and Burt (1975) extended their study to include 536 Spanish- and Chinese-speaking children of varying levels of proficiency in English as a second language, and they investigated 13 of Brown's original morphemes. They found a clear hierarchy for the acquisition of these morphemes, with four different groups of morphemes being acquired in a set order, no matter the L1, as shown in Figure 2.1 (from Dulay, Burt and Krashen 1982, p. 208). They conclude: 'It is highly probable that *children of different language backgrounds learning English in a variety of host country environments acquire eleven grammatical morphemes in a similar order*' (Dulay *et al.* 1982, pp. 207–9). If the results seem clear as far as child L2 learners are concerned, it does not necessarily follow that adults would also exhibit

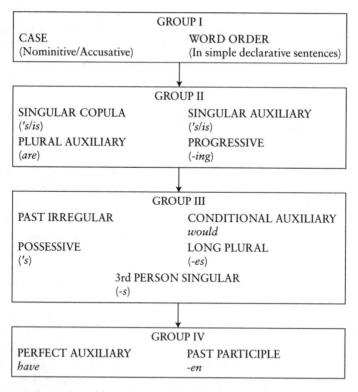

SAMPLE:

N:	536	Research design:	Cross-sectional
Age:	5–9 years old	Elicitation technique:	Structured conversation
L1:	461 Spanish		
	55 Chinese	L2 environment:	Host
L2:	English		

Acquisition Hierarchy Observed

GROUP I

CASE
(Nominitive/Accusative)

WORD ORDER
(In simple declarative sentences)

GROUP II

SINGULAR COPULA
('s/is)

SINGULAR AUXILIARY
('s/is)

PLURAL AUXILIARY
(are)

PROGRESSIVE
(-ing)

GROUP III

PAST IRREGULAR

CONDITIONAL AUXILIARY
would

POSSESSIVE
('s)

LONG PLURAL
(-es)

3rd PERSON SINGULAR
(-s)

GROUP IV

PERFECT AUXILIARY
have

PAST PARTICIPLE
-en

Fig. 2.1 Acquisition hierarchy for 13 English grammatical morphemes for Spanish-speaking and Cantonese-speaking children

the same order of acquisition. After all, children might approach the task of second language learning more like the learning of an L1 than adults do.

Bailey *et al.* (1974) conducted a similar study with adults. They used the same elicitation method (Bilingual Syntax Measure) in order to investigate the accuracy of production of the eight morphemes studied in Dulay and Burt (1973), in 73 adult learners of English from twelve different L1 backgrounds. Their results were very similar to those reported in the case of children by Dulay and Burt (1973, 1974c), as shown in Figure 2.2, taken from Dulay and Burt 1982, p. 210.

These morpheme acquisition studies attracted criticism, both at the time and subsequently; this critique is reviewed for example by Gass and Selinker (1994, pp. 84–7). (The criticisms are mainly about the elicitation technique used in these early studies which was thought to bias the results, and also about the assumption that relative accuracy of production reflects acquisition sequences.)[5] However, the basic argument that both child and adult learners of English as an L2 developed accuracy in a number of grammatical morphemes in a set order, no matter what the context of learning (classroom, naturalistic, mixed), survived the critique. The fact that this set order did not match the order found by Brown or de Villiers and de Villiers for first language acquisition is neither here nor there. The existence of such an order suggested that L2 learners are guided by internal principles which are largely independent of their first language; this was a strong blow for any proponents of Contrastive Analysis.

Moreover, soon after, a number of studies were reported which strongly suggested that systematic staged development could be found in a number of syntactic domains as well. For example, the acquisition of negative structures in English L2 was shown to occur in well-defined stages, by several early studies (cited in Adams 1978; Butterworth and Hatch 1978; Cazden *et al.* 1975; Ellis 1994, p. 99; Milon 1974; Ravem 1968; Wode 1978, 1981). Similar stages were also noted in the acquisition of negatives in German as a second language (Clahsen 1982; Felix 1978; Lange 1979; Pienemann 1981). In summary: 'Despite the differences in the final states towards which learners of English and German are targeted, marked similarities in the sequence of acquisition of negatives in the two languages can be seen' (Ellis 1994, p. 101). Moreover, the acquisition of negatives in English by L2 learners is not dissimilar to that of children acquiring English as their L1 (see Section 2.2.1).

The acquisition of other syntactic structures such as interrogatives, relative clauses, German word order, etc. are also well documented as exhibiting uniform patterns of acquisition, whatever the L1 of the learner (Ellis 1994, pp. 99–105, provides a comprehensive review of early studies). Moreover, the stages followed by L2 learners in the acquisition of these other areas of syntax show corresponding similarities to those followed by children learning their first language.

Thus, the 1970s witnessed a wealth of studies investigating development in L2 learners which seemed to show convincingly that it is systematic, that it is

SAMPLE:

N: 73

Age: *17–55 years old*

L1:   *Greek, Persian, Italian, Turkish,*
            Japanese, Chinese, Thai, Afghani,
            Hebrew, Arabic, Vietnamese

L2:   *English*

Research
design: *Cross-sectional*

Elicitation
technique: *Structured conversation*

L2
environment: *Host*

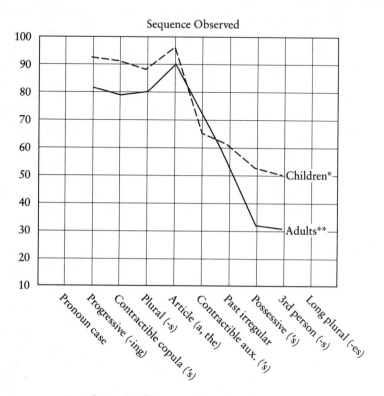

Sequence Observed

Correlation Coefficients and Significance Levels:

	Adults (Spanish Ss)
Children	$rho = .976$ (p < .01)
	(Spearman)

Fig. 2.2 Comparison of adult and child acquisition sequences

largely independent of the L1 of the learner, and that it presents many similarities with L1 acquisition, even though there are differences. These were
major empirical findings which undermined contemporary beliefs about how
second languages are acquired.

Before moving on to examine the theoretical proposals advanced to explain such findings, let us pause for an instant on the last point, namely the finding that acquisitional patterns in L1 and L2 learning were both similar and different, as it is still today an issue which is fiercely debated and highly controversial. Remember that the discovery of acquisition sequences in first language acquisition was linked to the theory that children are endowed with a language faculty which guides them in the hypotheses they make about the language around them. Brown's order of acquisition of grammatical morphemes was seen as evidence to support this view. So, what can we make of the finding that L2 learners also follow an order of acquisition, but that this order is different? The fact that they do follow such an order suggests that they are indeed guided by some set of internal principles, as children are. On the other hand, the fact that this order varies from that found for L1 suggests that these internal principles are different, in some respects at least.

A somewhat confused picture therefore emerges from the empirical work characteristic of the 1970s, and the 1980s' research agenda has tried to address some of these issues. But before we turn to the 1980s, we need to consider a highly influential attempt to conceptualize these issues in the first comprehensive model of second language acquisition, Krashen's Monitor Model.

2.3.4 Krashen's Monitor Model

Krashen's theory evolved in the late 1970s in a series of articles (1977a, 1977b, 1978), as a result of the findings outlined above. Krashen thereafter refined and expanded his ideas in the early 1980s in a series of books (Krashen 1981, 1983, 1985).[6] Krashen based his general theory on a set of five basic hypotheses:

1 the Acquisition-Learning Hypothesis;
2 the Monitor Hypothesis;
3 the Natural Order Hypothesis;
4 the Input Hypothesis;
5 the Affective Filter Hypothesis.

We shall briefly outline each of these in turn.

2.3.4.1 THE ACQUISITION-LEARNING HYPOTHESIS

This hypothesis has been highly influential, and, albeit in a different form, still remains the source of much debate today. The basic premise is that language *acquisition*, on the one hand, and *learning* on the other, are separate processes. Acquisition refers to the 'subconscious process identical in all important ways to the process children utilize in acquiring their first language' (Krashen 1985, p. 1), and learning refers to the 'conscious process that results in "knowing about" language' (1985, p. 1). In other words, acquisition is the result of natural interaction with the language via meaningful communication, which sets in motion developmental processes akin to those outlined in first language acquisition, and learning is the result of classroom experience, in which the learner is made to focus on form and to learn about the linguistic rules of the target language.

The contrast between the naturalistic environment and the classroom environment is not the crucial issue, however. What is claimed to be important is the difference between meaningful communication on the one hand, which can very well take place in the language classroom and which will trigger subconscious processes, and conscious attention to form on the other hand, which can also take place in naturalistic settings, especially with older learners who might explicitly request grammatical information from people around them. Krashen has been criticised for his vague definition of what constitutes conscious versus subconscious processes, as they are very difficult to test in practice: how can we tell when a learner's production is the result of a conscious process and when it is not? None the less, this contrast between acquisition and learning has been very influential, especially among foreign language teachers who saw it as an explanation of the lack of correspondence between error correction and direct teaching on one hand, and their students' accuracy of performance on the other. If there was some kind of internal mechanism constraining learners' development, then it could account for the fact that some structures, even simple ones like the third person singular -*s* in English (*he likes*), can be so frustrating to teach, with learners knowing the rule consciously, but often being unable to apply it in spontaneous conversation. In Krashen's terminology, learners would have learned the rule, but not acquired it.

What is also very problematic in this distinction is Krashen's claim that learning cannot turn into acquisition, i.e. that language knowledge acquired/learned by these different routes cannot eventually become integrated into a unified whole (Krashen and Scarcella 1978). Other researchers disagree (e.g. Gregg 1984; McLaughlin 1987), and the debate about whether different kinds of knowledge interact or remain separate, is still alive today, even though the terms used might differ (e.g. Schwartz 1993; Towell and Hawkins 1994; Myles, Hooper and Mitchell, forthcoming; Zobl 1995).

2.3.4.2   THE MONITOR HYPOTHESIS

According to Krashen, 'learning' and 'acquisition' are used in very specific ways in second-language performance. The Monitor Hypothesis states that 'learning has only one function, and that is as a Monitor or editor' and that learning comes into play only to 'make changes in the form of our utterance, after it has been "produced" by the acquired system' (1982, 15). Acquisition 'initiates' the speaker's utterances and is responsible for fluency. Thus the Monitor is thought to alter the output of the acquired system before or after the utterance is actually written or spoken, but the utterance is initiated entirely by the acquired system.

(McLaughlin, 1987, p. 24)

It is quite clear from the above that the Monitor does not operate all the time. Given enough time, when a focus on form is important for the learner, and when the learner knows the grammatical rule needed, they might make use of the Monitor in order to consciously modify the output produced by the acquired system. Needless to say, the pressures and demands of conversing in the second language in real time do not often allow for such monitoring to take place. Krashen's Monitor has been criticized for that reason, and also for the fact that attempts to test its predictions have been unsuccessful, for example in studies comparing learners when given more time (Hulstijn and Hulstijn 1984), or being made to focus on form (Houck *et al.* 1978; Krashen and Scarcella 1978), or checking whether learners who are able to explain the rules perform better than learners who do not (Hulstijn and Hulstijn 1984).

Krashen used the Monitor in order to explain individual differences in learners. He suggests that it is possible to find Monitor 'over-users' who do not like making mistakes and are therefore constantly checking what they produce against the conscious stock of rules they possess. Their speech is consequently very halting and non-fluent. On the other hand, Monitor 'under-users' do not seem to care very much about the errors they make, and for them, speed and fluency are more important. Such learners rely exclusively on the acquired system and do not seem able or willing to consciously apply anything they have learnt to their output. In between the two are the supposed 'optimal' Monitor users, who use the Monitor when it is appropriate, that is when it does not interfere with communication.

The problem with such claims, even though they might have some intuitive appeal, is that they are at present impossible to test empirically: how do we know when a learner is consciously applying a rule or not, or, in other words, whether the source of the rule that has been applied is the acquired system or the learned system?

2.3.4.3   THE NATURAL ORDER HYPOTHESIS

We acquire the rules of language in a predictable order, some rules tending to come early and others late. The order does not appear to be determined solely by formal simplicity and there is evidence that it is independent of the order in which rules are taught in language classes.

(Krashen 1985, p. 1)

Although there is evidently some truth in such a statement, it has been criticized for being too strong. It ignores well-documented cases of language transfer, or of individual variability. Not only are such cases ignored, but there is no place for them in Krashen's theory. Krashen's Natural Order Hypothesis has also been criticized for being based almost exclusively on the morpheme studies with their known methodological problems, and which, in any case, reflect accuracy of production rather than acquisition sequences.

A weak version of the Natural Order Hypothesis is undoubtedly supported by the kind of empirical evidence on L2 learning which we reviewed in Sections 2.3.2 and 2.3.3. However, Krashen gives us little help in under-standing why this should be the case.

2.3.4.4 THE INPUT HYPOTHESIS

The Input Hypothesis is linked to the Natural Order Hypothesis in that it claims that we move along the developmental continuum by receiving *comprehensible input*. Comprehensible input is defined as L2 input just beyond the learner's current L2 competence, in terms of its syntactic complexity. If a learner's current competence is i, then comprehensible input is $i + 1$, the next step in the developmental sequence. Input which is either too simple (already acquired) or too complex ($i + 2/3/4 \dots$) will not be useful for acquisition. Krashen views the Input Hypothesis as central to his model of second language acquisition:

> a) Speaking is a result of acquisition and not its cause. Speech cannot be taught directly but 'emerges' on its own as a result of building competence via comprehensible input.
>
> b) If input is understood, and there is enough of it, the necessary grammar is automatically provided. The language teacher need not attempt deliberately to teach the next structure along the natural order – it will be provided in just the right quantities and automatically reviewed if the student receives a sufficient amount of comprehensible input.

(Krashen 1985, p. 2)

Krashen's Input Hypothesis has been frequently criticized for being vague and imprecise: how do we determine level i, and level $i + 1$? Nowhere is this vital point made clear. Moreover, Krashen's claim is somewhat circular: acquisition takes place if the learner receives comprehensible input, and comprehensible input is claimed to have been provided if acquisition takes place. The theory becomes impossible to verify, as no independently testable definition is given of what comprehensible input actually consists of, and therefore of how it might relate to acquisition. Nor, of course, does the theory specify the internal workings of the 'Language Acquisition Device' where acquisition actually takes place – this remains a total black box.

2.3.4.5 THE AFFECTIVE FILTER HYPOTHESIS

As we have just seen, Krashen believes that learners need to receive comprehensible input for language acquisition to take place. This is not sufficient, however. Learners also need to 'let that input in', as it were. This is the role of the so-called Affective Filter, which supposedly determines how receptive to comprehensible input a learner is going to be.

> The Affective Filter Hypothesis captures the relationship between affective variables and the process of second language acquisition by positing that acquirers vary with respect to the strength or level of their affective filters. Those whose attitudes are not optimal for second language acquisition will not only tend to

seek less input, but they will also have a high or strong affective filter – even if they understand the message, the input will not reach that part of the brain responsible for language acquisition, or the Language Acquisition Device. Those with attitudes more conducive to second language acquisition will not only seek and obtain more input, they will also have a lower or weaker filter. They will be more open to the input, and it will strike 'deeper'.

(Krashen 1982, p. 31)

Although both researchers and teachers would agree that affective variables play an important role in second language acquisition, Krashen's Affective Filter remains vague and atheoretical. For example, many self-conscious adolescents suffer from low self-esteem and therefore presumably have a 'high' filter. Are they therefore all bad language learners? And are all confident and extrovert adults (with a 'low' filter) good language learners? Clearly not. Moreover, how does the Affective Filter actually work? All these issues remain vague and unexplored.

To conclude, in this brief account we have reflected criticisms of Krashen's five hypotheses and of his overall model which have been current almost since Krashen first advanced them. It remains true none the less that Krashen's ideas have been highly influential in shaping many research agendas and projects, and in so doing, considerably advancing our understanding of second language acquisition. Krashen's main overall weakness was the presentation of what were just hypotheses that remained to be tested, as a comprehensive model that had empirical validity. He then used his hypotheses prematurely as a basis for drawing pedagogical implications.

2.3.5 *Schumann's pidginization/acculturation model*

Other models appeared in the 1970s which attempted similarly to theorise SLA findings. We will mention very briefly here one other model, as it views second language acquisition from a radically different angle, and has also remained influential during the following two decades.

Schumann first proposed his pidginization/acculturation model in the late 1970s (1978a, 1978b, 1978c). On the basis of naturalistic studies of untutored learners, he noticed that early interlanguages resemble pidgin languages (i.e. simplified trading languages which lack native speakers: Sebba 1997), with characteristic features such as fixed word order and lack of inflections. Second language acquisition was compared to the complexification of pidgins, and this process was linked to degree of acculturation of the learners. The closer they feel to the target language speech community, the better learners will 'acculturate', and the more successful their L2 learning will be. The more alienated from that community they perceive themselves to be, the more pidgin-like their L2 will remain.

This model was influential in opening up alternative lines of research comparing SLA with pidginization and creolization, and in bringing to the fore social psychological variables and their role in SLA. For a substantial period of time, Schumann's proposals were the most theoretically ambitious claims about SLA which drew on sociolinguistic thinking. In Chapter 8 we revisit this model in more detail, and reassess it alongside other, newer sociolinguistic approaches.

2.4 The 1980s

We will not review this period in detail here, as the rest of the book is devoted to outlining the different approaches and the empirical work attached to them which followed in the 1980s and 1990s. In this section, we will briefly summarize the ongoing research agenda which arose from the major developments of the 1970s.

By the mid-1980s, the field of second language learning research was no longer subordinate to the immediate practical requirements of curriculum planning and language pedagogy. Instead it had matured into a much more autonomous field of enquiry, encompassing a number of substantial programmes of research, with their distinctive theoretical orientations and methodologies. The links with other related disciplines have by no means disappeared, however, and we will see throughout this book that many new links have developed. Research into the structure of language(s) and its use continues to be extensively drawn upon, and so is research into language variation and change. New links have emerged with cognitive science (e.g. the development of fluency; the role of consciousness), with neuropsychology (e.g. connectionist models; modularity of the brain), and with sociocultural frameworks (Vygotskian learning theory) which have greatly enriched our perception of the many facets of second language acquisition. But the SLA research agenda continues to focus on a number of fundamental issues carried forward from the 1970s, as follows.

1 The role of internal mechanisms.
   (a) Language specific: how similar are the first and second language acquisition processes, and how far are the similarities due to language specific mechanisms still being activated? If language-specific mechanisms are important, how can they best be modelled? How relevant is the current Chomskyan conception of Universal Grammar?
   (b) Cognitive: in what respects are second language learning and processing similar to the learning and processing of any other complex skill?
2 The role of the first language. It is clear that cross-linguistic influences from the first and other languages are operating in second language acquisition, but it is also clear that such language transfer is selective: some L1 properties transfer and others do not. An important aspect of today's research agenda is still to understand better the phenomenon of transfer.
3 The role of psychological variables. How do individual characteristics of the learner, such as motivation, personality, language aptitude, etc. affect the learning process?
4 The role of social and environmental factors. How similar is the learning

of a second language to the creation of pidgins and creoles? How does the overall socialization of the second language learner relate to the language learning process?

We will now turn to examine how these issues have been tackled across the range of current perspectives on L2 learning, starting in Chapter 3 with linguistics-inspired attempts to model the contents of the 'black box' of the Language Acquisition Device, left largely unexplored in the proposals of Krashen.

Notes

1 Asterisks are traditionally used in linguistics in order to indicate ungrammatical sentences.

2 The ages are given as a very rough guideline only; children vary considerably both in the age of onset of a given phase, and in how fast they proceed from one phase to another. All children normally go through the stages in the order indicated, however.

3 It is important to note that a large proportion of the verbs which are commonplace in the linguistic environment of the child have irregular past tense forms. For example, verbs such as *give, run, do, come, sit, sleep, fall, find, eat, hit, break*, will form part of both the early vocabulary used by the child, and of the typical verbs used by adults when addressing children.

4 A longitudinal study is where a (usually small) group of subjects is studied over a period of time. A cross-sectional study on the other hand investigates a (usually large) group of subjects at one point in time. In the case of developmental studies, cross-sectional studies take representative samples of subjects at different stages of development and compare their behaviour, inferring development when behaviour changes between two stages. Both types of studies have their advantages and disadvantages, and have been used extensively in language acquisition research.

5 The morpheme studies measured the accuracy of production of their subjects on the grammatical morphemes studied. Subjects were deemed to have acquired a morpheme if they supplied it correctly in at least 90 per cent of the obligatory contexts (e.g. if they produced the morpheme -*s* in at least 90 per cent of the cases when the context required a plural noun). Researchers then equated accuracy of production with acquisition, and have been criticised for doing that.

6 For a useful and comprehensive critique of Krashen's work, see McLaughlin (1987, pp. 19–58).

|3|

Linguistics and language learning

The Universal Grammar approach

> Universal Grammar is the black box responsible for language acquisition. It is the mechanism in the mind which allows children to construct a grammar out of the raw language materials supplied by their parents.
>
> (Cook 1997, p. 262)

3.1 Introduction

In following chapters, we shall consider individual theoretical perspectives on second language learning in greater detail. Our first topic is the Universal Grammar approach, inspired by contemporary linguistic theory, as formulated by the American linguist Noam Chomsky. We have concentrated on this particular linguistic approach because it has been much the strongest linguistic influence on second language acquisition research in recent years, and has inspired a great wealth of studies, articles and books on SLA, both empirical and theoretical.

The main aim of linguistic theory is twofold: first, to characterize what human languages look like and, second, to explain why they are that way. In terms of second language acquisition, what a linguistic approach attempts to do is no different; its aims are to describe the language produced by second language learners, and to explain why the language they produce is the way it is. The main emphasis of the research reviewed in this chapter is therefore on the product(s) of the acquisition process, from a descriptive as well as an explanatory point of view. In contrast, a detailed examination of the acquisition process itself will be the main concern of the cognitive approaches which we describe in Chapter 4.

First in this chapter, we will give a broad definition of the aims of the Chomskyan tradition in linguistic research, in order to delimit the aspects of second language acquisition to which this tradition is most relevant. Second, we will examine the concept of Universal Grammar itself in some detail, and finally we will move on to consider its application in second language learning research.

3.2　Why a Universal Grammar?

3.2.1　*Aims of linguistic research*

Linguistic theory is not primarily concerned with second language acquisition. Its main goals, as defined for example in Chomsky (1986a)[1] are to answer three basic questions about human language.

1　What constitutes knowledge of language?
2　How is knowledge of language acquired?
3　How is knowledge of language put to use?

('Knowledge of language' is an ambiguous term. Here, it means the subconscious mental representation of language which underlies all language use.) All three questions are also of concern to SLA researchers, and can briefly be developed as follows.

3.2.1.1　WHAT CONSTITUTES KNOWLEDGE OF LANGUAGE?

Linguistic theory aims to describe the mental representations of language which are stored in the human mind. It aims to define what all human languages have in common, as well as the distinctive characteristics which make human language different from other systems of communication. It also needs to specify in what way individual human languages can differ from one another. Although all human languages have a great deal in common, which enables us to translate from one language to another without too many difficulties, it is equally obvious that they are also very different from one another, as our struggle to learn foreign languages clearly shows.

The Universal Grammar (UG) approach claims that all human beings inherit a universal set of *principles* and *parameters* which control the shape human languages can take, and which are what make human languages similar to one another. In his *Government and Binding* theory, Chomsky (1981, 1986a, 1986b) argues that the core of human language must comprise these two components. His proposed principles are unvarying and apply to all natural languages; in contrast, parameters possess a limited number of open values which characterize differences between languages. Examples of such principles and parameters will be given later on in this chapter.

One of the main interests of this approach for SLA research is that it provides a detailed descriptive framework enabling researchers to formulate well-defined hypotheses about the task facing the learner, and to analyse learner language in a more focused manner. Moreover, it is a general theory of language, which should therefore encompass any theory dealing specifically with SLA.

3.2.1.2 HOW IS KNOWLEDGE OF LANGUAGE ACQUIRED?

How does the child create the mental construct that is language? Chomsky first resorted to this concept of Universal Grammar because he believes that children could not learn their first language so quickly and effortlessly without the help of an innate language faculty to guide them. The arguments put forward, often referred to as the 'logical problem of language learning', are that on the basis of degenerate input (spoken language is full of false starts, slips of the tongue, etc.), children create a mental representation of language which is not only much more complex than could be expected, but also strikingly similar to that of other native speakers of the same language variety. Children achieve this at an age when they have difficulty grasping abstract concepts, yet language is probably the most abstract piece of knowledge they will ever possess. This biologically endowed Universal Grammar would make the task facing the child much easier, by equipping them in advance with a clear set of expectations about the shape which language will take. This would also explain why the different languages of the world are strikingly similar in many respects.

If we now turn to the problem of second language learning, learners are faced with the same logical problem of having to construct a grammar of the second language on the basis of more or less fragmentary input, and of having to construct abstract representations on the basis of the samples of language they actually encounter. But although the task facing them is the same, this does not mean to say that L2 learners set about tackling it in the same way as children. After all, their needs are very different, if only because they are already successful communicators in one language, and because they already have a mental representation of language, with the parameters set to the values of their native language. Moreover, second language learners are cognitively mature and therefore presumably much more resourceful as far as their ability to solve problems and to deal with abstract concepts is concerned. From a theoretical point of view, therefore, different possible scenarios are open to consideration.

- L2 learners still have access to UG in the same way as children do, and the fact that they do not typically achieve full mastery of the second language is due to their different needs.
- L2 learners still access UG, but via their first language, with parameter values already set for that language.
- The language faculty in children, because it is biologically triggered according to a predetermined timetable, atrophies with age and is not available to adult L2 learners who then have to resort to general problem-solving devices.

- L2 learners only have access to part of UG; some parameters are no longer available.

There is considerable controversy about all these issues, and proponents of each of these positions abound in the literature about SLA. We revisit them in Section 3.5.

3.2.1.3   HOW IS KNOWLEDGE OF LANGUAGE PUT TO USE?

The UG approach to language is concerned with knowledge of language, i.e. with the abstract mental representation of language which all human beings possess, with *competence*. It is not about *performance*, about how language is used in real life, given the time constraints and competing demands on the brain's information-processing facilities. Performance is the domain of a theory of language use, in which linguistic competence is only one aspect. A complete theory of language use also has to define how we access our knowledge base, and how it is affected by a number of sociolinguistic and psycholinguistic variables. Although Chomsky acknowledges that this is an important area for research, he has been concerned almost exclusively with addressing the first two issues, and this is also true for UG-inspired research in SLA.

3.2.2   *Arguments from L1 acquisition*

In this section, we will review in some more detail the arguments which support the existence of an inborn language faculty in children. We will base our discussion on the brief outline presented in Chapter 2 of what we know about L1 acquisition, the main characteristics of which are summarized succinctly below.

1 Children go through stages.
2 These stages are very similar across children for a given language, although the rate at which individual children progress through them is variable.
3 These stages are similar across languages.
4 Child language is rule-governed and systematic, and the rules created by the child do not necessarily correspond to adult ones.
5 Children are resistant to correction.
6 Children's processing capacity limits the number of rules they can apply at any one time, and they will revert to earlier hypotheses when two or more rules compete.

Universalists could not conclude from the evidence presented above alone that there must be a specific language module in the brain; these regularities, although very striking, could be due to the more general cognitive make-up of human beings which leads them to process information, whether linguistic or not, in the way they do. After all, children learning maths or learning to play the piano also go through fairly well defined stages, although not at such a young age.

However, another striking feature of child language is that it does not seem to be linked in any clear way to intelligence. In fact, children vary greatly in the age at which they go through each developmental step in the sequence outlined above, and in how fast they go through each stage. By age three or four, though, individual differences have largely disappeared, and the late starter has usually caught up with the precocious child. Moreover, early onset of language is not linked to intelligence; Steinberg (1993) states that 'many very famous people, including Albert Einstein, are reputed to have been slow to talk'.

Not only is language development not directly linked to intelligence, but it is also one of the most complex and abstract pieces of knowledge children have to cope with at such an early age, not to say during the entire course of their life. To give an example of the complexities of language children have to disentangle, just consider the following sentences, some of them grammatical and others ungrammatical.

1 *John* saw *himself.*
2 **Himself* saw *John.*[2]
3 Looking after *himself* bores *John.*
4 John said that *Fred* liked *himself.*
5 **John* said that Fred liked *himself.*
6 John told *Bill* to wash *himself.*
7 **John* told Bill to wash *himself.*
8 *John* promised Bill to wash *himself.*
9 *John* believes *himself* to be intelligent.
10 **John* believes that *himself* is intelligent.
11 *John* showed *Bill* a picture of *himself.*

These examples are taken from White (1989), cited in Lightbown and Spada (1993, pp. 9–10). In all these sentences, the noun and the pronoun which refer to the same person are printed in italics.

Now imagine you are the child trying to work out what the relationship between the reflexive pronoun and its antecedent is; you might conclude from 1 and 2 that the reflexive pronoun must follow the noun it refers to, but 3 disproves this. Sentences 4, 5, 6 and 7 might lead you to believe that the closest noun is the antecedent, but 8 shows that this cannot be right either. It is also evident from 8 that the rule cannot be either that the reflexive and its antecedent have to be in the same clause. Furthermore, the reflexive can be in subject position in 9, an untensed clause, but not in 10, a tensed clause. Moreover, the reflexive can sometimes have two possible antecedents, as in (k) where *himself* can refer to either *John* or *Bill*. These few sentences should be enough to convince you of the magnitude of the task facing children; how can they make sense of this, and invariably arrive at the correct rule?

In support of the view that language is not linked to intelligence, there is also a large body of evidence from children with cognitive deficits who develop language normally (Bishop and Mogford 1993). For example, Bellugi *et al.* (1993) have studied children suffering from Williams syndrome, a rare metabolic disorder which causes heart defects, mental retardation and a distinctive facial appearance. They demonstrate that these children show a dissociation between language development and the kind of supposed cognitive prerequisites which Piaget and his followers would argue are necessary for language development. Sophisticated use of language with complex syntax and adult-like vocabulary is found in individuals whose overall level of mental development is below that of a 7 year old.

Smith and Tsimpli (1995) have studied in detail the extraordinary case of a brain-damaged man who is institutionalized because he is unable to look after himself, but who can read, write and communicate in any of fifteen to twenty languages.

> The most salient feature is a striking mismatch between his verbal and non-verbal abilities, supported by test results over a prolonged period and with recent documentation across a wide range of different tests. The basic generalization is that he combines a relatively low performance IQ with an average or above average verbal IQ.
>
> (Smith and Tsimpli, 1995, p. 4)

Evidence of the opposite is also found: children who are cognitively 'normal', but whose language is impaired, sometimes severely. This condition, known as SLI (Specific Language Impairment), is characterized by language being deficient in specific ways. One English-speaking family has been studied recently, in which 16 out of 30 members in the last three generations suffer from SLI, suggesting that it is an inherited disorder, and that some aspects of language at least might be genetically controlled (Cook 1997; Gopnik and Crago 1991; Pinker 1994).

Not only does language seem to be largely separate from other aspects of cognition – although the two interact of course – but within language itself, different modules also seem to be relatively independent of one another. We also find evidence in brain-damaged adults that language is separate from other kinds of cognitive faculties; people who suffer strokes or other localized injuries to the brain will exhibit very different symptoms depending on the location of their injury. Damage to the left hemisphere of the brain will usually result in language deficit, as in the vast majority of people (around 90 per cent) it is the left hemisphere which controls language. Moreover, the exact location of the injury within the left hemisphere is often linked to the kind of language deficit. Damage to the region in front of and just above the left ear (Broca's area) usually results in impaired speech production, sometimes very severe, characterized by effortful, hesitant and very non-fluent speech, with virtually no grammatical structure in evidence, consisting largely of specific nouns with few verbs, and poorly articulated. The comprehension of speech, in contrast, usually remains good. This condition is called Broca's aphasia, and is in many respects the mirror image of Wernicke's aphasia, which usually results from an injury to the region of the brain around and under the left ear (Wernicke's area). In the case of Wernicke's aphasia, patients produce effortless, fluent and rapid speech which is generally grammatically complex and well structured, but which is lacking in content words with specific meaning; these patients produce very general nouns and verbs such as *something, stuff, got, put* or *did*, and their speech is so vague that it is usually totally incomprehensible. In this condition, the comprehension of speech is severely impaired.

The picture we have just outlined of the relationship between brain and language is necessarily very oversimplified. (For more detailed accounts, see for example Caplan 1987, 1992; Harris and Coltheart 1986; Sabouraud 1995.) None the less it shows clearly that specific areas of the brain deal with specific aspects of language, and that suffering from a language deficit does not necessarily mean having lost language completely, but usually means having problems with one or more aspects of language.

All this evidence put together has been used by universalists to posit that there must be some kind of innate language faculty which is biologically triggered, in order to explain why language in children just seems to 'grow', in the same way as teeth develop and children start walking.

An influential book by Lenneberg (1967) called *Biological Foundations of Language* outlined the characteristics which are typical of biologically triggered behaviour and argued that language conforms to the criteria used in order to define such behaviour.

Aitchison (1989, p. 67) presents Lenneberg's four criteria as a list of six features, as follows.

1 'The behaviour emerges before it is necessary.' Children start talking long before they need to: they are still being fed and looked after, and therefore do not need language for their survival.
2 'Its appearance is not the result of a conscious decision.' It is quite obvious that children do not get up one morning and decide to start talking, whereas they might consciously decide to learn to ride a bike or play the piano.
3 'Its emergence is not triggered by external events (though the surrounding environment must be sufficiently "rich" for it to develop adequately).' Although children need language around them in order to learn it, there is no single event which will suddenly trigger language development.
4 'Direct teaching and intensive practice have relatively little effect.' We have seen how oblivious children seem to be to correction.
5 'There is a regular sequence of "milestones" as the behaviour develops, and these can usually be correlated with age and other aspects of development.' In the same way as a baby will sit up before standing up before walking before running, we have seen how children go through well-defined stages in their language development, which tend to run parallel to

physical development. The onset of the first words usually roughly corresponds to the onset of walking for example, although nobody would like to claim that there is any cause and effect correlation between the two, as it is obvious that some children never learn to talk but learn to walk and vice versa.

6 'There may be a "critical period" for the acquisition of the behaviour.' It is often argued that, in the same way as some species of birds have to be exposed to their species' song in order to learn it before a certain age, human beings have to be exposed to language before puberty in order for language to develop. This is a controversial issue; the evidence from children who have been deprived of language in their early years is difficult to interpret, as it is not usually known whether they were normal at birth or had suffered some kind of brain damage. We will examine later in this chapter the evidence that adult second language learners bring to this debate which is difficult to resolve.

After having reviewed the kind of argumentation used by universalists in order to propose the existence of a language-specific module in the brain which allows the child to learn language so easily and effortlessly, let us now turn to the question of what this so-called language faculty or Universal Grammar might be like.

3.3   What does UG consist of?

3.3.1   Principles

We have seen earlier that, according to this view of language learning, 'the learner's initial state is supposed to consist of a set of universal principles which specify some limited possibilities of variation, expressible in terms of parameters which need to be fixed in one of the few possible ways' (Saleemi 1992, p. 58). What does this mean in practice? The general idea is that language learning is highly constrained, thus making the task for the child much more manageable. In the following section, we will work our way through one concrete example of a principle and its associated parameters, in order to see how this theory has been applied to the problem of language learning.

The principle we are going to concentrate on is the principle of *structure-dependency* which states that language is organized in such a way that it crucially depends on the structural relationships between elements in a sentence (such as words, morphemes, etc.). What this means is that words are regrouped into higher-level structures which are the units which form the basis of language. Intuitively, we know that this is the case; in the following sentences.

(a) *She bought a new car yesterday.*
(b) *My friend bought a new car yesterday.*

(c) *The friend that I met in Australia last year bought a new car yesterday.*
(d) *The friend I am closest to and who was so supportive when I lost my job two years ago bought a new car yesterday.*

We know that '*she*', '*my friend*', '*the friend that I met in Australia last year*', and '*the friend I am closest to and who was so supportive when I lost my job two years ago*', are the same kind of groupings and perform the same role in the sentence, and in fact might refer to one single individual. Moreover, we also know that we could carry on adding details about this friend more or less *ad infinitum* by using devices such as *and*, or *that, which,* etc., running the risk of boring our listener to tears! We also know that the crucial word in these groupings is *friend*, or *she* if we have already referred to this person earlier in the conversation. This kind of structural grouping is called a *Phrase*, and in the examples above, we are dealing with a *Noun-Phrase*, as the main or central element (the head) of this phrase is a noun (or pronoun). In fact, all languages in the world are structured in that way, and are made up of sentences which consist of at least a Noun-Phrase (NP) and a Verb-Phrase (VP), as in [$_{NP}$Paul][$_{VP}$sings], which in turn optionally contain other phrases or even whole sentences, as (d) in the examples above shows.

This knowledge – that languages are structure-dependent – is a crucial aspect of all human languages which has many implications; it is a principle of Universal Grammar which explains many of the operations we routinely perform on language. For example, when we ask a question in English, we change the canonical order of the sentence (Subject-Verb-Object in English).

Your cat is friendly
▲*Is your cat friendly?*

The way in which we do that is not based on the linear order of the sentence, but is structure-dependent. We do not move the first auxiliary we encounter, or, say, the third word in the sentence, rules which would work in the above example, but would generate ungrammatical sentences in the following example.

The cat who is friendly is ginger
*Is the cat who friendly is ginger?
*Who the cat is friendly is ginger?

The correct answer is of course *Is the cat who is friendly ginger?*, where the second *is* is moved to the beginning of the sentence. Note that there is no immediately obvious reason why this should be the case; computers would have no problems dealing with either of the two artificial rules above. In fact, computers find it considerably more difficult to apply a rule which is based on a hierarchical structure as is the case in this natural-language example. As Cook and Newson put it: 'Movement in the sentence is not just a matter of recognising phrases and then of moving the *right* element in the *right* phrase: movement depends on the structure of the sentence' (1996, p. 8). In our example, the *is* which moves is the one belonging to the main clause, not the one in the relative clause.

The same restrictions apply to passive sentences. The sentence *The car hit the girl* can be made into a passive by raising the object Noun-Phrase to the subject position *The girl was hit by the car*. Notice that it is the whole NP which is moved to the front; it could just as well have been *Lisa*, or *The girl with the blue trousers*, or *The girl who won first prize in the creative writing competition*. French passive constructions work in exactly the same way: *L'enfant chatouille le nounours* (the child tickles the teddy) becoming *Le nounours est chatouillé par l'enfant* (the teddy is tickled by the child). In fact,

> structure-dependency can therefore be put forward as a universal principle of language: whenever elements of the sentence are moved to form passives, questions, or whatever, such movement takes account of the structural relationships of the sentence rather than the linear order of words.
>
> (Cook and Newson 1996, p. 11)

The UG theory claims that the fact that children never use computationally simple rules based on linear ordering, but instead use computationally complex structure-dependent rules, is because the hierarchical nature of human language is part of the human mind, and does not have to be learnt as such.

3.3.2   Parameters

If the structure-dependency principle seems common to all languages, which are all organized hierarchically in terms of phrases (Noun-Phrases, Verb-Phrase, Prepositional-Phrases, etc.), there are many other rules which differ between languages. Otherwise, all languages would work in the same way, which is obviously not the case. This is where *parameters* come in. Let us now turn our attention to an example of a parameter, also to do with language structure, which is going to determine one of the ways in which languages can vary. This particular parameter, called the *head parameter*, specifies the position of the head in relation to its complement(s) within phrases for different languages. (For more detailed analyses of both the structure-dependency principle and the head parameter, see for example Cook and Newson 1996, or Towell and Hawkins 1994, who apply them specifically to the study of second language acquisition.)

The head parameter deals with the way in which phrases themselves are structured. Each phrase has a central element, called a *head*; in the case of a Noun-Phrase, the head is the noun, in the case of a Verb-Phrase it is the verb, in the case of a Prepositional-Phrase, it is the preposition, and so on. One dimension along which languages vary is the position of the head in relation to other elements inside the phrase, called complements. For example, in the Noun-Phrase *the girl with blue trousers*, the head-noun *girl* appears to the left of the complement *with blue trousers*; in the Verb-Phrase *hit the girl*, the head *hit* appears to the left of its complement *the girl*; similarly, in the

Prepositional-Phrase *with blue trousers*, the head *with* is on the left of its complement *blue trousers*. In fact English is a *head-first* language, because the head of the phrase always appears before its complements. Japanese, on the other hand, is a *head-last* language, because the complements precede the head inside phrases.

> *E wa kabe ni kakatte imasu*
> (picture wall on is hanging)
> 'The picture is hanging on the wall.'
> The head verb *kakatte imasu* occurs on the right of the verb complement
> *kabe ni*, and the *post*position *ni* (on) comes on the right of the PP
> complement *kabe* (example from Cook and Newson 1996, p. 14).

Japanese is a head-last language, and all Japanese phrases will be ordered in that way. This parameter, which tells us how the head and its complements are ordered in relation to one another in a given language, is called the head-parameter, with two possible settings: head-first (like English), or head-last (like Japanese). So, on the one hand, we have a universal principle which tells us that languages are structured into phrases containing a head and optional complements, and on the other hand, we have a parameter which constrains the possible ordering of constituents within the phrase in relation to the head. This parameter has only two possible settings: head-first or head-last. From an acquisitional point of view, what all this means is that children, equipped with Universal Grammar, do not need to discover that language is structured into phrases, as this principle forms part of the blueprint for language in their mind. They also 'know' that all phrases in the language they are learning are going to be consistently ordered in relation to the head. The only task remaining is to learn which parameter-setting actually applies in the language which the child is learning. (In this case, is it head-first, or head-last?) In theory, the only input the child needs in order to set the head parameter to the correct value is one example of one phrase, and they will then automatically know the internal structure of all other phrases. In this view, the task facing children is considerably simpler than if they had to work out for themselves the extremely complex and abstract structure of natural language, and if they also had to discover the order of constituents within each type of phrase. Moreover, they need only minimal exposure on the basis of which they are able to make wide-ranging generalizations which affect different parts of the syntax of the language they are learning. In fact, Radford claims that:

> young children acquiring English as their native language seem to set the head parameter at its appropriate *head-first* setting from the very earliest multiword utterances they produce (at around age 18 months), and seem to know (tacitly, not explicitly, of course) that English is a *head-first* language.
>
> (1997, p. 22)

Remember also the puzzle which we posed in Section 3.2.2, when we asked how children could possibly figure out the precise relationships which apply between reflexives such as *himself* and their NP antecedents, in English? The answer offered by UG theory to this problem is that a principle, the Binding principle, and its associated parameter, the Governing Category parameter, are pre-existing in the child's language module, and only need to be 'set' in a certain way to generate this particular bit of language-specific knowledge. (In a language like Korean, this parameter is set another way: Schachter 1996, p. 178.)

According to Chomsky, 'a language is not, then, a system of rules, but a set of specifications for parameters in an invariant system of principles of Universal Grammar' (1995, p. 388). He proposes a network metaphor for the whole 'language faculty'.

> The initial state of the language faculty consists of a collection of subsystems, or modules as they are called, each of which is based on certain very general principles. Each of these principles admits of a certain very limited possibility of variation. We may think of the system as a complex network, associated with a switch box that contains a finite number of switches. The network is invariant, but each switch can be set in one of two positions, on or off. Unless the switches are set, nothing happens. But when the switches are set in one of the permissible ways, the system functions, yielding the entire infinite array of interpretation for linguistic expressions. A slight change in switch settings can yield complex and varied phenomenal consequences as its effects filter through the network.... To acquire a language, the child's mind must determine how the switches are set.
>
> (Chomsky, 1987, p. 68)

> Acquisition of language is in part a process of setting the switches one way or another on the basis of the presented data, a process of fixing the values of the parameters.
>
> (Chomsky, 1988, p. 63; both quotations taken from Lust, *et al.* 1994)

3.3.3   New developments: minimalism, functional categories

The aim of this chapter is not to give a full account of Universal Grammar and all its principles and parameters, but to understand how it has been applied to the study of language acquisition. Before leaving this descriptive section, however, it is important to outline briefly some recent developments in UG theory. We need to say a few words about the Minimalist Programme (Chomsky 1995; Cook and Newson 1996; Radford 1997), and about work undertaken on so-called functional categories, which has been highly influential recently, and makes a number of powerful predictions.

3.3.3.1   MINIMALISM

In the Minimalist Programme, 'Chomsky has proposed principles that are still more powerful and abstract in their effects on language knowledge' (Cook 1997, p. 259). But probably the biggest challenge to current thinking that Chomsky's minimalist programme is proposing concerns parameters.

Instead of being linked to specific principles and contained in the structural part of the grammar, parameters would now be contained within the lexicon. In fact, in this view, languages are different from one another only because their lexicons are different, and all that language acquisition involves is the learning of the lexicon. How can we then account for parameter setting in this framework?

The abstract principles underlying all human languages will already be specified (as before), and the task facing children (or L2 learners) is therefore to learn the vocabulary of the language around them, as well as the settings of the parameters applying to that language. What the 'lexical parameterization hypothesis', as it is called, suggests, is that the parameters are contained in a specific type of category in the lexicon, called *functional categories*.

3.3.3.2   FUNCTIONAL CATEGORIES

The term 'functional' is used in a number of different senses in linguistics. Crystal (1991 pp. 145–7) offers definitions of a range of traditional meanings of the term, as in 'functional grammar' etc. In Chapter 5 below, we ourselves use the term in a more traditional way. In this chapter, however, we follow current usage among Universal Grammar theorists. As defined by these theorists, functional categories have been playing an important part in UG-based language acquisition studies since the beginning of the 1990s, and have been influential in accounting for some aspects of child grammars, and more recently of L2 learners' grammars.

Functional categories are perhaps best explained by contrast to lexical categories which we are already familiar with. What we call lexical categories are groups of so-called 'content words' such as Nouns, Verbs, Adjectives, etc., that is, words that carry a specific meaning and clearly belong to the lexicon rather than the grammar. The kind of words we are now turning our attention to are grammatical words or 'function' words, such as determiners (e.g. *the, my*, etc.), complementizers (e.g. *whether*), or grammatical morphemes such as plural *-s*, past tense *-ed*, etc. Another way of conceptualizing the difference between lexical and functional categories is in terms of an open class of words, and a closed class of words. An open class of words (lexical categories) is one in which you can add elements quite freely; for example, in the lexical categories Noun or Verb, words such as *e-mail, microchip, to e-mail, to computerize*, etc. are being added all the time. A closed class of words (functional categories) is one to which elements cannot easily be added, but instead has a fixed number of members which do not vary. For example, you cannot add new determiners or new past-tense morphemes to a language in the straightforward way in which you can add new nouns or new adjectives.

In itself, this distinction between content and function words is not by any means new to linguistics. However, recent theory claims that these 'function' words or morphemes also have phrases attached to them in the same way as 'lexical' words do. In fact, these functional phrases are organized in the same way as any other phrase, with the function word or morpheme as head of that phrase. We will therefore have Determiner Phrases (DP), and Complementizer Phrases (CP), with determiners such as *the* or complementizers such as *whether* as their heads, but also Inflection Phrases (IP) made up of Tense Phrases (TP) and Agreement Phrases (AgrP), which carry tense and agreement markers such as past tense -*ed* or third person singular -*s* in English. The structure of these functional phrases is basically the same as that of lexical phrases, and they can be represented in the same way.

To take just one example, the structure of the Determiner Phrase within this framework is as shown in Figure 3.1. The determiner *this* is the head of the DP, and the NP *child* is the complement of the head (the determiner). Note that the complement is to the right of the head, as in all phrases in English, whether they are lexical phrases or functional phrases.

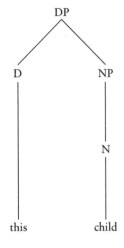

Fig. 3.1

We do not need to worry too much here about the technicalities of such an analysis; what is important to us is what this means in acquisitional terms. In the minimalist framework, all this information is now contained in the lexicon, which is made up of both lexical categories and functional categories. It therefore follows that a great deal of the grammatical information concerning a language will now be stored in the lexicon, as it will be contained in these functional categories. Similarly, a great deal of the variation which exists between the world's languages can therefore be accounted for by differences in the way in which functional categories are realized in the different languages, or in other words, by the different settings of the parameters attached to these functional categories.

Before turning to the relationship between UG and language acquisition, it is important to point out that, in fact, a strong motivation behind functional categories comes from L1 acquisition studies. In this model, children learning their mother tongue have to learn the lexicon of their language, which means learning both the lexical categories contained in it, and the functional categories, with their associated parameters. It has been claimed that children go through a stage of having acquired the lexical categories, but not the functional ones (for a detailed discussion of this phenomenon, see Radford 1990). Around the two-word stage, sometimes also termed the tele-graphic stage for the obvious reason that the child's language contains almost exclusively 'content' words, children show no surface evidence of having acquired functional categories. Their language is devoid of such elements as determiners or tense markings, and this phase has sometimes been termed the 'pre-grammatical' stage for that reason (e.g. *play ball; dolly drink; daddy gar-den*, etc.). From this theoretical viewpoint, the explanation is that the under-lying functional categories, which control much surface 'grammar', have not yet been acquired. But let us now turn specifically to the way in which UG explains language acquisition data.

3.4   UG and L1 acquisition

So, what is the evidence in the child acquisition literature for the UG view-point: do children indeed build phrase-structure by applying principles and setting parameters in the way we have described above?

Before we can deal with this question, let us first examine in more detail the structure of phrases. (In this section we draw on the more detailed account given by Towell and Hawkins, 1994, pp. 61–8). So far, we have only mentioned heads and complements, and we have not explained in any detail the hierarchical structure of phrases. We have seen already that the world's languages are made up of phrases which have an invariant structure consist-ing of a head category (the core element of the phrase) and of complements

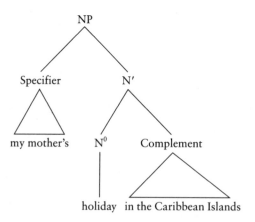

Fig. 3.2 [_NP_ ***my mother's holiday in the Caribbean Islands***][_VP_ *was fantastic*]

which optionally modify the head. Another type of modifier – also optional – is called a *Specifier*, as shown in the example of a Noun-Phrase in English given in Figure 3.2. Here the head Noun *holiday* is modified by its complement *in the Caribbean Islands*, and the grouping *holiday in the Caribbean Island* is itself modified by the Specifier *my mother's*. It is claimed in UG theory that the same underlying structural configuration of head, complement and specifier applies to all phrases in a given language. The following examples show how this works in English for the Verb-Phrase (Figure 3.3), the Adjectival-Phrase (Figure 3.4), and the Prepositional-Phrase (Figure 3.5).

All phrases are organized in this hierarchical manner, with an optional Specifier modifying an X', itself consisting of an X^0 (the head) modified by an optional Complement, where X can be any of the head-categories: N^0 (Noun), V^0 (Verb), A^0 (Adjective), P^0 (Preposition), D^0 (Determiner), $INFL^0$ (Inflection). (The notation X', X^0 is used to indicate the different levels in the

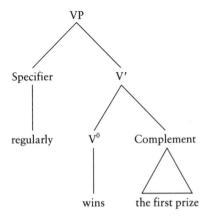

Fig. 3.3 [$_{NP}$*My brother*][$_{VP}$*regularly wins the first prize*]

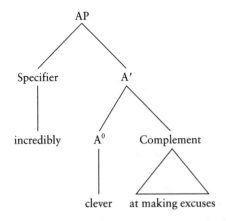

Fig. 3.4 *She became* [$_{AP}$*incredibly clever at making excuses*]

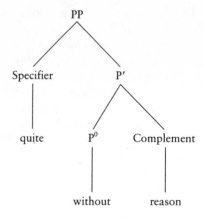

Fig. 3.5 *He did this* [PP *quite without reason*]

hierarchical structure of phrases, with X^0 representing the head element on its own, X' representing the unit 'head-element + complement' and so on.) The only possible variant is the situation of Head, Specifier and Complement in relation to one another. Thus in a language such as English, the general configuration illustrated in Figures 3.2–3.5 above can be summed up as shown in Fig. 3.6 (Towell and Hawkins 1994, p. 64).

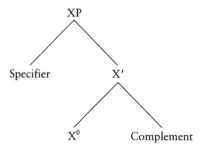

Fig. 3.6

In this case, in all types of phrase, the specifier typically precedes the head element, and the complement follows it. However, in a language such as Japanese, both specifier and complement precede the head as shown in Figure 3.7. Following this pattern, the examples given above would become *my mother's in the Caribbean Islands holiday, incredibly at making excuses clever,* and *quite reason without.*

The last possible ordering which is found in natural languages comprises head followed by both complement and specifier *see* Figure 3.8. This would give rise to the following re-ordering of our examples: *holiday in the Caribbean Islands my mother's, clever at making excuses incredibly,* and *without reason quite.* This configuration is found in languages such as Malagasy and Fijian (Towell and Hawkins 1994, p. 64).

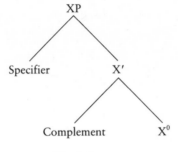

Fig. 3.7

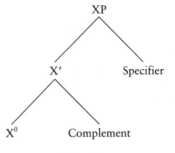

Fig. 3.8

In terms of first language acquisition, what does this mean? Remember that we have said that the structure of phrases is an invariant principle of Universal Grammar. Children would therefore know, rather than have to work it out, that sentences are made of phrases which consist of (Specifier)–Head–(Complement). However, they would not know the precise ordering of these elements which is found in their own language; that is, they would have to set the head parameter on the basis of language input. Notice, though, that the number of possibilities is constrained: Specifier–Head–Complement, Specifier–Complement–Head, or Head–Complement–Specifier.

There is indeed evidence from first language acquisition research that children have set the head parameter as early as the two-word stage (Radford 1997, p. 22), and that they 'know how to project productively X^0 categories into X' categories, and X' categories into XP categories' (Towell and Hawkins 1994, p. 65). This is shown in the examples below, taken from Radford (1990, cited in Towell and Hawkins 1994, p. 66).

	X^0	*Complement*		
	cup	tea	(N')	'a cup of tea'
	ball	wool	(N')	'a ball of wool'
	open	box	(V')	'open the box'
	get	toys	(V')	'get my toys'
(put)	in	there	(P')	'put it in there'
(get)	out	cot	(P')	'I want to get out of the cot'

Specifier	X'		
Mummy	car	(NP)	'Mummy's car'
Hayley	dress	(NP)	'Hayley's dress'
Dolly	hat	(NP)	'Dolly's hat'
Daddy	gone	(VP)	'Daddy has gone'
Hayley	draw (boat)	(VP)	'Hayley is drawing (a boat)'
Paula	play (with ball)	(VP)	'Paula is playing (with a ball)'

Radford suggests on the basis of this type of evidence that:

> the initial grammars formulated by young children show clear evidence of the acquisition of a well-developed set of symmetrical lexical category systems, in that young children at the relevant stage (typically between the ages of 20 and 23 months +/- 20 per cent) seem to 'know' how to project head nouns, verbs, prepositions and adjectives into the corresponding single-bar and [XP] categories.
>
> (1990, p. 81, cited in Towell and Hawkins 1994, p. 66)

Universal Grammar theory would predict this to be the case, as the result of the general principle underlying phrase-structure. It would also predict that children have to set the parameters for the particular language they are exposed to in order to learn the linear ordering of constituents within the phrase; because this has to be learnt on the basis of language input rather than being 'inbuilt', it might appear later in the production of children, who have to work out what that order is. In fact, Tsimpli has argued this to be the case when studying the early development of young children in a range of first languages (1991, quoted in Towell and Hawkins 1994, p. 66). For example, she found utterances produced by children learning French exhibiting the following orders: Spec X^0; X^0 Spec; Spec X^0 Comp; X^0 Spec, showing that the order is variable at this stage and the parameter not yet consistently set to the correct value for French.[3]

This simplified account has enabled us to see, with the help of a concrete example, the kinds of predictions a Universal Grammar approach enables us to make in the context of children acquiring their mother tongue. This kind of account has been advanced to account for the rapid, effortless and uniform acquisition of the extremely abstract and complex system that language is.

> The *principles and parameters* model of acquisition enables us to provide an explanation for why children manage to learn the relative ordering of heads and complements in such a *rapid* and *error-free* fashion. The answer provided by the model is that learning this aspect of word order involves the comparatively simple task of setting a binary parameter at its appropriate value. This task will be a relatively straightforward one if UG tells the child that the only possible choices are for a language to be uniformly *head-first* or uniformly *head-last*. Given such an assumption, the child could set the parameter correctly on the basis of minimal linguistic experience.
>
> (Radford 1997, p. 22)

How far can such an approach enlighten our understanding of second language acquisition, a phenomenon which shares some similarities with L1 acquisition, but which is also different in many ways?

3.5   UG and L2 acquisition

3.5.1   *Theoretical relevance of UG to L2 learning*

If the above sections have made clear what the appeal of the UG model has been in the field of first language acquisition, it might not be so obvious at first sight what its usefulness might be in the field of second language acquisition.

We need to go back to the developments that took place in the 1970s which we outlined in Chapter 2. Remember that a major impetus for second language acquisition research then was the discovery that L1 and L2 acquisition were similar in many ways. For example, we outlined the similarities in the development of a number of morphemes and of negative and interrogative structures in English in first and second language acquisition. Not only do children learning negative (or interrogative) constructions in their first language go through well-defined stages, but their productions are also unlike the language around them. In L1 acquisition, the explanation which generated most enthusiasm and therefore a wealth of theoretical and empirical work, was that there was some kind of language blueprint in the brain. This is the work we have summarized so far in this chapter.

If, as we have seen, L2 learners also go through fairly rigid stages when acquiring certain constructions in the L2, which are unlike both their L1 and the L2 they are exposed to, and which are not unlike the stages children go through, then a similar explanation is surely worth investigating. From a theoretical point of view, however, the situation is even more complicated than is the case for L1 acquisition. It is complicated by a number of factors, such as:

- L2 learners are cognitively mature;
- L2 learners already know at least one other language;
- L2 learners have different motivations for learning a L2 (language learning does not take place in order to answer the basic human need to communicate).

These points have important implications which will need addressing. In fact, even if the UG hypothesis is correct for L1 learning, there are still a number of logical possibilities concerning its role in L2 learning.

1 *No access hypothesis*: UG is not involved in L2 acquisition; it atrophies with age, and L2 learners have to resort to more general problem-solving skills.
2 *Full access hypothesis*: UG is accessed directly in L2 acquisition, and L1 and L2 acquisition are basically similar processes, the differences observed being due to the difference in cognitive maturity and in the needs of the learner.
3 *Indirect access hypothesis*: UG is not directly involved in L2 acquisition, but it is indirectly accessed via the L1; therefore, there will be just one

instantiation (i.e. one working example) of UG which will be available to the L2 learner, with the parameters already fixed to the settings which apply in the L1.

4 *Partial access hypothesis*: some aspects of UG are still available and others not; for examples, principles might still be available, but some parameter settings might not. This approach needs to be differentiated from the indirect access hypothesis, as it takes UG and its various subcomponents as the starting point, rather than the L1, hypothesising that some submodules of UG are more or less accessible to the L2 learner.

These possibilities can be summarized in diagram form as shown in Figure 3.9.

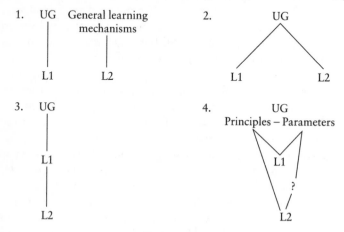

Fig. 3.9

It is obvious straight away that the situation is rendered more complicated by the presence of the L1 and its relationship with the L2 acquisition process. Moreover, Diagram 4 could be split into a variety of different diagrams each representing different modules of UG and their possible relationship with SLA; for example, UG could be split into principles and lexicon, which in turn would be split into lexical categories and functional categories, which in turn contain functional features which are parameterized. Each of these levels could be hypothesized to have a different role to play in the acquisition process. In fact, recent SLA studies increasingly adopt hypotheses which address such complications.

3.5.2 *Principles and parameters in SLA*

3.5.2.1 THE HEAD-PARAMETER

Let us return to the specific examples which we used to illustrate first language acquisition, namely the structure dependency principle and the head parameter. We saw that there are two possible settings for this parameter, head-first and head-last. Both French and English are head-first languages, i.e. the head precedes its complements. However, in French, although all phrases normally exhibit this order, there is one instance when this order is violated (Towell and Hawkins 1994, p. 68). This is in the case of unstressed object pronouns, as exemplified below.

1 *Le chat* [$_{VP}$*mange* [$_{NP}$*la souris*]] (the cat eats the mouse)
2 *Le chat* [$_{VP}$[$_{NP}$*la*] *mange*] (the cat it eats = 'the cat eats it')

Whereas in Verb-Phrases in French where the complement is a full Noun-Phrase (1), the head verb precedes its complement as normal, when the complement is an unstressed pronoun (2), the head verb follows it. Note that in English, the head direction is the same whether the complement is a full NP or a pronoun. From an acquisitional point of view, we have seen that children need minimal evidence in order to set the head-direction parameter, as all phrases in a given language normally follow the same order. For French children, there is ample evidence in the language around them that French is head-first. We would therefore expect French children to set the parameter early on (and we saw in Section 3.4 that they do, as early as the two-word stage), and to always place the head before its complement. This is in fact the case, and children produce utterances such as *Le chat mange la*, before going through a stage of omitting the pronoun altogether *Le chat mange* Ø, and later still inserting it in its target position *Le chat la mange* (Clark 1985).

If this developmental sequence is indeed due to the fact that French children have set the head-parameter and have thereafter to accommodate this particular structure which seems to violate it, then we should expect the same to happen for second language learners of French as an L2, as the task facing them is exactly the same. If UG is available to them, they would also find ample evidence in French for setting the head-direction parameter.

> In fact, the stages of development that L1 English speakers go through in acquiring this pattern in L2 French are very similar to the stages that child L1 learners of French go through in acquiring it. Following an initial stage where learners leave object pronouns postverbally in the position occupied by full noun phrases, e.g. *Le chien a mangé les*, 'The dog has eaten them' (Zobl 1980; Clark 1985), they go to a stage of omission of the pronoun: *Le chien a mangé* Ø (Adiv 1984; Schlyter 1986; Véronique 1986) before eventually acquiring preverbal object pronouns: *Le chien les a mangés*.
>
> (Towell and Hawkins 1994, p. 69)

It is interesting to note that French L1 learners of English L2 do not have problems in acquiring object pronouns in English, and do not go through a stage of preposing the pronoun (**the cat it eats*) nor through a stage of omitting the pronoun. This is to be expected if we assume that, on the basis of ample evidence in English that it is head-first, L2 learners set the head direction parameter early on and apply it consistently.

It is important to note at this stage that, because both French and English are head-first languages, we cannot say whether these observations are due to the fact that L2 learners reset the parameter to its correct value, or simply transfer their L1 parameter value. What is interesting, however, is that French learners do not transfer the idiosyncratic property of French for pronoun placement.

In order to know whether the head-parameter can be reset, we would have to investigate the acquisition of, say, a head-first language by learners whose L1 is head-last. Flynn (1983, 1984, 1987) has studied the role of this parameter in Japanese learners of English. (We have already seen that Japanese is a head-last language.) She concludes 'that, from the earliest stages of acquisition, Japanese speakers learning English as a Second Language (ESL), are able to acquire the English value of the head-direction parameter' (Flynn 1996, p. 135).

The evidence presented here therefore seems to suggest that, in the case of the head-parameter at least, L2 learners have access to Universal Grammar in the same way as children do. We have to be careful, however, not to draw hasty conclusions on the basis of evidence relating to one structure only, and we have to bear in mind that other explanations which do not involve UG might be possible, and have indeed been put forward.

3.5.2.2 FUNCTIONAL CATEGORIES

We have mentioned earlier that one of the recent developments in first language acquisition research has been the debate about whether children in early stages only have access to lexical categories and lack functional categories, which would explain the telegraphic nature of their early utterances. The same debate is also taking place in second language acquisition, and some researchers have argued also that functional categories are absent in the very early stages of adult L2 acquisition (Vainikka and Young-Scholten 1994), this phenomenon manifesting itself by a lack of morphological markings and of syntactic movement (Myles, Mitchell and Hooper forthcoming). Other researchers, however, have argued that functional categories are indeed present in the early stages in child L2 (Grondin and White 1996; Lakshmanan 1993; Lakshmanan and Selinker 1994) and also in adult L2 (Schwartz and Sprouse 1994). The debate is likely to go on for some time, complicated by the fact that functional categories themselves are not yet very clearly defined in UG theory.

What is becoming increasingly clear within the UG framework is that the question which has generated so much research over the last 15 years or so, namely whether UG is available to L2 learners or not, is now being replaced by more focused questions about which subcomponents of UG might be available or not to the second language learner. Principles are generally thought to be available, as L2 learners do not seem to produce interlanguages which violate them, and most of the work has concentrated on testing the availability of parameters, with as yet somewhat inconclusive results.

In a recent review, White suggests:

> that L2 learners often develop IL [interlanguage] grammars that are different from the grammars of NSs [native speakers] but that are nevertheless constrained by UG, and that this is due, in part, to properties of the L2 input interacting with UG and the L1 grammar. Many questions remain to be answered, including the question of why some learners 'fossilize' with these divergent IL grammars, whereas others successfully attain a nativelike grammar; why some parameters are successfully reset, whereas others are not, why positive L2 input is only sometimes successful as a trigger for grammar change.
>
> (1996, p. 115)

3.5.3 Empirical evidence

After having illustrated, in the context of SLA, how to apply a UG framework, taking the example of one principle (structure-dependency) and an associated parameter (head-direction), we can now turn to the re-assessment of the four theoretical positions we outlined in Section 3.5.1, in the light of an illustrative selection from the empirical evidence found in the literature.

3.5.3.1 HYPOTHESIS 1: NO ACCESS TO UG

The view that UG is no longer available to second language learners is still very much alive today. Proponents of this position argue that there is a critical period for language acquisition, and that adult L2 learners have to resort to other learning mechanisms. The reasons for adopting such a position are several (for a review, see Bley-Vroman 1989), but perhaps the most convincing one is the common-sense observation that immigrant children generally become native-like speakers of their L2, whereas their parents rarely do. For example, an influential study (Johnson and Newport 1989) found a correlation between age of arrival in the United States and native-like judgements on a number of grammatical properties of English. Immigrants who had arrived in the States before age seven performed in a native-like way, and the older a learner was on arrival, the more errors they made in the test. The correlation was not equally strong for all grammatical properties investigated, however.

Studies adopting this position tend to focus on differences between L1 and L2 acquisition, and on differences in the end result of the acquisition process. For example, in an extensive study of the acquisition of negation in French and German by L1 and L2 learners, Meisel concludes: 'I would like to hypothesize that second language learners, rather than using structure-dependent operations constrained by UG, resort to linear sequencing strategies which apply to surface strings' (1997, p. 258). Meisel therefore claims that one of the most fundamental principles of UG (structure-dependency) is no longer available to L2 learners.

3.5.3.2   HYPOTHESIS 2: FULL ACCESS TO UG

Flynn (1996) adopts this position. That is, she argues that UG continues to underpin L2 learning, for adults as well as children, and that there is no such thing as a 'critical period' after which UG ceases to operate. If it can be shown that learners can acquire principles and/or parameter settings of the L2, which differ from those characteristic of their L1, she claims, the best interpretation is the continuing operation of UG. She goes on to review a range of empirical work with L2 learners moving from a language such as Japanese to English (pp. 134–48). Thus, for example, we have already met her claim that adult Japanese learners of English L2 can successfully re-set the head-direction parameter (i.e. from head-last to head-first). She also claims that similar learners can instantiate principles which do not operate in Japanese, such as the Subjacency principle (which controls *wh*-movement in English); and can acquire functional categories, supposedly non-existent in Japanese. Flynn concludes her review thus:

> It appears that L2 learners do construct grammars of the new TLs [target languages] under the constraints imposed by UG; those principles of UG carefully investigated thus far indicate that those not instantiated or applying vacuously in the L1 but operative in the L2, are in fact acquirable by the L2 learner.
>
> We are thus forced to the conclusion that UG constrains L2 acquisition; the essential language faculty involved in L1 acquisition is also involved in adult L2 acquisition.
>
> (pp. 150–1)

Other researchers who believe that UG is still available to L2 learners include Thomas (1991), on the basis of work on the acquisition of reflexive binding, and White, Travis and Maclachlan (1992), also on the basis of work on *wh*-movement.

3.5.3.3   HYPOTHESIS 3: INDIRECT ACCESS

Proponents of this position claim that learners only have access to UG via their L1. They have already accessed the range of principles applying to their L1, and set parameters to the L1 values, and this is the basis for their L2 development. Other parameter-settings are not available to them, and if the L2 possesses parameter-settings which are different from those of their L1, they will have to resort to other mechanisms in order to make the L2 data fit their internal representations. These mechanisms will be rooted in general problem-solving strategies, based for example on the linear ordering of words, rather than UG-based. Bley-Vroman claims:

> Thus, the picture of the difference between child language development and foreign language learning as advocated here is the following:
>
> | *Child language development* | *Adult foreign language learning* |
> |---|---|
> | A. Universal Grammar | A. Native language knowledge |
> | B. Domain-specific learning procedures | B. General problem-solving systems |

This approach has attempted to account for the phenomena of transfer, and of the differences in the outcome of the learning process in L2 acquisition compared to L1 acquisition.

(1989, p. 51)

Schachter is also a supporter of the indirect access hypothesis, which she combines with the notion of a 'critical period' for L2 acquisition. In a recent review (1996), she cites a number of studies of adult L2 learners, claiming these show failure to acquire principles which are absent from the learners' L1, and/or failure to re-set particular parameters. For example, she cites her own work with Korean L1 learners of English as L2, who performed randomly in grammaticality judgement tests of *wh*-movement (1990). In English, *wh*-movement is allowed, but is restricted by the Subjacency principle (the extracted *wh*-word can move only across certain structural boundaries). In Korean, there is no *wh*-movement, so the Subjacency principle is presumably not operative. If all the principles of UG are still available to the learner, the absence of this particular principle from their L1 should not matter, and Subjacency should still be acquirable in English L2. Schachter claims that the Korean subjects' failure to recognize *wh*-movement problems reflects the non-availability to them of UG principles which were not already operative in their L1 – that is, that UG principles are accessible only as they have taken shape in L1.

Schachter does accept that UG may be available for child L2 learners, but argues that there is a critical period (or periods) for the successful acquisition of L2 principles and/or parameter settings, if these have not been operative in the learner's L1. She calls this critical period a Window of Opportunity, and argues that child L2 learners pass through different Windows for different modules of the target language (1996, p. 188). In support, she cites a study by Lee (1992) which tested Korean-English bilinguals on a particular parameter, the Governing Category (GC) parameter, which is set differently in the two languages involved. (As we have seen already, the GC parameter has to do with the binding of items such as reflexives; the English reflexive must refer to the subject within its own clause, while in Korean it may refer to a more remote subject: Schachter 1996, p. 178.)

In Lee's study, the Korean learners of English were of different ages; the youngest and oldest subjects had not acquired the English setting for the GC parameter, while the older children had apparently succeeded in doing so. Schachter concludes that these findings show the Window of Opportunity not yet operative for the youngest learners, but available to the older children. As far as adult learners are concerned, she concludes that 'UG . . . fails to shed light on adult L2 acquisition – either in terms of a biological perspective on maturation or in terms of the known linguistic achievements of adult L2 learners' (1996, p. 187). Instead, she believes, the only principles and parameter settings easily available to the adult L2 learner are those already activated in the course of L1 learning.

Another variant on the 'indirect access' hypothesis has recently been advanced by researchers such as Schwartz and Sprouse (1994). They argue that L2 learners transfer all the parameter-settings from their L1 in an initial stage, but that they revise their hypotheses when the L2 fails to conform to them. Learners then draw new hypotheses which are constrained by Universal Grammar. In this view, UG is accessed via the L1 in a first stage, and directly thereafter.

3.5.3.4   HYPOTHESIS 4: PARTIAL ACCESS

As we have already mentioned, this hypothesis has come to the fore recently, although which aspects of UG might be available and which not, is the subject of much debate. The strength (and weakness) of such a position, is that it attempts to reconcile somewhat contradictory facts about the second language acquisition process.

- Learners do not seem to produce 'wild' grammars, i.e. grammars which would not be constrained by UG. Does that suggest that at least principles of UG are available to them?
- Learners produce grammars which are not necessarily like either their L1 or their L2. Does this suggest that parameter-settings other than those realized in their L1 or L2 are available to them?
- Some principles and parameters seem to be unproblematic to reset (e.g. the head parameter), others more difficult, or even impossible (e.g. subjacency). Why?

Recent work in theoretical linguistics (for example, the work on functional categories mentioned earlier) has generated new and more detailed hypotheses about which particular aspects of UG might be transferred from the L1, and has been used to attempt to account for the facts mentioned above. This position has been adopted by researchers such as Martohardjono and Gair (1993), White (1992) and Hawkins and Chan (1997), on the basis of further consideration of the L2 acquisition of *wh*-movement by learners whose L1 does not have it (e.g. Korean and Chinese learners of English).

To round off this section, it is fair to say that the argument concerning access to UG in L2 learning is not concluded, and that strong defenders of all four positions can still be found. Often, they seem to be arguing about the best technical interpretation of admittedly indirect and tantalizing evidence gathered through grammaticality judgement tests, etc. None the less, our understanding of linguistic development in second language learners has been greatly enhanced by such debates. The direction of new research in this area seems to have shifted from the initial question of the availability versus non-availability of UG, towards a more modular view of language and the language faculty, with UG itself being modular (e.g. Smith and Tsimpli 1995). As a result, the questions that studies in second language acquisition have been addressing are becoming more focused, testing the availability of sub-modules of UG rather than UG itself.

Increasingly also, UG is being conceptualized within a modular view of the human mind, and the way in which it might interact with other modules has been the focus of much interest (Juffs and Harrington 1995; Myles 1995; Pinker 1994; Smith and Tsimpli 1995; Towell and Hawkins 1994).

3.6   Evaluation of UG-based approaches to SLA

3.6.1   *The UG theory*

It is important to remind ourselves in this section what the Universal Grammar theory is about, and what its aims are. It is not primarily a theory of second language learning, and therefore does not itself make any claims in this respect. It is a theory of language which aims to describe and explain human language. It is therefore only indirectly relevant to second language acquisition research. It is only relevant in so far as SLA researchers, in order to understand the acquisition process, need to understand what it is that learners have to acquire.

Although UG theory has been very influential in the field of second language acquisition, and it is this work which we have been concerned with in this chapter, we must be careful not to judge a *linguistic theory*, with its own aims and objectives, in terms of the aims and objectives of a *second language learning theory*.

As a theory of language, UG has been very influential, but not uncontroversial. This is partly due to its idealized view of language as being governed by an underlying framework or blueprint which allows for all human languages. In doing this, it focuses on some aspects of language and not others. Until very recently, syntax was the privileged object of study. Although this is changing, and phonology, morphology and more recently the lexicon have been the source of renewed interest, other areas such as semantics, pragmatics and discourse are still ignored. The object of study remains the sentence and its internal structure, rather than any larger unit of language. Work at the level of smaller units (words, morphemes, phonemes) has also been primarily concerned with structure and how different elements relate to one another. This is one of the major criticisms of work in this tradition; it studies language somewhat clinically, in a vacuum, as a mental object rather than a social or psychological one.

Similarly, the UG approach views the speaker/learner not as an individual with varied characteristics, nor as a social being, but as some kind of idealised receptacle for the UG blueprint. The emphasis is very much again here on language as the object of study, rather than on the speaker or learner as a social being. None the less, in spite of these criticisms, UG has been highly influential as a theory of language, and is probably the most sophisticated tool for analysing language today.

3.6.2   UG and second language acquisition

3.6.2.1   WEAKNESSES

When applied to SLA, how successful can the UG theory claim to be? UG-based approaches to SLA have been criticised for exactly the same reasons as the theory itself. It has left untouched a number of areas which are central to our understanding of the second language learning process. First, linguistically, this approach has in the past been almost exclusively concerned with syntax. Even if recent interest in phonology, morphology and the lexicon should redress the balance somewhat, semantics, pragmatics and discourse are excluded.

Second, the UG approach has been exclusively concerned with the developmental linguistic route followed by learners when learning an L2. The social and psychological variables which affect the rate of the learning process are beyond its remit and therefore ignored.

Another weakness of the UG approach is methodological. The theory is preoccupied with the modelling of linguistic competence, and the study of naturalistic performance is not seen as a suitable window into mental representations of language. However, tapping the underlying linguistic representations of L2 learners is even more difficult than in the case of native speakers, as L2 representations are less stable. We have seen (Chapter 1), that grammaticality judgement tests are thought to be the most appropriate methodology to access native speakers' intuitions about their native language, and that it is usually the case that native speakers agree about what is grammatical or ungrammatical in their language. L2 learners' intuitions, however, are much more likely to be unstable, and therefore less reliable. We have seen in earlier sections how often data on L2 competence deriving from grammaticality judgement tests are disputed and reinterpreted. (For a discussion of this problem, see Sorace 1996.)

3.6.2.2   STRENGTHS

While bearing the above in mind, there is still little doubt that the UG approach to research into second language acquisition has been highly influential and fruitful. First, it has been very useful as a sophisticated tool for linguistic analysis, enabling researchers to formulate well-defined and focused hypotheses which could then be tested in empirical work. This powerful linguistic tool has been useful in describing not only the language produced by learners, but also the language to be acquired as well as the first language of the learner. The work carried out by second language acquisition researchers within this framework is also feeding into our general understanding of human language, the principal aim of UG theory, as second languages are obviously examples (even if of a special kind) of such human languages.

Second, this approach has been useful, not only as a descriptive tool which contributed to establishing some of the facts about second language acquisition, but it has also met with some success in explaining those facts. For example, this approach has informed our understanding of the stages L2 learners go through, and of the systematicity shown by L2 learners; if learners are constrained by UG, we would expect their development to be staged and systematic, in the same way as children's L1 development is. UG has also enabled L2 researchers to draw up a principled view of language transfer/cross-linguistic influence, in terms of principles and parameters. As we have seen, they have then been able to test empirically whether parameters can be reset, for example.

Overall, there is little doubt that the UG approach to second language research meets the criteria of a good theory as defined in Chapter 1, by making clear and explicit statements of the ground it aims to cover and the claims it makes, by having systematic procedures for theory evaluation, by attempting to explain as well as describe at least some L2 phenomena, and finally by engaging increasingly with other theories in the field.

Notes

1 Chomsky (1988, p. 3) has added another question to this list which is of concern to the brain scientist rather than the linguist: 'What are the physical mechanisms that serve as the material basis for this system of knowledge and for the use of this knowledge?' (cited in Salkie 1990). This question is not directly relevant to the present discussion.

2 An asterisk in linguistics is traditionally used to indicate an ungrammatical sentence.

3 Although we will see later that all languages are not uniformly directional and French is a case in point. Languages appear to have a canonical order of constituents within the phrase which will apply to all phrase types; that is, if the Noun-Phrase exhibits a Specifier-N^0-Complement order, so will all other phrases in that language (VP, AP, PP, etc.). However, some languages such as French have a canonical order which has exceptions: the French clitic object pronoun appears before the Verb, giving the VP a Specifier-Complement-V^0 order. French children acquire this construction relatively late, and seem initially to rely on the canonical order for such constructions.

| 4 |

Cognitive approaches to second language learning

Human intelligence comes from both having the right knowledge and making it available at the right time.

(Anderson 1993, p. 69)

4.1   Introduction

In Chapter 3, we outlined the work of SLA researchers who are interested in the development of L2 grammars from a linguistic point of view. In that view, second language learning is seen as different from other kinds of learning, and a formal description of the linguistic systems involved (be they the L1, the L2 or the learner's interlanguage) is seen as crucial to our understanding of the task facing learners. UG-based researchers put the emphasis firmly on the *language* dimension of second language learning. The SLA researchers we are about to consider now, on the other hand, are primarily interested in the *learning* component of second language learning. They view second language learning as one instantiation of learning among many others, and they believe that we can understand the SLA process better by first understanding how the human brain processes and learns new information. The focus here is still very much on the learner as an individual (unlike the work of social theorists we will examine later), but unlike UG theorists who draw their hypotheses from the study of linguistic systems, the hypotheses they are investigating come from the field of cognitive psychology, and from what we know about the learning of complex skills generally.

Remember the distinction we have already discussed, between linguistic *competence* and linguistic *performance*. We said in Chapter 3 that UG theorists were interested primarily in competence, that is in the linguistic system underlying second language grammars, and in its construction. They are not interested in how learners access this linguistic knowledge in real time, or in the strategies they might employ when their incomplete linguistic system lets them down. Cognitivists are also interested in the construction of L2 grammars, but not exclusively so. In fact, they are just as interested in performance, if not more so. For example, recent work from cognitive psycholinguists has investigated the development of fluency in learners, and how learners improve access to their linguistic system with time and practice. Learning strategies have also been the focus of much attention. From this point of view, the learner is seen as operating a complex processing system which deals with linguistic information in similar ways to other kinds of information.

It would be wrong to suggest, however, that cognitivists are only interested in performance and not in competence. In fact, the line that they draw between the two (if they draw a line at all) is much more fuzzy than for theoretical linguists, and they see them as closely related and interacting aspects of the learning process, each driving the other forward in a dynamic tension.

The main difference between linguistic approaches and cognitive approaches to language learning is that whereas the former believe human beings to be endowed with a language-specific module in the mind, the latter do not believe that language is separate from other aspects of cognition; the human mind is geared to the processing of all kinds of information (information being understood in a broad sense), and linguistic information is just one type, albeit highly complex.

This dichotomy is of course somewhat caricatural, and you will find researchers who believe that there is a language-specific module for first language acquisition, but that the learning of second languages is different and relies on general cognitive mechanisms (see for example Bley-Vroman and his Fundamental Difference Hypothesis: 1989). You will also find that, even for L1 acquisition, some researchers believe that some aspects of language acquisition are innate and other aspects not, for example Butterworth and Harris:

> In some respects, both the claims of Piaget and Chomsky are correct. There is evidence that acquisition of some aspects of language, notably syntax, are independent of other aspects of cognitive development ... At the same time, however, there is no doubt that full understanding of a great deal of language requires other, more general, cognitive abilities.
>
> (1994, p. 124)

Some authors leave the question open.

> Related to this issue is that of the extent to which language acquisition depends upon innate language-specific principles. For example, it is not clear whether the way in which young children relate words to features of the world is constrained by specific innate limitations on the types of hypotheses which can be generated, or on more general principles such as 'attach words to whole objects in the first instance', or some combination of these.
>
> (Harley 1995, pp. 381–2)

As is clear from the above examples, the question of the specificity and innateness of the language faculty is far from resolved, in both the L1 and L2 acquisition fields, and the opposition between cognitivists and innatists should be seen more in terms of the two ends of a continuum rather than a dichotomy.

In this section, we will first investigate how cognitivists account for the learning of language, by reviewing three approaches: the *perceptual saliency* approach, *connectionism*, and the *information processing* approach. Thereafter, we will investigate the work of psychologists studying how the emerging linguistic knowledge is put to use in real time, by examining work on learning strategies and fluency development.

4.2 The perceptual saliency approach

This approach is largely based on the work of Dan Slobin in the 1970s and 1980s, culminating with the publication of a two-volume cross-linguistic study of child language development in 1985. He argues that the similarity in linguistic development across children and across languages is due to the fact that human beings are programmed to perceive and organize information in certain ways. It is this perceptual saliency which drives the learning process, rather than an innate language-specific module.

> I believe that we do not know enough yet about the LMC[1] [Language Making Capacity] to be very clear about the extent to which it is specifically tuned to the acquisition of language as opposed to other cognitive systems, or the degree to which LMC is specified at birth – prior to experience with the world of people and things, and prior to interaction with other developing cognitive systems.
>
> (Slobin 1985a, pp. 1158–9)

He has devised, added to and refined over the years a number of *operating principles* which guide children in their processing of the linguistic strings they encounter. His operating principles have been adapted to second language learning by Andersen (1984, 1990), and we will review this work shortly. Pienemann's learnability/teachability theory is also based on perceptual saliency, and will be explored thereafter.

4.2.1 Operating principles and first language acquisition

Slobin's (1973, 1979, 1985a,b) operating principles are based on the claim that 'certain linguistic forms are more "accessible" or more "salient" to the child than others' (1979, p. 107). The 1979 edition of his book *Psycholinguistics* lists five operating principles and five resulting universals; these are different from linguistic universals in that they are cognitive in nature and characterize the way in which children perceive their environment and try to make sense of it and organize it. These early principles are as follows (Slobin 1979, pp. 108–10).

Operating Principle A: Pay attention to the ends of words.
Operating Principle B: There are linguistic elements which encode relations between words.
Operating Principle C: Avoid exceptions.
Operating Principle D: Underlying semantic relations should be marked overtly and clearly.
Operating Principle E: The use of grammatical markers should make semantic sense.

Language acquisition universals are predicted from these principles in the following way.

- Universal 1 (based on principles A and B): for any given semantic notion, grammatical realizations as postposed forms will be acquired earlier than realizations as preposed forms.
- Universal 2 (based on C): the following stages of linguistic marking of a semantic notion are typically observed: (1) no marking, (2) appropriate marking in limited cases, (3) overgeneralization of marking, (4) full adult system.
- Universal 3 (based on D): the closer a grammatical system adheres to one-to-one mapping between semantic elements and surface elements, the earlier it will be acquired.
- Universal 4 (based on E): when selection of an appropriate inflection among a group of inflections performing the same semantic function is determined by arbitrary formal criteria (e.g. phonological shape of word stem, number of syllables in stem, arbitrary gender), the child initially tends to use a single form in all environments.
- Universal 5: semantically consistent grammatical rules are acquired early and without significant error.

By 1985, the list of operating principles had reached forty, and they had become much more sophisticated, using evidence from L1 acquisition in a range of languages. However, the above examples suffice to give us a picture of the approach adopted, as they represent the basis for further fine-tuning of the theory.

4.2.2 *Operating principles* **and** *second language acquisition*

In second language acquisition, operating principles have been investigated mainly by Andersen (see for example Andersen 1984, 1990; Andersen and Shirai 1994). Andersen's principles are based on Slobin's, but are then adapted to the learning of second languages (1990, pp. 51–63).

> The One-to-one principle: An interlanguage system should be constructed in such a way that an intended underlying meaning is expressed with one clear invariant surface form (or construction).

Example: Learners of German initially maintain an SVO word order in all contexts, in spite of the fact that German word order is not so consistent (Clahsen 1984).

> The multifunctionality principle: (a) Where there is clear evidence in the input that more than one form marks the meaning conveyed by only one form in the interlanguage, try to discover the distribution and additional meaning (if any) of the new form. (b) Where there is evidence in the input that an interlanguage form conveys only one of the meanings that the same form has in the input, try to discover the additional meanings of the form in the input.

Example: The one-to-one principle means that learners of English will often start with just one form for negation, e.g. *no the dog; he no go*, but once this form has been incorporated into their interlanguage, they are able to notice other forms and differentiate the environment in which they occur.

> The principle of formal determinism: When the form-meaning relationship is clearly and uniformly encoded in the input, the learner will discover it earlier than the other form-meaning relationships and will incorporate it more consistently within his interlanguage system. In short, the clear, transparent encoding of the linguistic feature in the input forces the learner to discover it.

Example: If we consider the example of English negation above, the learner will be driven from the use of a single form to the use of multiple forms because the distribution of such forms in English is transparent (*don't* in pre-verbal environments, *not* with noun phrases, adverbs, etc.).

> The principle of distributional bias: If both X and Y can occur in the same environments A and B, but a bias in the distribution of X and Y makes it appear that X only occurs in environment A and Y only occurs in environment B, when you acquire X and Y, restrict X to environment A and Y to environment B.

Example: In Spanish, punctual verbs (e.g. *break*) occur mainly in the preterite form, and verbs of states (e.g. *know*) mainly in the imperfect form, making the preterite much more common in the input. Second language learners of Spanish reproduce this bias, and acquire the preterite form earlier.

> The relevance principle (based on Bybee 1985 and presented by Slobin 1985, in the following way): If two or more functors apply to a content word, try to place them so that the more relevant the meaning of a functor is to the meaning of the content word, the closer it is placed to the content word. If you find that a Notion is marked in several places, at first mark it only in the position closest to the relevant content word.

Example: Andersen's research on SLA of Spanish verb morphology (see Andersen and Shirai 1994) broadly supports the prediction that aspect should be encoded before tense, as it is most relevant to the lexical item it is attached to (the verb), and that tense would be next since it has wider scope than aspect, but is more relevant to the verb than subject-verb agreement which would be last.

> The transfer to somewhere principle: A grammatical form or structure will occur consistently and to a significant extent in the interlanguage as a result of

transfer if and only if (1) natural acquisitional principles are consistent with the L1 structure or (2) there already exists within the L2 input the potential for (mis)generalization from the input to produce the same form or structure. Furthermore, in such transfer preference is given in the resulting interlanguage to free, invariant, functionally simple morphemes which are congruent with the L1 and L2 (or there is congruence between the L1 and natural acquisitional processes) and [to] morphemes [which] occur frequently in the L1 and/or the L2.

Example: Unlike English learners of French who follow English word order for the placement of French clitic object pronouns, French learners of English do not follow the French word order for clitic placement. This is because no model for such transfer is available in the input, whereas French provides a model for post-verbal placement of objects in the case of lexical noun-phrases.

> The relexification principle: When you cannot perceive the structural pattern used by the language you are trying to acquire, use your native language structure with lexical items from the second language.

Example: Japanese learners of English sometimes use Japanese SOV word order in English in the early stages, with English lexical items.

In a detailed review of both first and second language acquisition of tense and aspect, Andersen and Shirai (1994) conclude that the data can best be explained by just three principles (Relevance, Congruence and One-to-one).

> Learners restrict use of verb morphology such as past/perfective, progressive, and imperfective to a small subset of the verbs to which the morphology could be attached in fluent adult native speakers' language use. We attribute this early conservative use of verb morphology to adherence to (a) the Relevance principle (which guides learners to look for morphological marking relevant to the meaning of the verb), (b) the Congruence Principle (which guides learners to associate verb morphology with verb types most congruent with the aspectual meaning of the verb inflection), and (c) the One to One Principle (which causes learners to expect each newly discovered form to have one and only one meaning, function, and distribution).
>
> (1994, pp. 151–2)

4.2.3 *Learnability/Teachability theory*

There are other researchers who have appealed to similar psychological principles in order to explain SLA phenomena. Pienemann (1987, 1989, 1992a, 1992b) and Wolfe Quintero (1992), for example, have both proposed a number of learning principles which second language learners use and which supposedly explain developmental stages.

The notion of *learnability* arises from the well-documented observation (see Chapter 2) that second language learners follow a fairly rigid *route* in their acquisition of certain grammatical structures. This notion of route implies that structures only become 'learnable' when the previous steps on this acquisitional path have been acquired. In other words, learners cannot acquire a complex structure straight away, but have to follow the developmental route associated to this structure.

Moreover, in the *teachability* dimension of his theory, Pienemann considers the pedagogical implications of the learnability model, and draws precise conclusions about how some structures should be taught. If a structure only becomes learnable when the previous steps have been acquired, it follows that, by looking at the productions of a language learner and placing them on the developmental continuum for a given structure, the teacher can assess what this learner can be expected to learn next.

Pienemann's work on the teachability/learnability hypothesis is largely based on findings of the ZISA project (Zweitspracherwerb Italienischer, Spanischer und Portugiesischer Arbeiter: see for example Meisel *et al.* 1981). This project worked with Italian, Spanish, Portuguese and later Turkish (Clahsen and Muysken 1986) learners of German in an untutored setting (they were all migrant workers). One of the major findings is that there is a clear developmental route in the acquisition of German word order (a complex and much studied feature of the German language).

The developmental stages which Pienemann and his colleagues describe are as follows.[2]

Stage 1: Canonical Order (SVO)
          Die kinder spielen mim ball (= the children play with the ball)
          Learners' initial hypothesis is that German is SVO, with adverbials in sentence-final position. (This is true of Romance learners; Turkish learners' initial canonical order hypothesis reflects their L1.)
Stage 2: Adverb preposing
          Da kinder spielen (= there children play)
          Learners now place the adverb in sentence initial position, but keep the SVO order (no verb-subject inversion yet).
Stage 3: Verb separation
          Aller kinder muss die pause machen (= all children must the pause have)
          Learners place the non-finite verbal element in clause-final position.
Stage 4: Verb-second
          Dann hat sie wieder die knoch gebringt (= then has she again the bone brought)
          Learners now place the verb in sentence-second position, resulting in verb-subject inversion.
Stage 5: Verb-final in subordinate clauses
          Er sagte dass er nach hause kommt (= he said that he to home comes)
          Learners place the finite verb in clause-final position in subordinate clauses.

Pienemann's explanation of these stages is in terms of processing complexity. Learners first adopt a canonical order which reflects the way in which they perceive events (Actor – Action – Acted-upon). When learners realize that German does not consistently follow this canonical order, they are constrained by processing limitations in the hypotheses they can make. They are first able to move elements from inside the sentence to the outside, i.e. to sentence-initial or -final positions, then from outside to inside, and finally to move elements within the sentence. This is because the beginning and end of sentences are believed to be more salient perceptually. Within these general constraints, it is easier to move elements if they do not disrupt continuous constituents. That is the reason why adverb fronting happens before verb separation; both involve movement from inside to outside, but verb separation also involves separating finite and non-finite parts of the verb. Finally, learners assume that word order is invariant whatever the clause. German word order in subordinate clauses is different from that of main clauses, and is therefore acquired at a later stage.

In his teachability hypothesis, Pienemann argues that teaching can only be effective if learners have successfully passed through the preceding stages on the developmental route. When a learner shows signs of having reached a developmental stage, however, teaching can then speed up the acquisition process. The link Pienemann establishes between learning and teaching is interesting if only because SLA researchers rarely attempt to assess the pedagogical implications of their research, and researchers interested in pedagogy rarely assess language learning theories.

4.3 Connectionism or parallel distributed processing models

The *connectionist* (previously known as associationist) approach to learning has been around for some time, but it is only recently that advances in computer technology have given it a new breath of life. The 1980s and 1990s have witnessed an impressive wealth of studies adopting a connectionist framework to the study of memory and learning. Very recently, connectionism has been applied to L2 learning.

Connectionism, or parallel distributed processing (PDP) likens the brain to a computer which would consist of *neural networks*, complex clusters of links between information nodes. These links or connections become strengthened or weakened through activation or non-activation respectively. Learning in this view occurs on the basis of associative processes, rather than the construction of abstract rules. In other words, the human mind is predisposed to look for associations between elements and create links between them. These links become stronger as these associations keep recurring, and they also become part of larger networks as connections between elements become more numerous. When applied to the learning of language, connectionism claims that learners are sensitive to regularities in the language input (i.e. the regular co-occurrence of particular language forms), and extract probabilistic patterns on the basis of these regularities. Learning occurs as these patterns become strengthened by repeated activation.

> Connectionism attempts to develop computationally explicit parallel distrib-
> uted processing (PDP) models of implicit learning in well-understood, con-
> strained, and controllable experimental learning environments. The models
> allow the assessment of just how much of language acquisition can be done by
> extraction of probabilistic patterns of grammatical and morphological regu-
> larities. Because the only relation in connectionist models is strength of associ-
> ation between nodes, they are excellent modelling media in which to investigate
> the formation of associations as a result of exposure to language.
>
> (N. Ellis and Schmidt 1997, p. 153)

An example of a connectionist network from Elman *et al.* 1996, p. 51 is
shown in Figure 4.1. The connectionist approach differs strikingly from the
accounts we have reviewed so far, as it does not believe that the learning of
rules underlies the construction of linguistic knowledge, but rather that this
happens through the associative processes we have just described. This goes
against everything that linguists have taken as a starting point, namely that
language is a set of rules (syntax, morphology, phonology) with an accompanying lexicon, and that the task facing language learners is to extract those
rules from the language around them in order to build up their own mental
set of those rules, as well as learning the lexicon which will then fit into the
slots made available by the grammar. Saying, as connectionists do, that learning is not rule-governed, but is based on the construction of associative patterns, is a fundamental departure from currently held views. Connectionism
in that view is seen as an alternative to symbolic accounts of language acquisition: rule-like behaviour does not imply rule-governed behaviour (N. Ellis
1996b, p. 364).

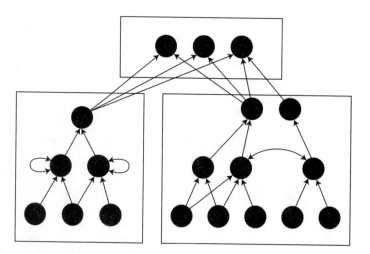

Fig. 4.1 A complex network consisting of several modules
Note: Arrows indicate the direction of flow of excitation/inhibition.

This approach does not deal exclusively with the construction of linguistic knowledge (or competence), but also with how this linguistic knowledge

is accessed and used (performance). In fact, it does not draw any distinction between the two. The creation and then the strengthening of interconnections are both seen as arising from the same associative processes.

4.3.1   *Connectionism and L1 acquisition*

Researchers working within this framework have been testing their hypotheses by designing computer models which are programmed to build the kind of neural networks which become established within the human mind as learning takes place. These models create networks on the basis of the input (linguistic or otherwise) they receive. The computer is then presented with novel input, and the output of the model is compared to natural (human) output. Let us illustrate what is meant with a concrete example, taken from the pioneering work of Rumelhart and McClelland (1986).

These researchers devised a computer model to simulate learning the regular versus irregular past tense in English, on the basis of associative patterns. It is well known that children go through three phases in the acquisition of irregular past tenses in English. In the first phase, they produce irregular past tense forms correctly (e.g. *went, fell*); in the second phase, they overgeneralize the regular past tense ending to irregular verbs (e.g. *goed, falled*); in the third phase they supply irregular forms correctly again. This pattern is usually explained by claiming that children start by rote-learning a few common past tense forms (many of the common verbs in early child language are irregular, e.g. *go, eat, fall, throw, sleep, come, give*, etc.), and only later extract from the linguistic input the rule that the past tense is most commonly formed by adding *-ed* to the verb. Children then apply this general rule to all verbs indiscriminately, before being able to allow exceptions.

Rumelhart and McClelland's simple learning model reproduced closely the way in which children acquire the past tense in English, including the typical U-shaped curve of learning for irregular verbs. The computer generalized on the basis of stored examples in a similar way to children. Although this early model was criticized (e.g. Pinker and Prince 1988), it has given rise to many further studies in recent years, which have addressed some of the criticisms (N. Ellis and Schmidt 1997; MacWhinney and Leinbach, 1991; Plunkett and Marchman 1991).

4.3.1   *Connectionism and L2 acquisition*

In second language acquisition, a number of researchers have explored connectionism recently (e.g. N. Ellis and Schmidt 1997; Gasser 1990; MacWhinney 1989; MacWhinney and Chang 1995; Sokolik 1990; Sokolik and Smith 1992). We will concentrate here on two studies, that of Sokolik and Smith (1992), and that of N. Ellis and Schmidt (1997).

Sokolik and Smith (1992) investigated the assignment of gender to French nouns using a connectionist framework. In French, nouns are marked for gender, either masculine or feminine, with little semantic basis for gender assignment. However, noun endings represent a good clue to their gender with, for example, nouns ending in *-ette* or *-tion* being feminine, and nouns ending in *-eur* or *-on* being generally masculine. Although noun endings are not a foolproof way of determining gender, they are none the less predictive, and young French-speaking children have been shown to assign gender to novel nouns as well as nonsense nouns on the basis of these regularities. In fact, children learning French as an L1 do not seem to have much problem with gender assignment, which is thought to be acquired by age three (Clark 1985). Gender assignment for L2 learners, on the other hand, seems to remain problematic for a substantial period of time.

Sokolik and Smith devised a computer-based connectionist-type network model which learned to identify correctly the gender of a set of French nouns. The model was then able to generalize from that learning experience and assign gender to previously unstudied nouns with a high degree of reliability. The model assigned gender by relying solely upon information inherent in the structure of the nouns themselves, i.e. it relied exclusively on the orthography of the noun itself, to the exclusion of any other clues such as adjective or pronoun agreement, or semantic clues. In other words, the computer seemed to be able to assign gender accurately to novel nouns on the basis of the regularities (associative patterns) it had 'observed' in the input.

Learning in this view is thought to take place as the strength of given interconnections between nodes increases as the associative patterns are repeated over time. What is important to remember from this type of account is that the learner does not extract rules and then apply them (in this case the fact that gender assignment in French is not random but obeys certain orthographic and phonetic rules), but merely registers associative patterns which become strengthened with use.

> We have outlined a relatively simple model that is capable of learning the gender of a large set of French nouns. It accomplished this without relying on article or adjective agreement, without knowledge of noun meaning, and without being programmed with (or inferring) explicit morphological or phonological rules of gender formation. Rather it 'learned' that certain features (in this case, orthographic) of French nouns are correlated with particular genders. Based only on this information, it was able to classify at a high rate of reliability the gender of nouns it had never before encountered.
>
> These studies provide evidence that gender can in principle be assigned during relatively low-level perceptual analysis without the application of explicit rules.
>
> (Sokolik and Smith 1992, p. 50)

The difference between L1 learners who do not seem to encounter problems with gender assignment, and L2 learners who persist in making gender assignment errors in advanced stages, is explained by changing two of the variables in the model. First, whereas the computer model assigned L1 learners a zero-state of connectivity (they have not formed any associative patterns yet and are therefore starting as a blank slate), it assumed that L2 learners come to the task with some pre-existing pattern of connectivity which interferes with the task in hand. Second, this particular model also assigned a lower learning rate to second language learners, to reflect the researchers' belief that children seem to be better language learners than adults. With these variables built into the programme, Sokolik and Smith were able to simulate the development of gender assignment in L1 and L2 learning.

If the acquisition of gender assignment can be explained quite successfully using a connectionist model (though see Carroll 1995 for a critique), it could be argued that it is not representative of rules of grammar generally. All the computer had to do was to assign gender; the accompanying agreement features were not part of the study. If we now turn to (arguably more complex) morphosyntactic rules, what have connectionist models to offer?

N. Ellis and Schmidt (1997) have investigated the claim made by Rumelhart and McClelland (1986) that a connectionist model reproduced very closely the way in which children acquire the past tense in English (discussed above) and the counter-claim made by Pinker (1991), who argued that only irregular verbs are retrieved from an associative memory (the kind of connectionist network we have described). For Pinker, regular verbs are produced as a result of a suffixation rule (i.e. a symbolic rule rather than merely an associative pattern).

Using an artificial language in a laboratory situation, so that exposure and proficiency could be monitored closely, they investigated the adult acquisition of plural morphology. Half of the plurals were regular, i.e. shared the same affix, and half were irregular. Frequency was also a variable built into the study, with half the plurals being five times more frequent than the other half. Exactly the same input was fed into a simple connectionist model. They found that the results obtained from their connectionist model accurately mirrored their human data, and they conclude that associative mechanisms are all that are needed in order to explain the acquisition of plural morphology, and that we do not need the hybrid system suggested by Pinker (1991) in which the regular would be rule-governed and the irregular associative: 'These effects are readily explained by simple associative theories of learning. It is not necessary to invoke underlying rule-governed processes' (N. Ellis and Schmidt 1997, p. 152).

4.3.3 *Evaluation of connectionism in SLA*

After this brief account of the connectionist framework as applied to second language acquisition, let us briefly point out its most distinctive methodological features, as it differs so fundamentally from the type of studies we consider elsewhere in this book. One obvious feature is connectionism's reliance on controlled laboratory research, often involving experiments with artificial languages or fragments of real languages. This is due to the fact that the connectionist approach stems directly from the field of psychology, where such a degree of control is common. From one point of view, that of control of extraneous variables, this can be seen as an advantage.

> Laboratory research offers a number of important advantages over research conducted with L2 learners in classrooms or with uninstructed, so-called natural learners: control of the language and the target structures to be learned, control of exposure, control of instruction (explanation), control of tasks, and control of response measurement.
>
> (Hulstijn 1997, pp. 139–40)

However, the controlled nature of laboratory research can also be seen as a disadvantage. It is questionable how far you can isolate variables which would interact in a natural context, and therefore how far results obtained in that way actually mirror what happens in real life. Moreover, because of the highly controlled nature of laboratory experiments, the questions being asked tend to be very specific and local, with the resulting danger of ignoring how different aspects of the learning process might interact. Connectionists have tended to concentrate on simple, discrete, language phenomena: 'However, the more controlled the design and the more specific the learning task, the more we bear the risk of not studying L2 acquisition any more, but only participants' capacity to carry out some kind of cognitive puzzle' (de Graaff 1997, p. 272).

A further distinctive feature of connectionism resides in the links it attempts to build with neurology and even neurobiology. Connectionists believe that we have to study learning within the actual architecture of the brain, and make use of neurological information. As N. Ellis and Schmidt put it:

> The advantages of connectionist models over traditional symbolic models are that (a) they are neurally inspired, (b) they incorporate distributed representation and control of information, (c) they are data-driven with prototypical representations emerging as a natural outcome of the learning process rather than being prespecified and innately given by the modelers as in more nativist cognitive accounts, (d) they show graceful degradation as do humans with language disorders, and (e) they are in essence models of learning and acquisition rather than static descriptions. Two distinctive aspects of the connectionist approach are its strong emphasis on general learning principles and its attempt to make contact with neurobiological as well as cognitive phenomena.
>
> (1997, p. 154)

We will certainly hear a lot more about connectionism applied to SLA, and it is an exciting and promising new avenue for research. However, at present, the models which have been applied to the study of second language acquisition have been concerned with the acquisition of very simple, often artificial data, far removed from the richness and complexity of natural languages, and it is still questionable how much we can learn from these experiments about language learning in 'real' situations.

4.4 Information processing models

The work we will be discussing under this heading originates from information processing models developed by cognitive psychologists, which have then been adapted to the treatment of language processing, both L1 and L2. First, we examine McLaughlin's (1987, 1990) information processing model. Second, we will turn our attention to Anderson's ACT* model (1983, 1985), paying particular attention to O'Malley and Chamot's application of the model in the field of learner strategies (1990) and to Towell and Hawkins' (1994) application in the development of fluency. We will then review the 'communication strategies' literature in a final section (Kasper and Kellerman 1997).

4.4.1 McLaughlin's information processing model

> In general, the fundamental notion of the information-processing approach to psychological inquiry is that complex behaviour builds on simple processes.
> (McLaughlin and Heredia, 1996, p. 213)

Moreover, these processes are modular and can therefore be studied independently of one another. The main characteristics of such an approach can be summarized as follows.

1 Humans are viewed as autonomous and active.
2 The mind is a general-purpose, symbol-processing system.
3 Complex behaviour is composed of simpler processes. These processes are modular.
4 Component processes can be isolated and studied independently of other processes.
5 Processes take time; therefore, predictions about reaction time can be made.
6 The mind is a limited-capacity processor.

When applied to second language learning, this approach can be summarized as follows.

> Within this framework, second language learning is viewed as the acquisition of a complex cognitive skill. To learn a second language is to learn a *skill*, because various aspects of the task must be practised and integrated into fluent performance. This requires the automatization of component sub-skills. Learning is a *cognitive* process, because it is thought to involve internal representations that regulate and guide performance ... As performance improves, there is constant restructuring as learners simplify, unify, and gain increasing control over their internal representations (Karmiloff-Smith 1986a). These two notions – automatization and restructuring – are central to cognitive theory.
> (McLaughlin 1987, pp. 133–4)

Automatization (McLaughlin 1987, 1990; McLaughlin and Heredia 1996) is a notion based on the work of psychologists such as Shiffrin and Schneider

(1977) who claim that the way in which we process information may be either controlled or automatic, and that learning involves a shift from controlled towards automatic processing. Applied to second language learning, such a model works as follows.

1 Learners first resort to *controlled processing* in the L2. This controlled processing involves the temporary activation of a selection of information nodes in the memory, in a new configuration. Such processing requires a lot of attentional control on the part of the subject, and is constrained by the limitations of the *Short-Term Memory* (STM).

2 Through repeated activation, sequences first produced by controlled processing become *automatic*. Automatized sequences are stored as units in the *Long-Term Memory* (LTM), which means that they can be made available very rapidly whenever the situation requires it, with minimal attentional control on the part of the subject. As a result, automatic processes can work in parallel, activating clusters of complex cognitive skills simultaneously. However, once acquired, such automatised skills are difficult to delete or modify.

3 *Learning* in this view is seen as the movement from controlled to automatic processing via practice (repeated activation). When this shift occurs, controlled processes are freed to deal with higher levels of processing (i.e. to the integration of more complex skill clusters), thus explaining the incremental (step by step) nature of learning. It is necessary for simple subskills and routines to become automatic before more complex ones can be tackled.

4 This continuing movement from controlled to automatic processing results in a constant *restructuring* of the linguistic system of the L2 learner. This phenomenon may account for the some of the variability characteristic of learner language; restructuring destabilizes some structures in the interlanguage, which seemed to have been previously acquired, and hence leads to the temporary reappearance of L2 errors.

This account is also especially convincing in its explanation of the vexed issue of *fossilization* which is so well documented in SLA studies. As we saw in Chapter 1, fossilization refers to the fact that L2 learners, unlike L1 learners, sometimes seem unable to get rid of non-native-like structures in their L2 in spite of abundant linguistic input over many years. Fossilization in this model would arise as a result of a controlled process becoming automatic before it is native-like. As we have seen, automatic processes are difficult to modify as they are outside the attentional control of the subject. Thus they are likely to remain in the learner's interlanguage, giving rise to a stable but erroneous construction.

4.4.2   Anderson's ACT* model

Another processing model from cognitive psychology which has also been applied to aspects of second language learning is Anderson's ACT* model (Adaptive Control of Thought: 1983, 1985).[3] This model is not dissimilar to McLaughlin's. It is more wide-ranging, and the terminology is different, but practice leading to automatization also plays a central role. It enables *declarative knowledge* (i.e. knowledge *that*, not unlike controlled processes) to become *procedural knowledge* (i.e. knowledge *how*, not unlike automatic knowledge). One of the major differences is that Anderson posits three kinds of memory: a working memory, similar to McLaughlin's short-term memory (STM) and therefore tightly capacity-limited, and two kinds of long-term memories (LTMs), a declarative LTM and a procedural LTM. Anderson believes that declarative and procedural knowledge are different kinds of knowledge which are stored differently.

But before outlining the way in which the different kinds of memories work and interact, let us illustrate with a simple example what is meant by declarative and procedural knowledge. If you are learning to drive for example, you will be told that if the engine is revving too much, you need to change to a higher gear; you will also be told how to change gear. In the early stages of learning to drive, however, *knowing that* (declarative knowledge) you have to do this does not necessarily mean that you *know how* (procedural knowledge) to do it successfully. In other words, you go through a declarative stage before acquiring the procedural knowledge linked with this situation. With practice, however, the mere noise of the engine getting louder will trigger your gear changing, without you even having to think about it. This is how learning takes place in this view, by declarative knowledge becoming procedural.

Anderson's application of his model to first language acquisition (1983) has been criticized for insisting that all knowledge starts out in declarative form (DeKeyser 1997); this is clearly problematic in the case of L1 learners (though Anderson has answered some of the early criticisms of his model's application to language learning and does not claim that all knowledge needs to start as declarative knowledge any more: Anderson and Fincham 1994; MacWhinney and Anderson 1986). However, other applications, e.g. to the learning of algebra, geometry or computer programming have been very successful. Indeed, it is the comparability of the teaching/learning of second languages in tutored environments with the teaching/learning of complex skills such as algebra which has attracted the attention of SLA researchers. Because Anderson's model is a general cognitive model of skill acquisition, it can be applied to those aspects of second language learning which require proceduralization and automatization (Johnson 1996; O'Malley and Chamot 1990; Raupach 1987; Schmidt 1992; Towell and Hawkins 1994).

Let us illustrate with an example how the notions of declarative versus procedural knowledge apply to second language learning. If we take the example of the third person singular -s marker on present tense verbs in English, the classroom learner might initially know, in the sense that they have consciously learnt the rule, that s/he + verb requires the addition of an -s to the stem of the verb. However, that same learner might not necessarily be able to consistently produce the -s in a conversation in real time. This is because this particular learner has declarative knowledge of that rule, but it has not yet been proceduralized. After much practice, this knowledge will hopefully become fully proceduralized, and the third person -s will be supplied when the conversation requires it. This dichotomy between, on the one hand, knowing a rule, and on the other, being able to apply it when needed, is all too familiar to second language learners and teachers.

According to Anderson, the move from declarative to procedural knowledge takes place in three stages (Anderson 1985, p. 232, cited in Towell and Hawkins 1994, p. 203) as follows.

1 *The cognitive stage*: A description of the procedure is learned.
2 *The associative stage*: A method for performing the skill is worked out.
3 *The autonomous stage*: The skill becomes more and more rapid and automatic.

In the examples outlined above, in the cognitive stage, the learner would learn that the clutch pedal has to be pushed down and the gear lever moved to the correct position or, in the case of the language example, that an -s must be added to the verb after a third person subject. In the associative stage, the learner would work out how to do it, i.e. how to press the pedal down and how to get the gear lever in the correct position, or how to add an -s when the context requires it. In other words, the learner learns to associate an action (or a set of actions) with the corresponding declarative knowledge. In the autonomous stage, our learner's actions (changing gear or adding an -s) become increasingly automatic, to the point that the corresponding declarative knowledge may (although not necessarily) be lost; in other words, our learner might not be able to explain or even be conscious of what they are doing.

In the same way as with McLaughlin's model, we can also see how this model would explain the incremental nature of learning. When tasks become proceduralized, they are accessed automatically, without having to resort to the working memory which is limited in its processing capacity. Therefore, new declarative knowledge can be attended to and thereafter proceed through the associative and eventually autonomous stages.

Proceduralization presents similar advantages and disadvantages as McLaughlin's automatization process. Procedularized knowledge is available quickly and efficiently, and does not make many demands on the working memory; it will be difficult to modify, however, and will be applicable only to the situation that gave rise to it. It will also need time and the same routine will have to be activated successfully a large number of times, in order to become proceduralized. Each time the procedure is applied successfully, it is strengthened and thereafter called upon more easily. To illustrate this shift from declarative to procedural knowledge in the context of L2 learning, Anderson himself speculated that:

> When we learn a foreign language in classroom situation, we are aware of the rules of the language, especially just after a lesson that spells them out. One might argue that our knowledge of the language at that time is declarative. We speak the learned language by using general rule-following procedures applied to the rules we have learned, rather than speaking directly, as we do in our native language. Not surprisingly, applying this knowledge is a much slower and painful process than applying the procedurally encoded knowledge of our own language. Eventually, if we are lucky, we can come to know a foreign language as well as we know our native language. At that point, we often forget the rules of the foreign language. It is as if the class-taught declarative knowledge had been transformed into a procedural form.
>
> (1980, p. 224)

Here we see the basic suggestion that the learner's speech becomes more fluent as more knowledge becomes proceduralized, and is therefore accessed more quickly and efficiently. We can also see how learning is an incremental process: as knowledge becomes proceduralized, the working memory is freed to work on higher-level knowledge.

Johnson (1996) has pursued the application of Anderson's model to explicit classroom instruction. However, most contemporary theorists of L2 learning, from whatever perspective, would not now agree with the implied position taken by Anderson (1980), that all or most of L2 grammar is initially learned through the conscious study and application of explicit rules. Even for classroom learners, there is a consensus that much grammar learning takes place without conscious awareness, whether by the operation of a specific language module, or by general cognitive processes. Some information processing theorists have responded to this problem by suggesting that the 'declarative knowledge' component can be subdivided into conscious and unconscious parts (e.g. Bialystok 1991). Others have argued that information processing models are most helpful in explaining complementary strands in L2 learning. In the following sections we see how Anderson's model has been applied to two such strands: to the application of learning strategies to the L2 learning problem, and to the development of L2 fluency.

4.5   Learning strategies

This section will examine how the ACT* model has been applied to the field of language learning strategies, by researchers such as O'Malley and Chamot (1990). Learning strategies are procedures undertaken by the learner, in order to make their own language learning as effective as possible. They may include:

> focusing on selected aspects of new information, analyzing and monitoring information during acquisition, organizing or elaborating on new information

during the encoding process, evaluating the learning when it is completed, or assuring oneself that the learning will be successful as a way to allay anxiety.

(O'Malley and Chamot 1990, p. 43)

Learning strategies must not be confused with communication strategies which we will discuss later, although there is some overlap; their focus is on facilitating learning, whereas communication strategies are used in order to overcome a specific communicative problem. Learning strategies can be classified into three categories, as exemplified in Table 4.1 (O'Malley and Chamot 1990, p. 46). In O'Malley and Chamot's view:

> learning strategies are complex procedures that individuals apply to tasks; consequently, they may be represented as procedural knowledge which may be acquired through cognitive, associative, and autonomous stages of learning. As with other procedural skills at the different stages of learning, the strategies may be conscious in early stages of learning and later be performed without the person's awareness.
>
> (1990, p. 52)

Thus, strategies have to be learned in exactly the same way as other complex cognitive skills. A good language learner will be a learner who has proceduralized the strategies described in Table 4.1. Remember that before a skill is proceduralized, it will have to compete for working memory space with other aspects of the task in hand; as the working memory is tightly capacity-limited, learning strategies which have not yet been fully proceduralized might not be applied because of competing demands.

An obvious pedagogical implication of such a view is that L2 learners would benefit from being taught learning strategies. If learning strategies are a skill, then they can be taught, with the advantage that they will become proceduralized more quickly, therefore freeing working-memory space for other aspects of learning. A problem raised by O'Malley and Chamot is that teaching strategies will involve a considerable investment of time and effort in order to be effective (before the skills taught can become proceduralized), and we therefore need long-term studies investigating the effect of strategy teaching. Their own research does suggest some positive effect of strategy teaching on vocabulary development, listening comprehension, and oral production.

O'Malley and Chamot (1990, p. 217) sum up the general benefits of applying cognitive theory to the field of second language acquisition as follows.

- Learning is an active and dynamic process in which individuals make use of a variety of information and strategic modes of processing.
- Language is a complex cognitive skill that has properties in common with other complex skills in terms of how information is stored and learned.
- Learning a language entails a stagewise progression from initial awareness and active manipulation of information and learning processes to full automaticity in language use; and
- Learning strategies parallel theoretically derived cognitive processes and have the potential to influence learning outcomes in a positive manner.

Table 4.1 Classification of learning strategies

Generic strategy classification	Representative strategies	Definitions
Metacognitive strategies	Selective attention	Focusing on special aspects of learning tasks, as in planning to listen for key words or phrases.
	Planning	Planning for the organization of either written or spoken discourse.
	Monitoring	Reviewing attention to a task, comprehension of information that should be remembered, or production while it is occurring.
	Evaluation	Checking comprehension after completion of a receptive language activity, or evaluating language production after it has taken place.
Cognitive strategies	Rehearsal	Repeating the names of items or objects to be remembered.
	Organization	Grouping and classifying words, terminology, or concepts according to their semantic or syntactic attributes.
	Inferencing	Using information in text to guess meanings of new linguistic items, predict outcomes, or complete missing parts.
	Summarizing	Intermittently synthesizing what one has heard to ensure the information has been retained.
	Deducing	Applying rules to the understanding of language.
	Imagery	Using visual images (either generated or actual) to understand and remember new verbal information.
	Transfer	Using known linguistic information to facilitate a new learning task.
	Elaboration	Linking ideas contained in new information, or integrating new ideas with known information.
Social/affective strategies	Co-operation	Working with peers to solve a problem, pool information, check notes, or get feedback on a learning activity.
	Questioning for clarification	Eliciting from a teacher or peer additional explanation, rephrasing, or examples.
	Self-talk	Using mental redirection of thinking to assure oneself that a learning activity will be successful or to reduce anxiety about a task.

Source: O'Malley and Chamot 1990, p. 43

O'Malley and Chamot are clear, however, that such an approach does not concern itself with the language learning route followed by learners. It deals exclusively with the rate of learning and how learning strategies can influence it.

> The cognitive theory described in this book is largely a theory of learning processes and not theory that specifies precisely what is learned, what content will be easiest (or most difficult) to learn, or what learners will select to learn at different stages of development or levels of mastery of a complex skill.
>
> (O'Malley and Chamot 1990, p. 216)

4.6   Fluency development in SLA

In a comprehensive review of the psychological mechanisms underlying fluency, Schmidt (1992) analyses and evaluates how well a range of current psychological models account for fluency and fluency development in learners. We refer the reader to this work for an insightful overview, and we will concentrate here on one illustration of the application of psychological models to the development of fluency. We will outline how Towell and Hawkins (1994) have incorporated aspects of the ACT* model into their overall model of second language learning, in order to account for fluency development.

Towell and Hawkins (1994) reject the idea that Anderson's model can account for all aspects of L2 learning, notably the acquisition of 'core' grammatical knowledge. They have used models of natural language processing such as Anderson's and Levelt's (1989) primarily in order to explain how grammatical knowledge becomes transformed into fluent performance in the second language. Their model (Towell and Hawkins 1994, p. 248, shown here as Figure 4.2) attempts to integrate how learners learn the L2 system with how they learn to use the system. In order to explain why certain grammatical structures appear before others, and why learners go through fairly rigid stages in their acquisition of second languages, they resort to a Universal Grammar approach. In order to understand how learners use this grammatical knowledge in increasingly efficient ways (hopefully!), Towell and Hawkins appeal to an information processing account.

As can be seen from Figure 4.2, the internally derived hypotheses about L2 structure (shaped by UG and the L1) are stored in different ways in the mind at different stages of the learning process. In a first stage, a hypothesis will be stored in the declarative long-term memory (controlled). (In Towell and Hawkins' account, declarative knowledge may be implicit or explicit, and the learner will not normally have any conscious analysed knowledge of such UG-derived hypotheses.) When put to use, this kind of internally derived knowledge will give rise to a production stored in the procedural long-term memory, initially in 'associative' form (i.e. under attentional control from the learner). The hypothesis may then be revised and cause some reorganization of the declarative knowledge, which will then give rise to other revised productions. Eventually, after successive reorganizations, these productions will

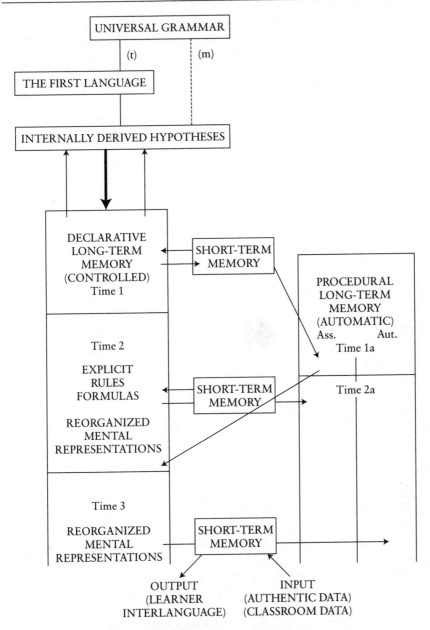

Fig. 4.2 Towell and Hawkins' model of second language acquisition

become autonomous (i.e. automatized and free from attentional control) and are stored as such in the 'autonomous' part of the procedural memory. This model allows Towell and Hawkins to make a number of specific claims concerning different kinds of learning (1994, pp. 250–1).

- Internally-derived hypotheses about L2 structure, if confirmed by external data, will give rise to a production which will be stored in procedural memory, first in associative form and eventually in autonomous form.
- Formulas, that is form-function pairs which have been learned as routines (e.g. *What's your name?* produced in the absence of a creative rule for the formation of interrogatives), can be stored in the procedural memory at the associative level, before going back to declarative memory for re-analysis under controlled processes, and can finally be stored as an autonomous procedure when all stages of analysis and re-analysis have been completed.
- Explicit rules (e.g. verb conjugations) can be learned and stored as proce-duralized knowledge. As such, they will only be recalled as a list of verb-endings. But, if they can go back to the declarative memory in order to undergo a controlled process of analysis by interacting with internally derived hypotheses, they might eventually also give rise to autonomous productions available for language use.
- Learning strategies, by facilitating the proceduralization of mechanisms for faster processing of linguistic input, are incorporated in the information processing part of the model, without having to interact with internal hypotheses.

This model attempts to reconcile internal, UG-derived hypotheses about L2 structure with what actually happens to these hypotheses during the processes of language learning and language use. It thus represents an ambitious attempt to link together linguistic and cognitive approaches to the study of second language learning.

4.7   Communication strategies in L2 use

While learning strategies are the means adopted by the learner to maximize the effectiveness of the overall learning process, *communication strategies* are tactics used by the non-fluent learner during L2 interaction, in order to overcome specific communicative problems. The study of communication strategies (CS) is a relative newcomer in the field of SLA research. For a comprehensive review of recent work on communication strategies, see the collection edited by Kasper and Kellerman (1997), on which a substantial part of this section is based.

Initially, work within the field of communication strategies concentrated on primarily descriptive issues, to do with definition, identification and classification. More recently, explanation of CS in terms of psychological models has come to the fore. Early *definitions* tended to focus on the notion of *problem-solving*: what does a learner do when encountering a communicative difficulty? The learner resorts to mental plans or strategies in order to overcome the problem. For some researchers, communication strategies tend to be seen as some kind of 'self-help' module within the learner, located within models of speech production (e.g. Dechert 1983; Færch and Kasper 1983b), or within general models of cognitive organization and processing (Bialystok 1990).

For other researchers, CS are seen as a much more interactional, inter-individual activity in which learners solve problems by negotiating meaning (e.g. Tarone 1983). CS for these researchers are seen within the framework of conversational analysis (e.g. Wagner and Firth 1997) or sociolinguistics (e.g. Rampton 1997).

The methodology used by those two distinct approaches will also be different, with the sociolinguists tending to observe natural phenomena, while the psychologists experiment with controlled variables. Given the focus of this chapter on psychological, intra-individual approaches, we will not consider further here the sociolinguistic approach to L2 communication, which is discussed in Chapter 8.

Identification of CS usually relies on two methodological approaches, often used in parallel. The first of these is the study of *explicit strategy markers*, such as increased hesitation, or metalinguistic comments such as *I am not sure how to say this*. This is often complemented by *retrospective protocols*, in which learners are played back a tape of their own speech and are asked to identify problems they encountered and indicate how they solved them.

Classification of CS probably formed the most important part of early CS work. Early approaches tended to be taxonomic, and concentrated on the characterization of differences in strategy output, for example in terms of paraphrase, use of L1, use of L3, gestures, mime, etc.

4.7.1   A sample taxonomy of communication strategies

The focus of CS studies has been largely on the lexicon, as word-finding difficulties are much easier to identify and investigate than other communication problems, and CS taxonomies reflect this. In this section, we present one recent classification of lexical communication strategies offered by Yule and Tarone (1997). This classification is shown in Figure 4.3, (from Kasper and Kellerman 1997, p. 20).

The L2 French examples given below (taken from Bialystok 1990, p. 62) help to illustrate some of the different types of CS in the taxonomy.

- Message abandonment: 'garden hose': *Le l'eau vient de ça. C'est attaché à* ... (= The water comes out of it. It is attached to ...)
- Approximation: 'playpen': *On peut mettre un bébé dedans. Il y a comme un trou.* (= You put a baby in it. There is like a hole.)
- Word coinage: 'wooden spoon': *C'est une cuiller en bois.* (= It's a spoon of wood.)
- Circumlocution: 'can opener': *Quelque chose que tu utilises dans la cuisine quand tu veux ouvrir des bouteilles.* (= Something you use in the kitchen when you want to open bottles.)

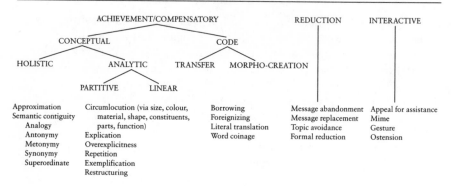

Fig. 4.3 Types of communication strategy

- Literal translation: 'beater': *C'est pour si on veut 'mixer'*. (= It's for if you want to mix.)
- Language switch: 'child's car seat': *C'est une chaise pour bébé que tu mets dans la voiture pour tu sois 'safe', sauf*. (= It's a chair for a baby that you put in a car to keep you safe.)
- Appeal for assistance: 'nail': *Je ne sais pas qu'est-ce que c'est un clou*. (= I don't know what a nail is.)

(Some of these examples show that it can be difficult to classify some of the strategies, and that they sometimes belong to more than one type, e.g. the example given for 'language switch' above is also a 'circumlocution'.)

The authors of this taxonomy are representative of researchers who are primarily interested in variability in learners and therefore in expanding and refining the list of strategies learners resort to (see also Tarone 1984; Yule and Tarone 1990). They see CS as playing an important role in second language learning, as good strategy users are seen as maximizing their learning opportunities. The teaching of CS to learners is therefore considered useful and to be encouraged. At a conceptual level, this approach is based on the belief that the study of performance, i.e. learner output, is a window on to their competence, and moreover, that performance creates competence. At a methodological level, what is of interest to these researchers is the comparison of the strategies used by L2 learners when performing a task with the strategies used by native speakers when performing the same task. This view assumes that, as L2 learners' use of CS moves closer to that of native speakers, so does their competence.

The other main psycholinguistic perspective on CS argues that taxonomies need to be both *generalizable* and *psychologically plausible*, and therefore need to be reduced to their underlying processing mechanisms. The belief in this approach is that the CS used by L2 learners are no different from the CS used by any language user, and that L2 learners will make use of the same set of CS when using their L1 and their L2 (with the obvious difference, of course, that they will encounter more difficulties in the L2 and therefore resort to CS more often). Strategic language use is part of adult competence; it has already matured and is therefore available to adults when they are learning an L2. It is part of the cognitive make-up of the individual, and as such, any taxonomy must reflect this cognitive underpinning. As strategies are already present in learners, they therefore do not need to be taught.

In the next section, we see how a model of language processing can be applied in order to account for these common features of L1 and L2 communication strategies.

4.7.2   *Communication strategies and language processing*

As we have mentioned before, CS are usually resorted to when the learner has word-finding difficulties. Any account of CS therefore has to be placed in the context of what is known about the way in which we access words in our mental lexicon. Poulisse (1993) has used a model of lexical access and applied it to the study of CS. She bases her work on Levelt's (1989) model of lexical access in monolingual speakers, and its adaptation to bilingual lexical access by De Groot (1992). The model Poulisse uses is a 'spreading activation' model of lexical access. In a very simplified manner, we can explain such a model in terms of lexical items having a list of features characterizing them. For example, a word such as *shark* might have the features [+ noun], [+ animate], [+ fish], [+ grey], [+ man-eater], and a word such as *elephant* might consist of the features [+ noun], [+ animate], [+ mammal], [+ grey], [+ enormous]. Lexical retrieval in this view consists of the narrowing of possible candidates to just the one needed. In other words, accessing the word *elephant* will involve the activation of all the words sharing some of its features: all nouns, all animates, all mammals, everything grey and everything enormous. The more features are shared, the stronger the activation; therefore, a *mouse* should be activated more strongly than, say, a *cat*, as it shares more features with *elephant* (four rather than just three). The reason for positing such a model of lexical access is that we know that accessing words in our mental lexicon activates other words in semantically related fields. The mental lexicon is seen as a complex network with words linked together not only by semantic similarities, but also by their phonological and syntactic properties.

(There are some simple tests which can show such properties of the mental lexicon convincingly. If you ask a group of people to say which word comes to their mind when you say the word, say, *egg*, you will get a limited number of answers, and the connection with the word *egg* will usually be obvious; this is because the accessing of the word *egg* has partially activated words linked to it, i.e. sharing features with it.)

An important feature of this model, therefore, is that the lexical items sharing features with the word searched for will also be activated, and increasingly so the more features they share. Applied to bilingual lexical access, a communicative strategy when access is denied is to use a lexical item which is just one feature short of the target. For example, an English learner of French trying to access the lexical item with the feature specifications [+ noun], [+ human], [+ male], [+ young], [+ in French], should ideally activate *garçon*, but also *boy* as well as *homme*, as both are only one feature away. If *garçon* is not available for any reason, the learner in this view will resort to the nearest item, in this case an item sharing all features but one. In this view, using either *boy* or *homme* would be considered as the same strategy of substituting the target item with the closest one available. This kind of strategy is termed a 'substitution' by Poulisse (1993).

The work of Poulisse is just one example of researchers having applied models of language processing to the study of communication strategies. This particular model is concerned specifically with lexical access, but other models, such as for example Bialystok's (1990) model of second language proficiency have also been applied to the study of CS (e.g. Kellerman and Bialystok 1997).

4.8 Evaluation of cognitive approaches to second language learning

In conclusion, it is clear that a wealth of studies have been carried out recently from the angle of cognitive psychology. The methods used as well as the questions asked differ substantially from more traditional second language acquisition studies which stem directly from the field of linguistics, or from a more socially oriented approach.

Psychologists make use of laboratory techniques in order to measure accurately performance indicators such as length of pauses, priming effects, etc. Linguists, on the whole, tend to apply linguistic analysis techniques to the study of second language learners' productions or intuitions. Both methodologies have their advantages and disadvantages. We have seen earlier how laboratory studies have the benefit of being able to control in a precise way the variables under study. This very fact can also be seen as a disadvantage, as it assumes one can study discrete aspects of language in isolation, without taking account of the interaction between the different language modules. Linguists, on the other hand, tend to consider language outside of the mechanisms underlying its use.

The ultimate goal of any second language acquisition model, that of better understanding the second language acquisition process, has undoubtedly been much enriched by studies of the cognitive processes involved, and we have gained new insights into the SLA process. It is clear that our understanding of how L2 learners use and process language has greatly increased, and that the development of fluency has received well-deserved attention. Cognitive approaches have also been able to enlighten us on what processes are involved in the speeding up of the acquisition process; this should of course enable us to draw pedagogical implications from such findings.

It is much less obvious whether cognitive approaches can explain adequately at the present time what the mental grammar of the learner consists of, and what constrains learners' hypotheses about the language system, although connectionist models are clearly attempting to do just that. But at the moment, the route followed by L2 learners is not convincingly explained by such approaches.

The dichotomy (between linguistic versus cognitive approaches) is somewhat crude, however, and different aspects of the second language learning process, such as the development of linguistic competence as well as the ability to use language, are increasingly becoming integrated in more complex models which take account of linguistic development as well as cognitive development.

Notes

1 Language Making Capacity: Slobin's version of Chomsky's LAD (Language Acquisition Device).
2 Pienemann cites learners without using capitals for German nouns, maybe because it is a transcription of spoken, non-standard German. NB: *mim* is the contracted form of *mit dem*.
3 The star refers to a revised and updated version of Anderson's initial ACT model. A more recent version of the ACT model is ACT-R (Anderson 1993), which we will not be discussing here.

|5|

Functional/pragmatic perspectives on second language learning

You won't understand adult language acquisition if you don't understand discourse activity.

(Perdue and Klein 1993, p. 263)

5.1 Introduction

Where do grammars come from? In Chapter 3, we encountered theorists whose main concern was with this particular question, and who have argued that because of its complexity as a formal system, the natural grammar of human language cannot be learned in its entirety, from scratch, by each individual human being, but must at least to some extent be innate. We went on to examine the work of SLA researchers who see as their central concern the understanding of how this inbuilt grammatical system develops in learners.

In this chapter, we review the work of another group of SLA researchers, who take a somewhat broader approach to the study of learners' interlanguage development. These are the researchers who adopt a functional/pragmatic approach to the study of second language learning. They typically start with the ways in which L2 learners set about making meaning, and achieving their personal communicative goals; they argue that the great variety of interlanguage forms produced by second language learners cannot be sensibly interpreted, unless we pay attention also to the functions which learners are seeking to perform. Further, it is argued that these meaning-making efforts on the part of the learner are a driving force in ongoing second language development, not excluding the development of formal grammatical systems. (The reader should note that the term 'functionalist' is being used here in a different sense from the way it is used in recent Chomskyan theory, discussed in Chapter 3.)

We begin the chapter with a brief consideration of the place of this kind of functionalist analysis in research on L1 acquisition. We then examine a number of small-scale functionalist case studies of second language learning, selected so as to illustrate key issues and principles of this approach. We then review a major research programme of the European Science Foundation (ESF), which examined second language learning by adult immigrants in a range of European countries, and finally evaluate the overall contribution so far of this tradition to our understanding of L2 development.

5.2 Functional perspectives on first language development

Researchers studying child language have been interested for many years in the meanings which children are trying to convey, and the possible relationship between developments in children's messages, and developments in the formal systems through which they are expressed. Table 5.1 is drawn from one of the best-known 1970s' child language studies, already referred to in Chapter 1 (Brown 1973); here we see children's two-word utterances being interpreted as expressing a range of semantic relations. For example, in Brown's data the utterance *Daddy hit* is interpreted not as an expression of the formal syntactic relationship Subject + Verb, but as a combination of semantic categories of 'Agent' (or 'doer'), plus 'Action'. As the examples show, the child's language at this point is lacking in the morphological markers of case, tense, number, etc.; this is one key reason why formal categories devised to describe the mature adult system are not seen as useful at this developmental stage. Researchers in this tradition have argued essentially 'that syntactic categories develop as prototypes based on semantic information' (Harley 1995, p. 371).

Table 5.1 Eleven important early semantic relations and examples

Relation	Example
Attributive	'big house'
Agent–Action	'Daddy hit'
Action–Object	'hit ball'
Agent–Object	'Daddy ball'
Nominative	'that ball'
Demonstrative	'there ball'
Recurrence	'more ball'
Non-existence	'all-gone ball'
Possessive	'Daddy chair'
Entity + Locative	'book table'
Action + Locative	'go store'

Source: Brown 1973

Budwig (1995) has produced a useful recent survey of broadly functionalist approaches to the study of child language development. She brings together a wide range of perspectives on the relationship between form and function in child language, and on development in this relationship over time. She divides them into four main 'orientations' (pp. 3–13): *cognitive orientation, textual orientation, social orientation* and *multifunctional orientation.*

5.2.1   *The cognitive orientation*

The cognitive orientation is typified by the work of Slobin (1985a), which we have already referred to in Chapter 4. Slobin proposes the existence of a 'basic child grammar', in which children construct their own form–function relationships to reflect a child's-eye view of the world. For example, Slobin suggests on the basis of cross-linguistic comparisons that regardless of the particular target language which is being acquired, 'one of the opening wedges for grammar is the linguistic encoding of a scene in which an *agent* brings about a *change of state* in an *object*' (Budwig 1995, p. 10).

5.2.2   *The textual orientation*

As far as the textual orientation is concerned, 'the issue of central importance is the extent to which particular linguistic devices are employed to help organize stretches of discourse both intrasententially and across broader stretches of text' (Budwig 1995, p. 11). This approach has its roots in functional-systemic linguistics, e.g. the work of the Prague school, or of Michael Halliday. At the level of the individual sentence, theorists in this tradition are interested in how the underlying information structure (whether labelled as *topic–comment, theme–rheme,* or *given–new information*) is reflected in surface syntax. At the level of discourse, functional-systemic linguists are interested in how lexis and grammar (e.g. conjuncts, deictic elements, pronominal systems) are deployed to create textual cohesion.

In child language studies, functionally oriented research concerned with textual matters has mostly concentrated on the systems used by older children to establish cohesion in narratives (e.g. Karmiloff-Smith 1987). Again, it has been argued that children begin by deploying forms adopted from adult input, for their own distinctive set of textual functions.

5.2.3   *The social orientation*

Functionalist child language research with a social orientation is interested in relationships between the development of the child's formal language system, and aspects of their social world. Some of this work examines the speech acts which children perform, and their relationships with lexical/grammatical choices. For example, Deutsch and Budwig (1983) re-analysed some of the data gathered by Brown (1973), arguing that expressions involving first person possessive determiners (*my pencil*) consistently expressed different speech acts from expressions involving the child's own name (*Adam pencil*) – the first group were *indicative* ('That's my pencil'), while the second group were *volitional* ('I, Adam, want a pencil'). Other work looks much more broadly at the social context within which children interact, and the types of speech events in which they are engaged, and seeks to link these wider influences to grammatical development. A striking example is the work of Ochs in Samoa (1988), where she argues for a link between children's acquisition of inflectional morphology, and socially patterned variation in adults' usage. (The specific example analysed by Ochs concerns the acquisition of ergative case marking. In Samoan, ergative marking is optional, and rare in women's domestic talk. Samoan children seem to acquire this feature much later than do children learning other ergative languages. This social orientation on child language acquisition is revisited more fully in Chapter 8.)

5.2.4   *The multifunctional orientation*

The functional approaches to child language studies which have been briefly outlined pay attention respectively to the relations between grammatical development and event schemata; between grammar and text organization; and between grammar and the social world. Budwig points out (1995, p. 13) that there has so far been little work on child language which seeks to integrate the study of these different sets of relationships in a multifunctional orientation. However, she cites the work of Gee/Gerhardt (the same person) as an exception (e.g. Gee and Savasir 1985; Gerhardt 1990). For example, Gerhardt studied the use of the forms *will* and *gonna* by 3-year-old children, and argues that they are used in different discourse contexts, with distinctive illocutionary force.

> *Gonna* appears in discourse in which the children were planning and organizing; it implies a more distant intention to act in a particular way. In contrast, *will* appears in the context of ongoing cooperative peer play, and refers to an immediate intentional stance.
>
> (Budwig 1995, p. 13)

In her own longitudinal research, Budwig (1995) examines the self-reference forms (*I, me, my, Own Name,* etc.) used by a group of 2-year-old children to express the semantic notions of *agentivity* and *control,* and also seeks to explain variability in usage in terms of the different pragmatic functions which are being expressed. For example, at 20 months, Megan used the three forms *I, my* and *Meggie* for self-reference; *my* was seen as expressing high agentivity (*my open that*), while *I* and *Meggie* expressed mid/low agentivity (*Meggie swinging*), with *I* typically being used for mental state verbs (*I wanna wear that*). There were also differences in usage which could be related to pragmatic function, e.g. *my* typically appeared in disputes over control of objects (*my cups!*, said as Megan grabs cups from another child). Over time, however, Megan extended the use of *I* to perform a wider range of functions, and use of *my* and *Own Name* became more target-like.

Budwig's 1995 study is typical of recent research on form–function relationships in child language. It has a number of characteristics which we will see repeated in second language learning research in the functional tradition.

1 Her data comprise longitudinal case studies of a small number of individual children; her prime concern is to trace the evolving patterns of relationships between language form and function over time.
2 That is, her research is interested in the evolving developmental *process*, rather than in end states; acquisition is viewed as a slow, incremental business, rather than an all-or-none achievement. (In some more form-oriented research, for example, a form is considered to have been acquired only when it is supplied in over 90 per cent of 'obligatory contexts'; for researchers like Budwig, such a definition of acquisition is unacceptably product-oriented.)
3 She is concerned to link different levels of analysis of learner language (e.g. paying attention to intonation as a signal of pragmatic function); and she is concerned to collect data from a variety of social settings, e.g. peer interactions as well as caretaker–child interactions, in the interest of accessing a wide range of pragmatic functions.

In conclusion, Budwig reviews possible factors which may drive children forward to continually reorganize their systems of form–function relationships, along the documented developmental path; linguistic maturation, cognitive development, encounters with target input, and communicative need. As yet, she argues, child language data do not offer definitive support to any one theoretical position: 'the specific mechanisms guiding the reorganization process are ... quite vague' (1995, p. 197). We will review below the efforts of functionalist SLL researchers to address the same fundamental problem.

5.3   Early functionalist studies of second language learning

In the historical overview of second language learning research given in Chapter 2, we have already reviewed the emergence during the 1970s of the concept of *interlanguage* in second language research (Corder 1967; Selinker 1972). This involved a major shift away from viewing learner language essentially as a defective version of the target language, or as a mixture of L1 and L2, as the earlier tradition of *error analysis* had done, towards viewing it as an organic system with its own internal structure. Researchers concerned primarily with the development of learner syntax moved on from the methodology of the morpheme acquisition order studies (Dulay *et al.* 1982), to the study of developmental sequences in linguistic subsystems such as negation or word order (e.g. in the ZISA Project on the acquisition of target language German, which we have discussed in Chapter 4: Meisel *et al.* 1981).

5.3.1   *Pragmatic* vs *syntactic modes of expression*

Within interlanguage research, functionalist approaches to the study of second language communication and development soon appeared. For example, Dittmar (1984) presents a re-analysis of data collected for an earlier, grammar-oriented study of adult Spanish L1 migrants' L2 German. This is a cross-sectional study of learners at a very elementary level, who make little use of the morphology of standard German, and typically express semantic concepts like temporality and modality either lexically or through contextual inference, rather than through grammatical encoding.

For example, the following learner utterance involving code switching between German and Spanish (in parentheses) was interpreted in context as expressing a promise:

Ich morgen /a/España /y/sage bei dir: zuruck España, eine /botella de coñac/bei dir
I tomorrow to Spain and say with you: back Spain, one bottle of cognac with you
'I am going to Spain tomorrow and promise to bring back a bottle of cognac for you.'

(after Dittmar 1984, p. 243)

Here the only explicit reference to future time is expressed in the lexical item *morgen* (tomorrow); modality and the notion of 'promising' have to be inferred from context; the inflected second person pronoun *dir* seems to be produced as part of an unanalysed chunk, *bei dir*, etc. Dittmar argues that the interpretation of data like this is helped by the theoretical distinction drawn by Givón (1979) between pragmatic and syntactic 'modes of expression'. Givón has argued that both informal speech and learner speech (whether L1 or L2) convey meaning through a relatively heavy reliance on context, whereas more formal styles of language rely on more explicit language coding, with reduced dependence on contextual meaning. For Givón, these *pragmatic* and *syntactic* 'modes' are the ends of a continuum, rather than discrete categories; as well as language acquisition, he interprets language change and synchronic variation in terms of movement along this continuum.

Table 5.2 shows the main features of the pragmatic and syntactic modes proposed by Givón. Dittmar (1984) argues that the conversational talk of his elementary adult learners shows many characteristics of the pragmatic mode. In particular, he argues that their utterances are typified by a *theme–rheme* (or topic–comment) structure, delineated by a single intonation curve, rather than by a grammar-based subject–predicate structure. Typical examples from his German interlanguage data are:

> *ich alleine – nicht gut*
> I alone – not good
> *immer arbeite – nicht krank*
> always work(ing) – not ill
> *ich vier Jahre – Papa tot*
> I four years – father dead

However, Dittmar's analysis in this early study was somewhat impressionistic, and he made no attempt to trace development in the learners' 'basilang' (or basic language variety) over time. The issue of how learners' utterances might move from topic–comment structure to conventional target language sentence syntax was not addressed in any detail. Altogether, while this study appealed to the theoretical framework of Givón, by showing that learners start at the pragmatic end of the continuum, it did not yet offer any very rigorous test of it, as it does not tell us what happens after these very early stages. (In later work, e.g. that of the P-MoLL Project investigating modality in learner varieties of German, Dittmar adopts a longitudinal case study approach, and together with colleagues, performs a variety of more detailed form-to-function and function-to-form analyses: see various papers in Dittmar and Reich 1993.)

Table 5.2 Pragmatic and syntactic modes of expression

Pragmatic mode	Syntactic mode
a. Topic-comment structure	Subject-predicate structure
b. Loose conjunction	Tight subordination
c. Slow rate of delivery (under several intonation contours)	Fast rate of delivery (under a single intonational contour)
d. Word order is governed mostly by one PRAGMATIC principle: old information goes first, new information follows	Word order is used to signal SEMANTIC case functions (though it may also be used to indicate pragmatic-topicality relations)
e. Roughly one-to-one ratio of verbs to nouns in discourse, with the verbs being semantically simple	A larger ratio of nouns over verbs in discourse, with the verbs being semantically complex
f. No use of grammatical morphology	Elaborate use of grammatical morphology
g. Prominent intonation-stress marks the focus of new information; topic intonation is less prominent	Very much the same, but perhaps not exhibiting as high a functional load, and, at least in some languages, totally absent

Source: Givón 1979, p. 98

5.3.2   *Form-to-function analysis*

Some other early functionalist studies did take a longitudinal approach, e.g. the well-known year-long case study conducted by Huebner (1983) of a

Hmong L1 speaker, Ge, learning English as L2. Ge arrived as an adult in Hawaii with no English (but bilingual in two topic-prominent languages, Hmong and Lao) and was contacted within a few weeks by Huebner, who audio-recorded informal conversations with him at 3-week intervals. Ge was working full time in a garden centre to support relatives, and attended no language classes. Huebner's first intention was to study the developing tense-aspect system in Ge's English interlanguage. However, over the 12-month period, there was little evidence of formal development within the internal structure of the verb phrase; unlike Dittmar, Huebner did not pursue the means, presumably semantic/pragmatic, by which Ge located his utterances in time. Instead, he redirected his attention to a number of forms in Ge's interlanguage where development was more apparent, all of them important for the management of information in discourse.

For example, Huebner studied the changing functions of the form *is(a)* in Ge's interlanguage, over time. This form served initially as a general marker for topic–comment boundaries, and developed over time into a copula (as in standard English). Initially, therefore, *is(a)* was used in many 'ungrammatical' environments.

> *ai werk everdei, + isa woter da trii*
> 'As for the work I do everyday, it involves watering the plants' (p. 74).

The course of development evident in Ge's use of the *is(a)* form was not straightforward. From using it frequently as a topic boundary marker, he moved to much less frequent use of the form, in both grammatical and ungrammatical environments, according to the norms of Standard English (SE). Finally, Ge 'gradually and systematically re-inserted the form in SE grammatical environments' (p. 205), i.e. those where it performed the copula function.

Huebner describes similar patterns of development for the evolution of the functional distribution of article *da,* and the development of pronominal anaphora. Thus, he identified all possible contexts for production of *da*, and examined its actual frequency distribution over time. This analysis showed that:

> Ge's use of the article *da* shifts from an almost SE one but one which is dominated by the notion of topic, to one in which the form marks virtually all noun phrases. From that point, Ge's use of *da* is first phased out of environments which share no common feature values with SE definite noun phrases, followed by those environments that share one of the two feature values with SE definite noun phrases.
>
> (p. 130)

Huebner's study thus provides further evidence that early learner utterances may be characterized by topic–comment (theme–rheme) organization; 'the rules governing various aspects of the interlanguage grammar were influenced by the structure of discourse' (p. 203). He also documents the complexity of grammatical development in Ge's interlanguage, arguing that apparent variability is due to gradual, systematic shifts in function for particular forms, which may include apparent 'backtracking' away from target language norms. Finally, his study illustrates the need to pay attention to more than one level of language to make sense of interlanguage development; in order to pinpoint the functions of the forms *isa* and *da*, his analyses begin at the level of discourse/pragmatics, and move to an examination of syntax and morphology.

An important limitation of his study, however, lies in the fact that the languages in which Ge was already fluent (Lao and Hmong) are both topic-prominent languages. Therefore, Huebner recognizes, it is impossible to tell whether the topic-comment structure found in Ge's early English interlanguage is the product of L1 transfer, rather than a more universal characteristic of learner language. Another limitation has to do with the small number of subsystems actually studied; Huebner can only speculate on possible linkages across the interlanguage system as a whole, where a redistribution of functions within one subsystem may trigger change in other domains (p. 210). Finally, of course, Huebner's work has all the limitations of a single-subject case study, as he himself recognized (p. 209).

5.3.3 Function-to-form analysis: a fuller test of Givón

Another longitudinal case study conducted by Sato (1990), working with two Vietnamese L1 boys Thanh and Tai, draws (like the work of Dittmar 1984) on the theoretical contrast proposed by Givón between pragmatic and syntactic modes of expression. However, Sato is critical of much earlier work in this functionalist/textual tradition, on the grounds of vagueness in the operationalization and identification of topic–comment (theme–rheme) structures in learner language (pp. 29–39). Indeed, she questions the opposition between topic–comment and subject–predicate patterns, which SLA researchers have borrowed from Givón (*see* Table 5.2).

> Topic-comment structure, the most extensively studied feature to date, has proved difficult to analyze and the available results cannot be interpreted as strong evidence of the existence of topic-comment *as opposed to* subject-predicate structure. This is not to argue that topic-comment structure does not characterize the pragmatic mode. Rather, it seems to be the case that analysis has not gone very much beyond sentence-based, NP-focused quantification, where syntactic, semantic and pragmatic dimensions of topic-comment structure have been inappropriately conflated.
>
> (Sato 1990, pp. 45–6)

Sato argues that for the purposes of interlanguage research, Givón's framework must be adapted in a variety of ways. Her own study did not pursue the topic–comment problem further. Instead, it was designed to explore the extent to which her subjects' interlanguage moved from *parataxis* (adapted from Givón's 'pragmatic mode of expression') to *syntacticization* (from Givón's 'syntactic mode'). These concepts are redefined by Sato as follows.

1. Parataxis: extensive reliance on discourse-pragmatic factors in face-to-face communication and minimal use of target language (TL) morphosyntactic devices in expressing propositions. Discourse-pragmatic factors include shared knowledge between interlocutors, collaboration between interlocutors in the expression of propositions, and the distribution of propositional content over a sequence of utterances rather than within a single utterance.
2. Syntacticization: the process through which the use of morphosyntactic devices in IL increases over time, while the reliance on discourse-pragmatic context declines.

(Sato 1990, pp. 51–2)

Sato's two subjects were brothers in their early teens, who had arrived in the USA as 'boat people', and had been fostered in a white American family. They attended school, but received no specialist ESL instruction there. Over a period of ten months, Sato collected a range of informal conversational data from the boys at weekly intervals, visiting them at home: an example of talk between Sato (Ch) and Thanh (Th), in Sato's phonemic transcription, is given from Sato 1990, p. 125.

Th1: tudei ai ga muvi ın də ın də sku /
   'Today [I *got*] a movie in school'
C: You saw a movie?
Th2: tu au yæ /
   '[For] two hours, yeah'
C: of what?
Th3: muvi – ts əh (hʌv) yu si muvi / (1 sec. pause)
   '[A] movie – (unclear) you [seen this] movie?'
Th4: ɔnli bɔn pipol æn dei fait /
   'People only [made of bone] *were* fighting'
Th5: pipol ɔnli bɔn
   'People [who were] only [made of] bone'
C: Skeletons?   (Th/29/2)

The recorded speech of Thanh and Tai was divided into 'utterances' on the basis of phonological criteria ('an utterance being defined as a sequence of speech under a single intonation contour bounded by pauses', p. 58). To explore the nature and degree of parataxis/syntacticization, Sato concentrated on a *function-to-form* analysis of their IL talk. She first explored all means used by the boys to express *past time reference*, and second, examined the linguistic encoding of semantic *propositions*, both simple and complex. (A propositional utterance was defined as one which 'expressed at least one argument and a predication about that argument', p. 94.) We now look at how Sato has applied this approach to the development of these two areas of grammar.

5.3.3.1 THANH AND TAI: THE EXPRESSION OF PAST TIME REFERENCE

As far as past time reference was concerned, Sato found that over the ten months of the study, there was little development from a paratactic mode of expression in the direction of syntax. Throughout, the boys typically expressed past time either adverbially, or through pragmatic inference from the discourse context. A few irregular past tense forms (*bought, came*) appeared in course of time, but the regular -*ed* inflection was never detectable.

Sato comments that these findings are in line with many other studies which show that inflected past tense verb forms are slow to develop for naturalistic learners; ten months was just too short a time for syntacticization to take place in this domain. She points out how seldom the absence of formal past tense markers caused any communication difficulties (i.e. there was little *communicative pressure* on the subjects to include these). She also points out the necessity of a multilevel perspective on this issue; regular past tense inflections were not phonologically very salient in the documented TL input which the boys were receiving. Another complication was the fact that in the boys' own IL speech, because of L1 phonological influence, realizations of syllable-final consonant clusters remained distant from the English target.

5.3.3.2   THANH AND TAI: THE ENCODING OF PROPOSITIONS

As far as propositional encoding was concerned, Sato (1990, p. 93) hypothesised that parataxis would involve the following:

1 a predominance of non-propositional speech (i.e. a large proportion of non-propositional utterances);
2 a low proportion of multi-propositional utterances;
3 extensive reliance on interlocutor collaboration in the production of propositions;
4 little use of connective morphology in expressing inter-propositional relations).

On this dimension, syntacticization would appear through:

1 an increase in propositional speech;
2 an increase in multi-propositional utterances;
3 a decrease in reliance on interlocutor collaboration;
4 an increase in the use of connective morphology.

The actual results did not fit the expected pattern, however. From the beginning of the study, Thanh and Tai were found to be producing a high proportion of (single-)propositional utterances, with little need of scaffolding by their interlocutors; Sato attributes these findings to their relative 'cognitive maturity', compared with the younger subjects studied in L1 acquisition research and some child SLA research (such as Hatch 1978). Multi-propositional utterances were rare, however, and simple juxtaposition was the most important means of linking them; both learners were only beginning to use a variety of logical connectors other than *and*. (Table 5.3 shows some examples of what Sato calls 'paratactic precursors' for various target language constructions, from the speech of Tai.)

Table 5.3 Paratactic precursors of different TL constructions (examples from Tai)

Precursors	Examples	
Infinitival complement	hi wan mi go fɔɬbæk he-want-me-go-fullback 'He wanted me to [play] fullback'	(T/8/1)
WH-complement	noʷ aị pɪkɪdau̜? wʌt stɔri no-I-pick-it-out-what-story- aị wa æn ši rid mi I-want-and-she-read-me 'No I pick out which story I want and she reads it to me'	(T/35/26)
Relative clause	tan hi seị ə - də piβɬ deị sɪktin dei kæn go tu muvi a:r Thanh-he-say-the-people-they- sixteen-they-can-(?)-go-to-movie-R' 'Thanh says that people who are sixteen can go to R-rated movies'	(T/25/25)
Adverbial clause	wi wɔkin aị sɔ də di dɛd we-walking-I-saw-the-deer-dead 'When we were walking, I saw the dead deer'	(T/20/2)

Source: Sato 1990, p. 111

Where multi-propositional utterances (MPUs) were produced, many of them involved a small set of memorized phrases or 'chunks' as the starting point: the expressions /ai dono, hi dono, ai tin, hi sei, yu sei/(I don't know, he don't know, I think, he say, you say) were found in around 25 per cent of all such utterances. Sato argues here that particular lexical–semantic items may form important 'entry points' to aspects of TL syntax, again an instance of the general need for multi-level analysis.

Though Sato's study is once more small scale, and tantalizingly short, it has been treated at some length, because it raises a number of important theoretical issues for functionalist research in SLL.

1 She critiques and seeks to clarify the Givón distinction between pragmatic and syntactic modes of expression (though her own predictions about the relationship between parataxis and syntacticization are not fully borne out).
2 In her work on past time reference and propositional encoding, she offers a clear example of function-led analysis (in contrast with e.g. Huebner, who started with particular forms identified in the English IL of his subject Ge, and tried to track the changing functions they expressed).
3 She demonstrates important interrelationships between different levels of language (phonology, lexis and grammar), in particular highlighting the potential importance of particular chunks/lexical items as entry points into new syntactic patterns.

4 She highlights the need to take account of L2 learners' level of cognitive maturity, and offers a reminder of the limitations of conversational interaction as a 'driver' for syntactic development, because communication problems in this context can so routinely be solved through discourse-pragmatic means. (Indeed, she argues at one point that Thanh's greater mastery of syntactic means for expressing multi-propositional utterances may be due to his richer experience of English literacy at school: p. 117.)

5.4   Functionalism beyond the case study: the European Science Foundation project

The functionalist research studies which we have reviewed in detail up to this point have been small scale, taking the form of case studies of one or more learners, and typically involving just one source language and one target language (Spanish–English, for Dittmar 1984; Hmong–English, for Huebner 1983; Vietnamese–English, for Sato 1990). In small-scale work of this kind, the generalizability of results is obviously limited in a number of ways. The personal characteristics of the learner, as well as the unique pattern of their particular social encounters with the target language and its users, may affect the rate and/or route of L2 development, and these individual effects are not 'averaged out' in small-scale work. In studies involving single pairs of languages, it is also not possible to determine how far the particular characteristics of the learner's interlanguage are the product of L1 influence.

In this section we turn to a major project on the second language acquisition of adult migrants, which brought a functionalist perspective to bear on the problem of SLA on a much larger scale. This project has given rise to a large number of publications, but authoritative overviews can be found in volumes authored/edited by the project directors (Klein and Perdue 1992; Perdue 1993a, 1993b). The project was funded by the European Science Foundation over a period of six years (1982–88), and involved research teams in five European countries. These teams worked with groups of adult migrant subjects, both men and women, in process of acquiring one of five target languages (English, German, Dutch, French and Swedish). The migrants spoke a range of first languages, so that ten language pairs in all were explored, in the following pattern:

English	German	Dutch	French	Swedish
/ \	/ \	/ \	/ \	/ \
Punjabi	Italian	Turkish	Arabic	Spanish Finnish

In the end, a total of twenty-one L2 learners contributed substantially to the research. In selecting the participants, care was taken to avoid people currently attending language classes, as the aim was to study naturalistic development. The research teams kept in contact with the participants over a period of 2.5 years, by means of regular tape-recorded or video-recorded encounters at four- to six-week intervals. They were recorded undertaking a varied range of tasks which were regularly repeated, including informal conversation, picture description, role plays (e.g. of service encounters), and re-telling the story of a Charlie Chaplin film.

5.4.1   Aims and findings of the ESF Project

The ESF Project aimed to produce a comprehensive longitudinal account of both the rate and the route of naturalistic interlanguage development among adult learners. They also aimed to document the characteristics of NS-NNS communication, and to identify internal and external factors on which the rate and degree of success of the acquisition process might depend. Perdue and Klein argue very explicitly for a functional approach, as the basis for a theory of SLA which is independent of theoretical linguistics (Perdue and Klein 1993, pp. 266–9). Like Sato and others, they argue that only a broad discursive–pragmatic approach can capture the changing sequence of means used by the learner to express notions such as *temporality*, and therefore provide a complete, contextualized account of the origins of more narrowly linguistic means for encoding time reference (verb inflections to do with tense/aspect). Similarly, they argue that structuring within learners' utterances has its basic origins in the wish

> to refer to persons or objects. . . . Speakers do not learn – for example – N-bar structure. They learn to refer with varying means under varying conditions, and *the result of this acquisitional process is what theoretical linguists like to call N-bar structure.*
>
> (p. 269, emphasis in original)

Drawing especially on the Charlie Chaplin narratives, Klein and Perdue (1992) argue that through a functional analysis, three developmental levels in the basic organization of learners' utterances could be identified across all the linguistic groups which were studied. These were the following:

- Nominal utterance organization (NUO);
- Infinite utterance organization (IUO);
- Finite utterance organization (FUO).

The three types of utterance organization are distinguished as follows.

> In NUO, utterances are extremely simple and mainly consist of seemingly unconnected nouns, adverbs and particles (sometimes also adjectives and participles). What is largely missing in NUO is the structuring power of verbs – such as argument structure, case role assignment, etc (hence, 'preverbal utterance organization' might be a better term). This is different in IUO: The presence of verbs allows the learner to make use of the different types of valency which come with the (non-finite) verb; it allows, for example, a ranking of the actants of the verb along dimensions such as agentivity, and the assigning of positions according to this ranking. At this level, no distinction is made between the finite and non-finite component of the verb; such a distinction, which is of fundamental importance in all languages involved in this study, is

only made at the level of FUO, which is not attained by all our learners. Transition from NUO to IUO and from there to FUO is slow and gradual, and the coexistence of several types of utterance organization as well as backsliding is not uncommon.

(Klein and Perdue 1992, p. 302)

The IUO level is exemplified in an extract from a Charlie Chaplin film retelling by one of the Punjabi L1 learners of English, when Charlie Chaplin escapes from a police van.

(1) *Back door stand the policeman? right?*
(2) *she pushin policeman ...*
(3) *charlie and girl and policeman put on the floor*
(4) *car gone ...*
(5) *charlie get up first*
(6) *he say daughter/sorry +*
     he pickup girl + charlie +
(7) *say 'go on*
(8) *this time nobody see you'*
(9) *policeman get up*
(10) *charlie hittin the head*

(Klein and Perdue 1992, p. 76)

At all levels of proficiency, the ESF team argue learner utterances were produced under a range of competing constraints, *pragmatic*, *semantic* and *phrasal*. In proposing pragmatic constraints on the form of learner utterances, Klein and Perdue revisit the issue of topic–comment (theme–rheme) structure, originally proposed by Givón as typical of the pragmatic communication mode. They relabel and redefine the concepts of topic and comment as *topic* and *focus*, as follows.

> Very often, a statement is used to answer a specific question, this question raising an alternative, and the answer specifying one of the 'candidates' of that alternative. For example, the question 'Who won?' raises an alternative of 'candidate' persons – those who may have won on that occasion – and the answer specifies one of them. ... Let us call 'focus' that part of a statement which specifies the appropriate candidate of an alternative raised by the question, and 'topic' the remainder of the answer.

(1992, pp. 51–2)

They suggest that an important pragmatic constraint operates on learner utterances, which provides that the focus element in an utterance should normally come last, e.g. *Charlie* [topic] *get up first* [focus]).

The main semantic constraint has to do with the notion of *control*. For verbs which associate with more than one 'actant' (or argument),

> a semantic asymmetry is observed in that one actant has a higher, and the other(s) a lower degree of control over the situation.... This asymmetry is a continuum ranging from clear 'agent-patient' relations down to cases of real or intended possession'.

(p. 340)

The proposed semantic constraint on utterance structure is that the actant with highest control (the 'controller') should be mentioned first. Again, in the Charlie Chaplin example, we see this exemplified for two-place verbs such as *push*, *hit*.

These two constraints, *Focus last,* and *Controller first,* are said to interact with phrasal constraints which basically specify the range of syntactic resources available at a given developmental level, and their permitted sequences. Of course, these constraints are sometimes in competition (as when the 'controller' is 'in focus'), and Klein and Perdue see these conflicts as 'a major germ of development' (p. 303).

5.4.2   *The basic learner variety*

An important descriptive claim of the ESF project is that all the learners in the study, irrespective of language background, developed a particular way of structuring their utterances which seemed to represent a 'natural equilibrium' between the various phrasal, semantic and pragmatic constraints. This they termed a 'basic variety', mainly characterized by a small number of phrasal patterns, which were:

(a) NP1 – V – (NP2)
(b) NP1 – Cop – {NP2}
               {Adj}
               {PP}
(c) V – NP2.

In these phrases, NP2 must be lexical, while NP1 may be represented by a personal pronoun or an empty element. All patterns could be preceded or followed by adverbials of time or space; verbs are not inflected (i.e. are non-finite); 'Focus last' and 'Controller first' apply throughout. This basic variety was exemplified for English in the first Chaplin example above. Another example of basic variety German is given in another Chaplin example (here the source language is Italian); it must be emphasized that, lexis apart, the researchers see the basic variety as 'remarkably impermeable to the specifics of source language and target language' (Perdue and Klein 1993, p. 257).

(1) *jetzt charlie komme in eine restaurant*
    'now Charlie come in a restaurant'
(2) *und essen*
    'and eat'
(3) *und wann is fertig + *chiama**
    'and when is ready + *(calls)'
(4) *eine polizei komme*
    'a police come'
(5) *und charlie sage*
    'and Charlie say'
(6) *"bezahle"*
    '"pay"'
(7) *charlie sage de polizei*
    'Charlie say the police'

(8) *"bezahle was alles ich esse* [this is repeated, with slight variants]
   "'pay what all I eat'"
(9) *und die polizei jetzt bezahle*
   'and the police now pay'
(10) *nicht charlie + die polizei*
   'not Charlie + the police'
(11) *und fort brauchen die charlie*
   'and away bring the Charlie'
(12) *und jetzt komme eine auto*
   'and now come a car'
(13) *und charlie *sale**
   'and Charlie (leaves)'

                                        (Klein and Perdue 1992, pp. 152–3)

5.4.3   Development beyond the basic variety

Before arriving at the basic variety, the learners have passed through a pre-basic variety, which is largely noun-based; one noun is related to another through topic/focus organization, and temporality, etc. are inferred from context. All learners in the study appeared to achieve the basic variety, and some then fossilized, i.e. did not grammaticize their productions any further.

Others, however, did progress beyond the basic variety; the most important indicator of this development was the acquisition of 'finiteness', i.e. the gradual appearance of verb inflections (tense marking preceding aspect marking, irregular forms preceding regular ones). Parallel developments were identified in the pronoun system, in the acquisition of focalization devices such as cleft structures (*is not the man steal the bread, is the girl*: Klein and Perdue 1992, p. 321), and of means for subordination (*they think about one house for live together*, p. 322). Some learners made considerable progress towards TL syntactic norms, and the researchers conclude that they can see no reason in principle why L2 learners cannot achieve these in full. However, L1 background was now seen as influencing at least the rate of progress beyond the basic variety, and possibly as affecting the degree of ultimate success.

But what drives development? If the basic variety is effective for everyday communication, why move beyond it? At varying times, the ESF researchers propose somewhat different answers to this question. When discussing the acquisition of temporality they review two possible factors promoting the gradual development of verb inflection:

1 the subjective need to sound and to be like the social environment;
2 concrete communicative needs.

At this point, they argue that,

> Our observations about development beyond the basic variety clearly indicate that the first factor, the subjective need...outweighs the other factor... Learners try to imitate the input, irrespective of what the forms they use really mean, and it is only a slow and gradual adaptation process which eventually

leads them to express by these words and constructions what they mean to express in the TL.

(Klein *et al.* 1993, p. 112)

This view is repeated in the conclusions to a later, more detailed volume produced by members of the team, concentrating on the acquisition of temporality (Dietrich *et al.* 1995, p. 273). However, in their general conclusion to the overview volumes, Perdue and Klein seem to have changed their minds somewhat. Now, they give priority to 'communicative needs in discourse' (1993, p. 261): 'acquisition is pushed by the communicative tasks of the discourse activities that the learner takes part in' (p. 262). This is argued not only with reference to the acquisition of the basic variety, but also with reference to some post-basic features. However, it is recognized that learners cannot attend to all their communicative needs at once, and that 'you have to work new items and rules in' (p. 265): at particular times, particular interlanguage rules will become 'critical', i.e. open to change and reorganization.

(It is worth comparing the ESF team's views on this point with those of Dittmar, who argues that the shift from pragmatic and lexical modes of expression towards grammaticalization is motivated primarily by the learner's long-term need 'to look for economy and efficiency in language use and to stabilise the expressibility in the basic communicative functions': (Dittmar 1993, p. 216.)

At the same time, Perdue and Klein accord the source language some influence in determining the rate of development and degree of eventual success, beyond the basic variety. The extent of daily contact with the target language is also found to be generally predictive of rate of progress though a pessimistic view is taken of the role of instruction; however, these 'extrinsic' factors are discussed in fairly general terms. (See Chapter 8 for a fuller consideration of the distinctive ethnographic work of some subgroups within the ESF team: Bremer *et al.* 1993, 1996.)

5.5   Evaluation

What are the most important contributions of the functionalist tradition to our understanding of second language learning?

5.5.1   *The scope and achievements of the functionalist perspective*

The functionalist tradition is well established in second language learning theory. Its fundamental claim is that language development is driven by pragmatic communicative needs, and that the formal resources of language are elaborated in order to express more complex patterns of meaning. Functionalist research typically takes the form of naturalistic case studies of individuals or groups of learners; most often these have been adults in the early stages of L2 learning, who are acquiring the language in informal environments rather than in the classroom. These studies have offered us numerous rich accounts of both the rate and route of L2 learning, at least in the early stages.

Functionalist researchers vary, however, in the scope of their enquiries. Some have adopted a 'patch' approach, studying the use and evolution of selected L2 forms, or the development of L2 within a sub-domain such as 'time' or 'space'. On the other hand, the ESF team has made quite strong claims for their proposed L2 'basic variety', which represents a proto-grammar stage which all learners should pass through. Below, we summarize our overall view of their contributions to understandings of the nature of interlanguage, the learning process, and the language learner.

5.5.2   *Functionalism and the nature of interlanguage*

Descriptively, the functionalist tradition has added considerably to our understanding of interlanguage systems. By paying attention to function as well as form, functionalist researchers have promoted a more systematic and thorough treatment of interlanguage communication, demonstrating the wide range of devices (lexical and pragmatic) which IL users deploy in order to convey meaning. For example, the expanded treatment by functionalist researchers of the semantic notion of 'temporality' has taken the study of how IL users locate their utterances in time, well beyond a search for formal sequences in verb morphology. Functionalist research has thus contributed to our understanding of the internal workings and integrity of interlanguage.

Functionalist researchers have also drawn our attention to the issue of textual/discourse organization in learner language, and offered considerable evidence in support of the view that early learner varieties rely heavily on parataxis rather than on syntax in order to structure and express both individual propositions and inter-propositional relationships. However, so far, learner varieties have not been found to map neatly on to Givón's 'pragmatic mode of expression', nor have the various attempts to identify topic–comment type structuring in interlanguage utterances met with complete success.

A significant limitation on functionalists' characterization of interlanguage is the fact that up to now, this research perspective has concentrated on the early stages of development, describing IL grammars in their earliest forms. Comparatively little attention has been paid to the later stages, so that this tradition has little to say on the nature and development of more complex syntactic structures.

5.5.3   *Functionalism on language learning and development*

Functionalist researchers insist universally on the gradual nature of IL development and syntacticization, with learners working actively on only part of the system at any one time, but with possible reorganizational consequences which may spread widely through the system. At the same time, most functionalist researchers have so far adopted a 'patch' approach, working on basic utterance structure on the one hand, and on a range of sub-systems (temporality, modality, space, pronouns, articles ...) on the other. Linkages across and between these different sub-systems are often still tenuous.

Functionalist researchers argue consistently for a multilevel approach to the analysis of IL data – unsurprisingly, given their general interest in movement from pragmatic to lexical to syntactic modes of expression. Some valuable work has been done, e.g. demonstrating the role of intonation and prosody in demarcating utterances, or demonstrating how paratactic constructions mirror and prefigure their syntactic equivalents. However, the lexical level has as yet been relatively little studied, despite e.g. Sato's speculations about the potential significance of items such as *think* and *know* for the development of subordination.

While their contribution at a descriptive level has been very strong and varied, however, the contribution of functionalist studies to the explanation of IL development has so far been more limited. It has been amply shown how effective a basic or pidginized variety can be in meeting immediate communicative needs; thus far, discourse-based accounts of interlanguage seem firmly grounded. But it is less clearly established that communicative need is indeed the prime driver for syntacticization and development beyond the basic variety. As we have seen, even the ESF team wavers on this point; and Sato articulates a number of reasons, grounded in close examination of the interactions in which her child learners were engaged, why this might not be particularly effective. Her suggestion, that the literacy demands of formal schooling might be instrumental in promoting syntactic development, has not been taken further by other researchers; and it remains unclear why the ESF team eventually abandoned its interim suggestion that learners seek TL accuracy either for its own sake, or for integrationist reasons.

The treatment of input and interaction in functionalist research remains inconsistent. Sato pays some attention to the formal features of input received by her subjects during data collection sessions, e.g. noting the rarity and lack of phonological saliency in interlocutor speech of regular past tense forms. She also notes an unexpectedly low level of 'scaffolding', at least in terms of learners' individual propositional utterances; in her data, 'vertical constructions' were rare.

As far as the ESF research is concerned, the main research team pays little attention to the details of input and interaction in which its subjects were engaged. It asserts that quantity of TL contact was predictive of IL development, and also argues that communicative need was a prime driver in development up to and beyond the basic learner variety. However, it does not present any analyses of NS/NNS interaction, which provide any detailed evidence of how this might be taking place on an ongoing basis; at certain moments, new syntactic forms are documented in learner talk, but where they have arrived from remains obscure.

Within the ESF team there is of course a subgroup which provides very detailed commentaries on NS/NNS interaction: the ethnography group (Bremer *et al.* 1993, 1996), whose work is discussed further in Chapter 8. These researchers proclaim a general interest in Vygotskian perspectives on collaborative learning; however, their detailed commentaries on NS/NNS interaction are concerned with other forms of (un)co-operative behaviour and the immediate achievement of understanding, as we will see more fully below. They have not yet paid detailed or systematic attention to the microgenesis within interaction of new linguistic forms.

5.5.4   Functionalism on the language learner

Finally, functionalist research has typically interested itself in naturalistic adult learners, acquiring a socially dominant TL in the workplace and other non-domestic settings. To date, little interest has been shown in instructed second language learning. The ESF team are pessimistic about the contribution of instruction to learning, on the general *a priori* grounds that instruction is too clumsy an instrument to address those language issues which are 'critical' at a given moment for a given learner. Indeed, this project had tried to avoid selecting informants who had received TL instruction, to avoid classroom contamination. In the event, over half their informants had had 100+ hours instruction at some time, and it is clear from some marginal comments that in at least some cases, this had decisively affected the route of interlanguage development (Perdue 1993a, pp. 49–50). But the ESF team makes little of this, and in general, the possibility that functionalist explanations could account for classroom learning also has hardly been pursued.

6

Input and interaction in second language learning

6.1 Introduction

In previous chapters, we have reviewed a range of current perspectives on SLL which are concerned primarily with the language learner viewed as an autonomous individual. In Chapter 3, we investigated the view that human beings are individually endowed with a special language faculty, so that the core of the language learning process involves the setting/resetting of parameters within a hard-wired, genetically based Universal Grammar, of which every human being has their personal copy, as it were. For UG theorists, the language data encountered by the learner in the surrounding social environment of course has a role to play in language learning, in so far as it offers positive evidence of what is structurally possible within a particular natural language system, and thus guides the setting/resetting of UG parameters. However, the learner's encounter with users of the language being learned, and their resulting language experience, is useful primarily as a source of evidence which can stimulate or trigger internal mechanisms of growth and development.

In Chapter 4, we reviewed the work of theorists who believe that general learning mechanisms can account for much or all of the processes of language learning. However, the 'cognitive' perspective on second language learning also views the learner as an autonomous actor, processing language data available in the environment in order to restructure a range of internally generated hypotheses concerning language structure. For researchers in both these traditions, the language experience of the learner is viewed, on the one hand, as a source of 'input' on which internal learning mechanisms can get to work and, on the other, as an opportunity for testing structural hypotheses through language 'output'. It is assumed that all learners can/must process this 'input' in much the same way, with differences in its usability depending primarily on the current developmental stage at which the individual learner may have arrived. Even the 'Affective Filter' hypothesis proposed by Krashen, and discussed in Chapter 2, which argues that the learner must be in a relaxed and confident state in order to exploit available input most effectively, assumes an essentially individual state, which teachers and other language 'experts' can influence only in broad contextual terms.

In Chapter 5, we turned our attention to researchers who analyse the development of learners' ability in functional terms. From this perspective, as we have seen, the prime driving force behind language acquisition is commonly viewed as the urge to communicate meanings, in social settings. However, we noted in the conclusion to Chapter 5 that many researchers in this tradition have so far paid surprisingly little attention to the details of interactions in which their subjects were engaged, and certainly have not tried to trace in any detail how such interactions might provide evidence about/give rise to developing use and control of new target language forms.

In the next three chapters, we progressively turn our attention to theorists who view language learning in more social terms. In this chapter, we examine an empirical strand of SLA research originally inspired by another of Krashen's hypotheses, this time the *Input Hypothesis* (Krashen 1982, 1985; see Chapter 2 Section 2.3.4). In the early 1980s, the researcher Michael Long first advanced the argument that in order to understand more fully the nature and usefulness of input to second language learning, greater attention should be paid to the interactions in which learners were engaged (e.g. Long 1981, 1983a, 1983b). These interactions should be seen not only as a prime source of target language input, feeding into the learner's presumed internal acquisition device; it was argued by Long and others that when learners engaged with their interlocutors in negotiations around meaning, the nature of the input might be qualitatively changed. That is, the more the input was negotiated to increase its comprensibility, the greater its potential usefulness as input well targeted to the particular developmental level and acquisitional needs of the individual learner.

These theoretical claims have led, during the 1980s and early 1990s, to a rich vein of empirical work, examining the detail of target language interaction involving second language learners. (Useful overviews can be found in Chaudron 1988, Chapter 5; in Larsen-Freeman and Long 1991, Chapter 5; and in Pica 1994.) In this chapter we review and evaluate this work, which has taught us a great deal about the kinds of interaction in which learners typically engage, and about a range of variables which seem to influence the quality of these interactions. However, this tradition retains much in common with those reviewed in earlier chapters, in so far as it views the actual business of learning as something to be accomplished by the individual, who uses relatively autonomous internal mechanisms of some kind in order to exploit the varying spectrum of input data on offer in the interactive environment. It is in later chapters (Chapters 7 and 8) that we go on to examine the work of yet other groups of researchers, who claim that target language interaction cannot be viewed simply a source of 'input' for autonomous and internal learning mechanisms, but has a much more central role to play in learning.

6.2   Input and interaction in L1 acquisition

Before examining the L2 interactionist tradition in more detail, it will be help-ful to recap briefly on current understandings of the role of input and inter-action in the acquisition by young children of the L1. It is well known that adults and other caretakers commonly use 'special' speech styles when talk-ing with young children, and terms such as *baby talk* are current in common parlance to refer to this. The idea that 'baby talk' with its particular charac-teristics might actually be facilitative of language acquisition, and the empir-ical study from an acquisitionist perspective of caretakers' interactions with young children, or of *child directed speech* (CDS) as it is now known, dates back to the 1960s. This empirical research tradition was very active in the 1970s and 1980s, though dogged by criticism especially from Universal Grammar theorists; in 1986, for example, Noam Chomsky described as 'absurd' the notion that aspects of L1 acquisition could be related to the input (quoted in Snow 1994, p. 4). In turn, child language specialists have crit-icized parameter-setting models of acquisition as overly deterministic (e.g. Valian 1990), and ignoring substantial evidence of probabilistic learning from 'noisy' input (Sokolov and Snow 1994, p. 52).

A recent collection edited by Gallaway and Richards (1994) provides a use-ful overview of the interactionist tradition within L1 acquisition studies. Gallaway and Richards (1994, p. 264) point out that CDS might be expected to facilitate language acquisition in a wide variety of ways, including:

• managing attention;
• promoting positive affect;
• improving intelligibility;
• facilitating segmentation;
• providing feedback;
• provision of correct models;
• reducing processing load;
• encouraging conversational participation;
• explicit teaching of social routines.

However, the editors and contributors to the 1994 volume are cautious about the extent to which any of these possible CDS contributions to language acquisition have been solidly demonstrated. Some of the clearest findings and conclusions from the tradition, which are potentially relevant to second lan-guage learning, are the following.

1 CDS has mostly been studied in English-speaking contexts in the devel-oped world, and most usually in a middle-class family setting. In such con-texts, CDS is typically *semantically contingent* – that is, the caretaker talks with the child about objects and events to which the child is already paying attention. Richards and Gallaway comment that 'there is much evidence that semantic contingency...is facilitative, [though] the final

causal link is frequently lacking' (1994, p. 265). Also in CDS, explicit formal corrections of the child's productions are unusual, but *recasts* are
common – that is, utterances in which the caretaker produces an expanded
and grammatically correct version of a prior child utterance.

CHILD: Fix Lily
MOTHER: Oh ... Lily will fix it

(Sokolov and Snow 1994, p. 47)

Sokolov and Snow (1994) argue that these recasts offer the child potentially
useful *negative evidence* about their own hypotheses on the workings of
the target language, at least implicitly. There is also very substantial empirical evidence for positive correlations between the proportion of recasts
used by a child's caretakers, and its overall rate of development.

2 As well as more general claims about the overall contribution of semantic
   contingency and of recasts, there is evidence for some more specific claims
   about the relationship of particular formal characteristics of CDS and
   children's developing control of particular constraints. For example, there
   seems to be a relationship between the caretaker's use of inverted yes–no
   questions e.g. *Have you been sleeping?* and children's developing control
   of verbal auxiliaries in English L1, presumably because the fronted auxiliary is perceptually more salient than questions marked through intonation only (Pine 1994, pp. 25–33) However, such relationships are complex,
   and dependent on the precise developmental stage reached by the individual child. Again, we meet the notion of 'currently sensitive areas of development' already encountered in Chapter 5, or as some L1 researchers have
   expressed it: '"hot spots" of engagement and analysis that lead to a heavy
   concentration of available processing capacity on highly relevant exem-
   plars for stage-relevant acquisition' (Nelson *et al.* 1989, quoted in Richards
   and Gallaway 1994, p. 262).

3 In spite of the potential usefulness of CDS as input data, it is clear that
   CDS-using caretakers are not typically motivated by any prime language-
   teaching goal, nor is their speech in general specially adapted so as to
   model the target grammar. Instead, its special characteristics derive primarily from the communicative goal of engaging in conversation with a
   linguistically and cognitively less competent partner, and sustaining and
   directing their attention (Pine 1994, p. 19).

4 Cross-cultural studies of interaction with young children have made it
   clear that CDS is far from being a universal practice, and that societies can
   be found where pre-linguistic infants are not seen as conversation partners
   (see review by Lieven 1994). For example, in Trackton, a poor rural community studied by Heath (1983), in the south-eastern United States, children are hardly addressed directly by adults, until they can themselves
   produce multi-word utterances. Similarly, among the Kaluli of Papua New
   Guinea, infant babbling is seen as 'bird talk' and something to be discour-
   aged rather than engaged with (Schieffelin 1985). As children none the less
   learn to speak perfectly well under these widely differing conditions, this

cross-cultural evidence seems to challenge strongly environmentalist explanations of language learning, by weakening any notion that finely tuned CDS is actually necessary.

However, Lieven and others point out that even in cultures where CDS of the western type is rare or absent, children are constantly present in group settings, and surrounded by contextualized talk routines to which they can and do pay attention. In such settings, their early utterances frequently include partial imitations and the production of 'unanalysed and rote-learned segments, picked up in routinised situations' (Lieven 1994, p. 62). Indeed in some cultures, such as that of the Kaluli, adults actively teach language by requiring children to engage in direct imitation of conversational routines. We also know that children will not normally learn a language to which they are merely exposed in a decontextualized way e.g. on television (Snow *et al*, 1976, quoted in Lieven 1994, p. 59). As Lieven concludes:

> the study of child language development cross culturally supports the idea that children will only learn to talk in an environment of which they can make some sense and which has a structure of which the child is a part; on the other hand, children can clearly learn to talk in a much wider variety of environments than those largely studied to date. This is ... only partly because of the repertoire of skills that the child brings to the task of learning to talk. It is also because there are systematic ways in which the structure within which the child is growing up gives her/him access to ways of working out the language.
>
> (1994, p. 74)

From a wide-ranging review of the whole area, Snow concludes that,

> the normally developing child is well buffered against variation in the input ... buffering implies either that only a relatively small amount of social support of the right sort might be necessary, or alternatively that any of several different environmental events might be sufficient for some bit of learning to occur. Under these circumstances, variations at the margin in the quality of the linguistic environment a child is exposed to might not have any measurable effect on the speed or the ease of language acquisition.
>
> (1994, p. 11)

This naturally makes the study of environmental effects very difficult! And at present researchers in this field seem to agree on the following.

1 Multi-dimensional (modular?) models of acquisition are necessary, which will in some way reconcile a range of components which will include parental input, learning mechanisms and procedures, and innate (linguistic) constraints built into the child (Sokolov and Snow 1994, p. 51).
2 The way forward in clarifying just how it is that input and interaction may be facilitating language acquisition lies at present in close, detailed studies of relationships between particular features of the input, and of related features in the child's linguistic repertoire, as they evolve over time.

They remain hopeful that such studies will eventually demonstrate exactly how it is that environmental linguistic evidence interacts with and constrains the linguistic hypotheses under development by the child learner.

6.3 Input in second language acquisition: Krashen's 'Input Hypothesis'

Just as 'baby talk' was noted in the early work on child language development, as a simplified register used to talk to children, so a number of sociolinguists in the 1960s and 70s noticed and commented on what they called
foreigner talk, a simplified and pidgin-like variety sometimes used to address
strangers and foreigners (on *Me Tarzan, you Jane* lines: see review in Long
1996, pp. 414–18). It has always been obvious that comprehensible and appropriately contextualized L2 data is necessary for learning to take place.
However, the precise developmental contribution of the language used to
address L2 learners first attracted serious attention from psycholinguists and
second language researchers in the light of the *Input Hypothesis* proposed by
Stephen Krashen (1982, 1985: see also Chapter 2).

In its most developed form, the Input Hypothesis claims that exposure to
comprehensible input is both necessary and sufficient for second language
learning to take place. The hypothesis states that 'Humans acquire language
in only one way – by understanding messages, or by receiving "comprehensible input" ... We move from i, our current level, to i + 1, the next level along
the natural order, by understanding input containing i + 1' (Krashen 1985,
p. 2). Linked to the hypothesis are two further ideas:

1 speaking is a result of acquisition and not its cause; and
2 if input is understood, and there is enough of it, the necessary grammar is
  automatically provided (1985, p. 2).

According to this hypothesis, then, how exactly does acquisition take place?
At one point Krashen proposed three stages in turning input into *intake*:

1 understanding an L2 i + 1 form (that is, linking it to a meaning);
2 noticing a gap between the L2 i + 1 form, and the interlanguage rule which
  the learner currently controls;
3 the reappearance of the i + 1 form with minimal frequency (1983, pp.
  138–9).

In other versions of the hypothesis, however, the concept of 'noticing a gap'
is omitted, and it seems that acquisition takes place entirely incidentally/sub-
liminally.

As numerous critics have pointed out, the Input Hypothesis as originally
formulated by Krashen is supported by rather little empirical evidence, and is
not easily testable (e.g. McLaughlin 1987, pp. 36–51). The concepts of 'understanding' and 'noticing a gap' are not clearly operationalized, or consistently
proposed; it is not clear how the learner's present state of knowledge ('i') is
to be characterized, or indeed whether the 'i + 1' formula is intended to apply
to all aspects of language, from lexis to phonology and syntax.

The idea that 'comprehensible input' at the right level of difficulty is not
only necessary but sufficient to ensure acquisition has also been questioned.

There are many cases of L2 learners who have failed to progress beyond a fossilized and deviant interlanguage, at least as far as their own production is concerned, despite abundant meaning-oriented input. For example, in Canada in recent decades, many English L1 students have received French-medium education, in so-called *immersion programmes*. These students have been exposed to large amounts of French communicative input, in the school setting. Their progress has been extensively researched, and we know that in some respects these immersion students make very good progress (e.g. their comprehension of French approaches native speaker levels). However, many of these students seem to 'fossilize' as far as spoken French is concerned – that is, they fail to achieve productive control of many aspects of French grammar and lexis (see e.g. Swain 1985; Swain and Lapkin 1995). On the basis of such evidence, as we saw in Chapter 1, Swain argues in her *Comprehensible Output Hypothesis*, that comprehension of L2 input is often achievable by semantic/pragmatic means, making it unnecessary for the L2 listener (or reader) to struggle to process unfamiliar syntax in full. She suggests that it is the effort of composing new utterances which is more likely to drive learners to form new hypotheses about target language syntax, and to try them out. Thus she sees the acquisition of new syntactic structures in particular as more likely to result from learners' attempts at L2 production, than simply from the struggle to comprehend i +1 utterances. (Rivers 1994 makes similar arguments.)

Despite these problems, Krashen's proposals encouraged other researchers to examine more closely the character of the language data actually available as input to second language learners. A range of studies conducted in the 1970s and 1980s demonstrated that talk addressed to learners was in fact rarely of the *Me Tarzan, you Jane* type. Instead, it was typically grammatically regular, but often somewhat simplified linguistically by comparison with talk between native speakers (e.g. using shorter utterances and a narrower range of vocabulary, and/or less complex grammar: see review in Long 1983a). However, as Long showed, the degree of simplification reported in many descriptive studies was puzzlingly variable. Also, these studies typically stopped short at the description of distinctive features of Foreigner Talk Discourse (FTD), as it came to be known. They did not generally go on to demonstrate either that these special qualities made FTD more comprehensible, or that it actually promoted L2 acquisition.

Long was critical of the descriptivism of early studies, and proposed a more systematic approach to linking features of 'environmental' language, and learners' L2 development. He argued that this could be done in the following way.

Step 1: Show that (a) linguistic/conversational adjustments promote (b) comprehension of input.

Step 2: Show that (b) comprehensible input promotes (c) acquisition.

Step 3: Deduce that (a) linguistic/conversational adjustments promote (c) acquisition.

(Long 1985, p. 378)

In two quasi-experimental studies reported in the same 1985 paper, he showed that 'lecturettes' pre-scripted and delivered in a modified, FTD style were more comprehensible to adult L2 learners than were versions of the same talks delivered in an unmodified style, thus supporting the argument that linguistic modifications could promote comprehension of input. However, these lecturettes involved passive listening by the learners. In other work, Long shifted the attention of the SLA field towards more functional and interactive aspects of FTD, in parallel with developments in child language studies at the time.

6.4   Interaction in second language acquisition

6.4.1   Long's 'Interaction Hypothesis'

Long went on to propose an extension of Krashen's Input Hypothesis, which has come to be called the *Interaction Hypothesis*, and has attracted continuing attention (e.g. Long 1996). For his own doctoral research (1980, 1981, 1983a), Long conducted a study of sixteen NS–NS and sixteen NS–NNS pairs, carrying out the same set of face-to-face oral tasks (informal converson, giving instructions for games, playing the games, etc.). He showed that there was little linguistic difference between the talk produced by NS–NS and NS–NNS pairs, as shown on several measures of grammatical complexity. However, there were significant differences between the two sets of conversations, when these were analysed from the point of view of conversational management and language functions performed. Specifically, in order to solve ongoing communication difficulties, the NS–NNS pairs were much more likely to make use of conversational tactics such as *repetitions, confirmation checks, comprehension checks* or *clarification requests* (*see* Table 6.1 for examples).

As we noted in relation to child language research, NSs apparently resort to these tactics in order to solve communication problems when talking with less fluent learners, and not with any conscious motive to teach grammar. The prime trigger for interactional adjustments in both cases seems to be a perception that the interlocutor is experiencing ongoing comprehension problems (Long 1983b). However, from the perspective of the Interaction Hypothesis, such collaborative efforts between more and less fluent speakers should be very useful for language learning. As they struggle to maximize comprehension, and negotiate their way through trouble spots, the NS–NSS partnership is incidentally fine-tuning the L2 input, so as to make it more relevant to the current state of learner development. That is, they are collaborating to ensure that the learner is receiving i + 1, in Krashen's terms, rather than i + 3, or indeed i + 0. As Larsen-Freeman and Long put it:

> Modification of the interactional structure of conversation ... is a better candidate for a necessary (not sufficient) condition for acquisition. The role it plays in negotiation for meaning helps to make input comprehensible while

still containing unknown linguistic elements, and, hence, potential intake for
acquisition.

(1991, p. 144)

Following on Long's original descriptive studies, many others have followed
which have drawn on the Interaction Hypothesis and used a similar taxonomy of conversational moves to track meaning negotiations and conversational repair. These are usefully reviewed by Larsen-Freeman and Long (1991
pp. 120–8), and in Pica (1994). On the whole, these studies have followed
designs similar to that of Long (1980), tracking pairs of native and non-native
speakers in various combinations, undertaking a variety of semi-controlled
conversational tasks. These studies have taught us a good deal about the types
of task which are likely to promote extensive negotiation of meaning, inside
and outside the classroom. (For example, convergent, problem-solving tasks
in which both partners control necessary information are more likely to promote negotiation than are more open-ended discussions.) They have also
demonstrated that negotiation of meaning occurs within NS–NNS pairs and
groups, as well as between fluent and less fluent speakers, given the right task
conditions.

Table 6.1 Examples of interactional modifications in NS–NNS conversations

NS	NNS
And right on the roof of the truck place the duck. The duck. Duck.	I to take it? *Dog?*[a] Duck.
It's yellow and it's a small animal. It has two feet.	*I put where it?*[b]
You take the duck and put it on top of the truck. *Do you see the duck?*[c]	*Duck?*[a]
Yeah. Quack, quack, quack. That one. The one that makes that sound.	Ah yes. I see in the–in the head of him.
OK. *See?*[c]	*Put what?*[b]
OK. Put him on top of the truck.	*Truck?*[a]
The bus. Where the boy is.	Ah yes.

Notes

a Confirmation checks: Moves by which one speaker seeks confirmation of the other's preceding
   utterance through repetition, with rising intonation, of what was perceived to be all or part of
   the preceding utterance.

b Clarification requests: Moves by which one speaker seeks assistance in understanding the other
   speaker's preceding utterance through questions (including *wh*-, polar, disjunctive, uninverted
   with rising intonation, or tag), statements such as *I don't understand*, or imperatives such as
   Please repeat.

c Comprehension checks: Moves by which one speaker attempts to determine whether the other
   speaker has understood a preceding message.

Source: Pica *et al*. 1987, p. 74

However, as Long (1996) points out, these studies have mostly been undertaken in culturally homogeneous settings (western educational institutions), and we still know little about the kinds of negotiation and repair which may typify conversational interactions involving L2 learners in other contexts. It is also the case that until recently, not many studies of negotiation, etc. have gone beyond the first descriptive steps of establishing the existence and general patterning of conversational repair.

6.4.2 *Empirical studies linking interaction and comprehension*

One of the first studies which attempted to establish a link between interactional modifications and increased comprehension was carried out by Pica *et al.* (1987). Groups of L2 learners listened to different versions of a script instructing them to place coloured cut-outs on a landscape picture, and tried to complete the task. One group heard a linguistically modified version of the script (e.g. with increased redundancy and simplified grammar), but were not allowed to ask any questions as they carried out the instructions. The second group heard a version of the script originally recorded with native speakers, but were encouraged to ask for clarifications, etc. from the person reading the script. The main result of these requests was a great increase in repetitions of content words, rather than e.g. any particular simplification of grammar. Indeed, the authors note that 'interaction resulted in input that was more complex than input that was modified according to conventional criteria of linguistic simplification' (p. 750).

Pica *et al.* were none the less able to show that the learners allowed to negotiate the meaning of an unmodified script by their interlocutor were more successful on the task than those who simply heard the simplified script, and argued that this shows increased comprehension, due to interactional modifications of the input. This study, and others like it, are relevant to Long's Step 1 quoted above (1985); they seem to show that interactional adjustments (and the focused linguistic adjustments consequent on them) are more effective in promoting comprehension of input than are linguistic adjustments alone.

6.4.3 *Empirical studies linking interaction and acquisition*

In Long's Steps 2 and 3, he challenges researchers to link interactional modifications and learner comprehension to language acquisition. These links have been pursued in several studies reported in the 1990s, though with somewhat mixed results. Two examples will briefly be considered here.

A study by Loschky (1994) involved the administration of listening comprehension tasks to learners of Japanese as a foreign language. The learners heard individual locative sentences (in Japanese) such as 'To the right of the pen is a ruler', 'A big black circle is above the big black square', and had to locate and number the correct items on a range of picture sheets. One group of learners heard these sentences without any further support; a second group heard linguistically modified versions (with some added redundancy); and a third group was allowed to ask for clarifications, etc. as the sentences were presented.

As in earlier studies, Loschky found that the third condition was most helpful to the learners in successful task completion, and thus offers further evidence that interaction around meaning aids L2 comprehension. But Loschky also administered pre- and post-tests of language proficiency to his subjects, comprising a recognition test of relevant vocabulary, and a grammaticality judgement test on similar locative structures. Here, he found that all his subjects made significant gains in the course of study, but that no single group was advantaged over the others by the differing intervening treatment. Thus while his study showed interactional modifications leading to increased comprehension (Long's Step 1), it failed to show any clear link between increased comprehension and acquisition (Long's Step 2).

In a not dissimilar study, Gass and Varonis (1994) got NS–NNS pairs to undertake a problem-solving communication game. As in the Pica *et al.* (1987) study, this involved placing figures in particular locations on a landscape scene. The 'game' was run twice, first of all with the NS participants issuing instructions to their NNS interlocutors and, second, the other way around.

When the NS participants gave instructions on the first occasion, half were asked to follow a linguistically pre-modified script, and the other half followed an unmodified script. For each script, half the NS subjects were instructed to allow negotiation about meaning, and the other half were not. In this study, both the modified script WITHOUT interaction, and either script WITH interaction, seemed to increase NNS comprehension (as measured by success on the task), compared to those who heard the unmodified script and could not negotiate around it. This part of the study is obviously relevant once again to Long's Step 1.

In the second part of the experiment, however, when the NNS participants took responsibility for giving instructions, they were not given any scripts to follow. Once more, half of them were allowed to negotiate meaning with their NS interlocutor, the other half were not. (The design of this experiment is shown in Figure 6.1. taken from Gass and Varonis 1994, p. 290.)

Interestingly, this time around, it did not make any difference to the success of the NSs on the task (as measured by the proportion of objects correctly/incorrectly placed on the board), whether their NNS instructors were allowed to interact with them or not. It seemed that the quality/intelligibility of NS directions could not be improved significantly by ongoing interaction.

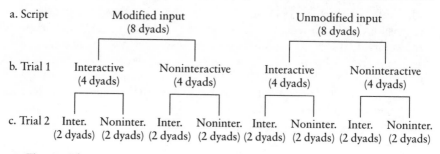

Fig. 6.1 The contributions of modified input and interaction to task success:
diagram of experimental design

Something else did make a difference, however. It turned out that those
NNS subjects who had been allowed to interact with their interlocutor during Trial 1, were significantly better at giving directions during Trial 2, than
those who had not had this earlier opportunity. In a qualitative analysis, Gass
and Varonis illustrate why this might be the case. They consider the possibility that the NNSs might have learned a larger number of useful vocabulary
items during their interactive experience of Trial 1, only to reject it. Instead,
they argue that the Trial 2 data show evidence of NNSs having internalized
various descriptive devices. Using the following data extract, the researchers
point out that the subject Hiroshi seems to have learned (or at least, to have
re-used), is not the lexical item *squirrel*, but a tactic for defining it, using more
basic vocabulary.

First trial
JANE: All right now, above the sun place the squirrel. He's right on top of
           the sun.
HIROSHI: What is ... the word?
JANE: OK. The sun.
HIROSHI: Yeah, sun, but ...
JANE: Do you know what the sun is?
HIROSHI: Yeah, of course. Wh-what's the
JANE: Squirrel. Do you know what a squirrel is?
HIROSHI: No.
JANE: OK. You've seen them running around on campus. They're little
           furry animals. They're short and brown and they *eat nuts* like
           crazy.

Second trial
HIROSHI: The second thing will be ... put here. This place is ... small
           animal which *eat nuts*.
JANE: Oh, squirrel?
HIROSHI: Yeah (laughter).

(Gass and Varonis 1994, p. 296)

Taken together, the results from the Loschky and Gass and Varonis studies
are tantalizing. Loschky is looking for impact of increased comprehensibility
on the acquisition of a small cluster of Japanese locative structures, and fails
to find it! Gass and Varonis do claim an effect for interaction on later

language use, but only having made far less specific predictions as to what that effect might be. In their commentary, all these researchers express the need for stronger theoretical models clarifying the precise nature of the supposed link between interaction and acquisition, if we are to make sense of such mixed results. (In fact, both research teams appeal to ideas of *noticing*, *consciousness-raising*, *attention*, etc., as an element to be added to the equation: see Section 6.6.)

6.5 A linguistic critique of input and interaction research

So far, we have reviewed current thinking about the contribution of 'environmental' language to second language learning mainly from the point of view of Krashen's original Input Hypothesis, and Long's earlier formulations of his Interaction Hypothesis. We have already noted that Krashen's Hypothesis came quickly under criticism for its extreme generality, and failure to specify the supposed psycholinguistic mechanisms by which comprehensible input might be analysed and integrated into the learner's developing L2 (e.g. Chaudron 1985). Somewhat similar criticisms have recently been expressed about the research tradition inspired by the Interaction Hypothesis, from a linguistic point of view (Braidi 1995).

Braidi believes that researchers in the interaction tradition (Long, Pica and others) have concentrated too one-sidedly on analysing functional aspects of interaction between NSs and NNSs, and in particular in developing elaborate taxonomies to document the negotiation of meaning in FTD. In comparison, she argues, they have paid rather little attention to grammatical aspects of FTD, and have analysed this dimension in very global terms (e.g. using general measures of complexity such as length of T-units, or type-token ratios: Braidi 1995, p. 142). Braidi notes the lack of success to date of this approach in establishing Long's Step 3: 'It is still unclear how interaction affects grammatical development' (p. 143). Indeed, she is sceptical that an approach concentrating on characterizing L2 interaction predominantly in terms of the negotiation of meaning can illuminate in any detail the processes by which input may be used to develop an L2 grammatical system over time.

Adopting the theoretical perspective of Universal Grammar, Braidi argues for a much more grammar-focused approach to the study of FTD. She points out that Universal Grammar permits the researcher to predict the kind of utterances which may act as *triggers* for the setting/resetting of particular parameters. (For example, a documented utterance such as *there's a chimney on the left*, Pica 1994 p. 511, might be usable as a trigger for the setting/resetting of the Pro-Drop Parameter.) Braidi believes that interactional research should concern itself with investigating the following:

1 the *availability* of such UG-related triggers in negotiated input;

2 the *accessibility* of such triggers to the learner (i.e. does the input have qualities which make particular grammatical features within the input comprehensible to the learner, and/or which highlight or make salient the required input?);

3 how *variability* of interactional input may affect the acquisition of these trigger structures.

She reviews existing international research from the point of view of these issues, arguing that in its present form, FTD research cannot provide any clear answers on the availability, accessibility, etc. of key structures. She goes on to argue for a new research agenda tracking individual grammatical structures in interactional FTD in much fuller detail (pp. 164–5).

6.6 Rethinking the Interaction Hypothesis

Despite the comments of critics such as Braidi, L2 input/interaction researchers have shown themselves responsive to the developing influence within SLA research of Universal Grammar and learnability theory (Pinker 1989), just as L1 interaction researchers have done. This is very evident in Long's recent reformulation of the Interaction Hypothesis (1996), which places much more emphasis on linking features of input and the linguistic environment with 'learner-internal factors', and explaining how such linkages may facilitate subsequent language development (1996, p. 454).

In his recent writing, Long re-defines the Interaction Hypothesis as follows.

> It is proposed that environmental contributions to acquisition are mediated by selective attention and the learner's developing L2 processing capacity, and that these resources are brought together most usefully, although not exclusively, during *negotiation for meaning*. Negative feedback obtained during negotiation work or elsewhere may be facilitative of L2 development, at least for vocabulary, morphology and language-specific syntax, and essential for learning certain specifiable L1–L2 contrasts.
>
> (1996, p. 414)

This new version of the hypothesis highlights the possible contribution to L2 learning of *negative evidence* as to the structure of the target language, derivable from environmental language (i.e. from FTD). It also highlights the attempt to clarify the processes by which input becomes intake, through introducing the notion of *selective attention*. In the next two sections, the usefulness of these concepts to interactive acquisition theory is discussed.

6.7 Feedback and negative evidence in second language acquisition

We saw in Section 6.2 that the existence and usability of negative evidence in Child-Directed Speech (CDS) have become important in debates on first language acquisition. The argument sharpened as studies of CDS revealed that caretakers' speech with young children was, in general, regular and well formed, i.e. it seemed to provide essentially *positive* evidence on the nature of the language system to be learned. Moreover, it seems that (at least in the well-studied English-speaking world), explicit negative evidence, in the form of parental correction of children's grammar mistakes, is rare.

Theorists arguing for a strongly innatist model of language learning have claimed that language is simply not learnable from input which provides only (or even mostly) positive evidence about the target language (e.g. Pinker 1989; Wexler and Culicover 1980). The logical reason is of course that a constant diet of well-formed utterances provides the learner with evidence on structures, etc. which the target language system does permit, but does not provide specific enough information on the limits to the system, i.e. it fails to rule out a number of generalizations which are compatible with the input received, but are actually incorrect. This is an important argument underlying claims that language must to a certain extent be 'hard wired' in order to be learnable, e.g. underlying Universal Grammar concepts of principles and parameters.

We saw in Section 6.2 that a number of child language researchers have responded to this view, by re-examining and reinterpreting CDS data. Researchers such as Bohannon et al. (1990) and Farrar (1992) assert that negative evidence is much more prevalent in CDS than was previously thought, particularly by asserting that caretakers' *recasts* of poorly formed child utterances offer implicit negative evidence about children's interim grammatical hypotheses. There is a continuing controversy among child language researchers on this issue, particularly concerning the standards to be applied to evidence supporting claims that recasts promote grammatical development (see e.g. Bohannon *et al.* 1996; Morgan *et al.* 1995). From his general review, Long (1996) concludes, however, that L1 acquisition researchers have generally succeeded in demonstrating that (implicit) negative evidence first, is regularly available in CDS, second, exists in usable form and, third, is picked up and used by child learners, at least in the short term. Whether negative evidence is necessary for the acquisition of core aspects of language (e.g. of the principles specified by Universal Grammar theory) still remains much less clear, however.

6.7.1   *Negative evidence in the L2 classroom*

As far as second language learning is concerned, most of the evidence regarding a possible role for negative evidence derives from classroom studies of instructed L2 learning. Here, some studies have suggested that active correction (i.e. provision of *explicit* negative evidence) contributes to increased accuracy in learners' target language production, at least in the short term (see reviews in Chaudron 1988, pp. 175–8, and DeKeyser 1993). A cluster of recent Canadian studies has taught us more about the kinds of explicit teacher feedback which are likely to promote accuracy. For example, Spada and Lightbown (1993) documented a teacher, included in a classroom quasi-experiment only as a control, whose pupils significantly out-performed those receiving an experimental treatment intended to promote their control of English L2 WH-interrogative structures. The experimental treatment provided a programme of explicit, form-focused instruction. The 'control' teacher did not follow the experimental programme; however, she regularly engaged in incidental correction of students who produced inaccurate WH-questions in the course of ongoing classroom interaction, and insisted on correct production.

Spada and Lightbown argue that these tactics were maximally effective because the corrections were regular, yet incidental and contextualized, assisting the students to form more correctly utterances which they were already motivated to produce for ongoing communicative ends. Presumably also, the students were at a developmental stage when they were likely to be receptive to/attend to such correction, on this particular cluster of structures (see Section 6.6 below).

Another recent classroom study (Lyster and Ranta 1997) looked at different types of error feedback offered by teachers, and noted that recasts were much the most common. However, recasts were much less likely to lead to immediate self-correction by the students, relatively speaking, than were other types of feedback (e.g. clarification requests, or metalinguistic feedback). These researchers argue that while recasts may offer valuable negative evidence, students are not put under pressure to attend it; they speculate that more interactive feedback modes may therefore be more effective in pushing classroom learners to amend their hypotheses about L2 structure.

Finally, a group of studies by White and colleagues (Trahey 1996; Trahey and White 1993; White 1991) have focused on the acquisition by French L1 children learning English as L2 of rules to do with adverb placement. (English allows SAV sentences such as *Helen rarely drinks orange juice*, which are not acceptable in French; however, English does *not* allow SVAO sentences such as **Helen drinks rarely orange juice*, while French permits this pattern. Native speakers of French must therefore learn the new SAV pattern, and also *un*learn the SVAO pattern, when mastering adverb placement in English).

At various times, different groups of classroom learners in these studies received either explicit instruction in English adverb placement (assumed to include systematic provision of negative evidence), or a so-called 'flood' of positive evidence on adverb placement, or instruction in other aspects of English. In 1996, Trahey reported a follow-up study looking for long-term effects in children's competence of these different treatments. She found that both the explicit instruction (negative evidence) group, and the flood (positive evidence) group, had apparently internalized the knowledge that SAV is permitted in English. However, it seemed that neither group had internalized the knowledge that SVAO is *not* permitted. (The instructed group had seemed to demonstrate proficiency on this point, in tests which took place shortly after the original period of instruction. However, in the long-term follow-up study, their ability to recognise SVAO as ungrammatical had significantly declined.)

In reviewing these equivocal results, Trahey speculates on similar lines to Spada and Lightbown (1993), that perhaps some mix of both positive and negative evidence may be required to ensure effective acquisition: 'An incorporation of attention to structure within the context of the flood may well have led to greater success' (1996, p. 136).

6.7.2 *Negative evidence in everyday FTD*

Much less work has so far been done even to document the existence of (implicit) negative evidence in FTD in non-classroom settings, far less to research its take-up in learners' interlanguage development. Of course, taxonomies developed to describe interactional modifications in FTD have always included categories such as 'semantic other-repetition'/'paraphrase' (Long 1983a, p. 138), which seem closely similar to the recasts treated in L1 research as sources of negative evidence. But these have not received special attention, so that e.g. Lakshmanan could conclude that: 'The role of indirect negative evidence (in contrast to direct negative evidence) has received hardly any attention in the child SLA and adult SLA literature' (1995, p. 318).

However, very recently a beginning has been made, on similar lines to earlier work in L1 acquisition. For example, Oliver (1995) recorded pairs of NS and NNS children carrying out one-way and two-way problem-solving tasks in English (both involving picture completion). In her data, over 60 per cent of NNS errors received some form of negative feedback from the NS children. Most frequent were *negotiations* of some kind (clarification requests, confirmation checks); these predominated where NNS utterances included multiple errors, and/or were semantically ambiguous. However, recasts also occurred, usually in response to utterances containing single errors, and also in association with particular types of grammar mistake.

The following example illustrates the pattern in which a native speaker responded with negotiation when the NNS's meaning was ambiguous, such as that caused by poor word choice:

(4) NNS   NS
     It go just one line.
                                            Just along the line?
     Yer.

In the next example, an error was recast as the meaning was transparent:

(5) NNS   NS
     And the . . . the boy is holding
     the girl hand and . . .
                                            Yer.
                                            The boy is holding the girl's hand.
                                                        (Oliver 1995, p. 473)

(See also Table 6.2 for the general relationships found in Oliver's data between error types and NS responses.)

Table 6.2 Child NS responses to different types of error

Error	Negotiate	Recast	Ignore	p
Article (n = 69)	32%	25%	43%	.1645
Aux/copula (n = 132)	54%	7%	39%	.0001***
Sing/pl/conc (n = 17)	18%	47%	35%	.007**
Pronoun (n = 27)	63%	7%	30%	.0399*
Tense (n = 19)	37%	16%	47%	.7853
Word order/omission (n = 77)	53%	14%	33%	.0364*
Word choice (n = 78)	54%	10%	36%	.0102*
No subject (n = 39)	64%	5%	31%	.0032**
Pronunciation (obvious error) (n = 42)	48%	26%	26%	.1245

Note: *p<◄.05. **p<◄.01. ***p = .001.
Source: Oliver 1995, p. 471

As well as documenting extensive negative feedback produced by her NS subjects, Oliver also showed that her NNS subjects incorporated just under 10 per cent of the recasts into their following utterances. This seems a low figure, but she argues that on many occasions, it was not conversationally appropriate/possible to do so. She also points out that the learners are operating under developmental constraints.

> NNSs can only incorporate structures when it is within their morphosyntactic ability to do so (Meisel *et al.* 1981; Pienemann 1989). That is to say, input, and in this case, recasts can only be usable if they are within the learnability range of the NNS ... It is quite probable that a substantial proportion of the recasts that were not incorporated were beyond the current L2 processing abilities of the NNSs.

> (Oliver 1995, p. 476)

Overall then, Oliver interprets her data optimistically as showing not only the availability of negative evidence in conversational FTD involving children, but showing also its usability and take-up, within the limits of the learners' current processing ability.

6.8 Attention, consciousness-raising and 'focus on form'

Finally, recent versions of the Interaction Hypothesis have tried to incorporate the idea that learners' processing capacities and degree of attention to matters of form may mediate the extent to which L2 *input* in the form of environmental language actually becomes L2 *intake*, i.e. becomes incorporated into the learner's developing L2 system.

As we have seen earlier, a number of researchers have argued in recent years that SLA cannot take place purely as a result of implicit and incidental learning. Remember that, according to Krashen's Input Hypothesis, it was sufficient for the learner to pay attention to the meaning embedded in comprehensible input, for the acquisition of language forms to take place. However, the mechanisms by which this was supposed to happen were never clearly specified.

Instead, researchers such as Sharwood Smith (1981, 1993), Schmidt (1990, 1994) and others have argued that learners need to pay some degree of attention to language forms if acquisition is to take place. Once again, this argument receives general support from the many examples of incomplete acquisition documented in the literature, in apparently input-rich environments (such as the Canadian immersion programmes).

Like others who have discussed this issue, Schmidt is careful to distinguish among different types of attention which learners might pay to language form. He uses the term *noticing* to refer to the process of bringing some stimulus into focal attention, i.e. registering its simple occurrence, whether voluntarily or involuntarily ('for example when one notices the odd spelling of a new vocabulary word', 1994, p. 17). He reserves the terms *understanding* and *awareness* for explicit knowledge: 'awareness of a rule or generalization' (1994, p. 18).

Schmidt is generally optimistic about the contribution of both kinds of attention to language learning. His main evidence is support of the significance of *noticing* comes from his own personal diary, kept while learning Portuguese (with accompanying tapes of his own conversational development: Schmidt and Frota 1986).

> Journal entry, Week 21 ... I'm suddenly hearing things I never heard before, including things mentioned in class. Way back in the beginning, when we learned question words, we were told that there are alternate long and short forms like *o que* and *o que é que*, *quem* or *quem é que*. I have never heard the long forms, ever, and concluded that they were just another classroom fiction. But today, just before we left Cabo Frio, M said something to me that I didn't catch right away. It sounded like French *que'est-ce que c'est*, only much abbreviated, approximately [kekse], which must be (o) *que* (é) *que* (vo)*cê* ...
>
> Journal entry, Week 22. I just said to N *o que é que você quer*, but quickly: [kekseker]. Previously, I would have said just *o que*. N didn't blink, so I guess I got it right.
>
> (Schmidt 1990, p. 14)

This is an extract from the diary, recording evidence of noticing for certain Portuguese question forms. Schmidt comments on this data extract as follows.

> In this particular case, it is very clear that these forms had been present in comprehensible input all along. *E que* variants of question words were used by my interlocutor on all the conversational tapes; 43 per cent of all question words on the first tape are of this type. I heard them and processed them for meaning from the beginning, but did not notice the form for five months. When I finally did notice the form, I began to use it.
>
> (Schmidt 1990, p. 141)

On the basis of this kind of evidence, Schmidt has argued that 'noticing is the necessary and sufficient condition for the conversion of input to intake for learning' (1994, p. 17), though he later modified this view to the weaker claim that 'more noticing leads to more learning' (1994: 18).

Regarding the possible contribution of explicit *awareness* of grammar rules to learning, Schmidt is more cautious. He points to a number of studies (e.g. Green and Hecht 1992) that show that learners can make judgements about what is 'right' and 'wrong' in target language data, without necessarily being able to state the relevant underlying rules. He also recalls that 'studies showing an advantage for explicit learning generally have not found a lasting effect for such learning' (1994, p. 19). (For example, this is borne out by the studies of adverb placement reported by Trahey, 1996, and discussed above.) None the less, he and others argue that tactics of *consciousness-raising* and *input enhancement*, through combinations of heightened saliency for target L2 items, metalinguistic commentary and/or negative feedback, may be important components of effective classroom learning, at least for some parts of the target language system (Sharwood Smith 1994, pp. 174–81).

It should be obvious by this point just how this developing concern with learner attention links up with revised forms of the Interaction Hypothesis. Recent commentators have pointed out that negotiation and modification of input in FTD may serve a broad purpose of making features of the target language more salient, and therefore more 'noticeable' by the language learner. For example, Pica (1994) points to the 'great number of opportunities that can arise during negotiation to draw learners' attention to both message meaning and L2 form' (p. 507). She quotes a range of examples from her own earlier studies to show how such negotiations can highlight phonological, lexical and structural features of the target language, presumably promoting their availability as potential intake.

NS: I have a piece of toast with a small pat of butter on it
NNS: hm hmm
NS: and above the plate
NNS: *what is buvdaplate?*
NS: **above**
NNS: *above the plate*
NS: **yeah not up as if you are sitting at the table it would be farther away from you than the plate**
NNS: hm hmm

(Pica 1992b, p. 225; Pica 1993, p. 440)

6.9 Evaluation: the scope of interactionist research

The Input and Interaction Hypotheses have led to very active strands of empirical research on Foreigner Talk Discourse (FTD). A first phase of research leaned heavily towards the general characterisation of FTD, and within it, towards documenting the phenomenon of meaning negotiation. If it could be shown that negotiation increased comprehensibility of TL input, it was assumed that this would also enhance L2 acquisition.

Later phases of FTD research have developed in at least two significant ways. First, FTD researchers have shown more concern to relate environmental factors in language learning to linguistic models of the language learning process, and in particular to the assumptions of Universal Grammar. Perhaps FTD is helpful primarily in learning those aspects of the target language which fall outside the Universal Grammar core (e.g. in learning vocabulary, or peripheral, language-specific features of syntax)? If on the other hand, FTD is helpful in promoting acquisition of core syntax (as conceptualized within UG), should it be viewed primarily as a source of positive evidence, and of triggers for parameter-setting, etc. within a UG framework? Or, does the pervasive discouraging evidence of incomplete learner success mean that a place for negative evidence has to be found in modelling any link-up between external and internal factors? Again, if negative evidence is being sought, FTD has been the place to look.

Second, FTD research has paid increased attention to a range of other specific claims about how individuals learn, and therefore, how input might be useful to them. In particular, recent FTD research has been influenced by new thinking about the role of attention in learning, and about the possible influence of a variety of processing constraints on intake.

The pace of change, and increased concern with theory-building, mean that FTD research is in a self-critical mood, with many researchers arguing for new directions in empirical research, for the adoption of alternative research methodologies, and greater agreement on the definition of constructs such as 'consciousness' – or indeed, 'acquisition' itself (Long 1996; Mellow *et al.* 1996; Pica 1994; Schmidt 1994). These can be compared interestingly with Richards 1994, raising similar methodological issues in respect of L1 input/interaction research.

6.9.1 *Achievements of interactionist research*

So what are the achievements to date of research in the Input/Interaction tradition? They may be summarized as follows.

1 It has been shown that NS and NNS interlocutors (child and adult) can and will work actively to achieve mutual understanding, at least within the framework of a fairly wide range of problem-solving tasks.
2 It has been shown that these negotiations involve both linguistic and interactional modifications, which together offer repeated opportunities to 'notice' aspects of target language form, whether from positive or negative evidence.
3 It has been shown that NNS participants in 'negotiations for meaning' can attend to, take up and use language items made available to them from their NS interlocutors' contributions to FTD.
4 It has been shown that learners receiving certain types of explicit instruction, and/or negative feedback, relating to particular target language

structures, can be significantly advantaged when later tested on those structures.

6.9.2　*Limitations of interactionist research*

However, the achievements of this tradition are constrained by a number of important limitations, which include the following.

1 Work on interaction has been carried out almost entirely within a western/ anglophone educational setting; extensive cross-cultural studies of inter-action between more and less fluent speakers will be needed before any claims can be made that 'negotiation for meaning' is a universal phenomenon.

2 All researchers in the Input/Interactionist tradition seem to accept in general terms that SLA must be the result of interaction between environ-mental factors and innate learning capabilities. Attempts at modelling this interaction are still very fragmentary and incomplete, however (even from the best-developed linguistic perspective, that of UG); this means that we are still far from identifying what may be the most productive research questions to ask, about the role of interaction etc. in learning.

3 A great deal of research on interaction, etc. has been of a broad brush kind, e.g. producing global characterizations of interactional modifica-tions, or demonstrating the existence of recasts or learners' re-use of nego-tiated items. There are relatively few studies which focus on particular language structures, tracking them through processes of instruction, nego-tiation and/or recasting, and documenting learners' subsequent use and control of these particular items. Such focused studies as exist (e.g. White 1991 on adverb placement, Loschky 1994 on locative structures) have widely differing theoretical motivations, and do not (yet) add up to a coherent and developmentally oriented treatment of different aspects of target language grammar.

4 We as yet have very little idea of the differential effectiveness of negotia-tion, etc. for acquisition, dependent on such key factors as the different components of the target language system, and the developmental stage of the learner. There are some suggestions in the literature, e.g. that negotia-tion may be more effective for aspects of phonology and lexis, less effec-tive for aspects of core syntax, but we do not really know. Similarly, as Pica (1994) puts it, citing Pienemann (1989): 'if learners are not ready for a new word, form or rule, they cannot acquire it, and thus negotiation will not help toward its internalisation'. But we still know very little about what might constitute 'readiness' to acquire any given item, either in terms of the necessary prerequisite state of the learner's interlanguage, or in terms of the degree of automaticity of processing, which might 'free up' the attentional space which is needed for 'noticing' something new.

But one thing is clear – while Input/Interaction research remains highly active, it cannot solve these difficulties alone. Its future is intertwined with the development of more comprehensive models of the learner-internal SLA process itself. (As we shall see, however, many of these comments apply not only to this particular research perspective, but to other primarily 'environmentalist' traditions to be explored in following chapters.)

7

Sociocultural perspectives on second language learning

7.1 Introduction

In this chapter and the next, we turn our attention to theorists who view language learning in essentially social terms. In both chapters, we examine the work of those who claim that target language interaction cannot be viewed simply as a source of 'input' for autonomous and internal learning mechanisms, but has a much more central role to play in learning. Indeed, for some researchers, interaction itself constitutes the learning process, which is quintessentially social rather than individual in nature. This is not a new view (see e.g. Hatch 1978), but it has been given extra impetus in the 1990s by the introduction of learning theory associated with the name of the Soviet developmental psychologist Lev S. Vygotsky to the domain of second language learning. In this chapter, we review and evaluate this relatively new strand of thinking, associated particularly with the work of James Lantolf, Richard Donato, Frank Brooks and others whose work is gathered together in two recent collections (Lantolf (ed.) 1994b; Lantolf and Appel 1994b).

7.2 Sociocultural theory

Lev Semeonovich Vygotsky was born in 1896, the same year as the Swiss developmental psychologist Jean Piaget whose views on language development were briefly mentioned in Chapter 1. Born in the Russian provinces, Vygotsky was active in Moscow between 1925 and his early death in 1934. Like Piaget, he was a researcher and theorist of child development; however, his work fell into disfavour within Soviet psychology, and the first of his many writings to be translated into English, *Thought and Language*, appeared only in 1962. Since then his sociocultural theories of child development have become increasingly influential, having been taken up and promoted by psychologists and child development theorists such as Jerome Bruner (1985), James Wertsch (1985) and Barbara Rogoff (1990), and applied in classroom studies by many educational researchers (e.g. Edwards and Mercer 1987; Mercer 1995). Many of his wide-ranging writings remain untranslated, and contemporary interpretations and modifications to Vygotskian theory have taken on an independent life of their own. Here, we will outline a number of key ideas current in contemporary interpretations/discussions of Vygotsky, which have recently been taken up by SLL theorists.

7.2.1   Mediation

Lantolf stresses that:

> Vygotsky's fundamental theoretical insight is that higher forms of human mental activity are always, and everywhere, *mediated* by symbolic means ... Mediation, whether physical or symbolic, is understood to be the introduction of an auxiliary device into an activity that then links humans to the world of objects or to the world of mental behaviour. Just as physical tools (e.g. hammers, bulldozer, computers etc.) allow humans to organize and alter their physical world, Vygotsky reasoned that symbolic tools empower humans to organize and control such mental processes as voluntary attention, logical problem-solving, planning and evaluation, voluntary memory, and voluntary learning ... Symbolic tools are the means through which humans are able to organize and maintain control over the self and its mental, and even physical, activity.
>
> (1994a, p. 418)

From a Vygotskian perspective, the prime symbolic tool available for the mediation of mental activity is, of course, language. Through language, for example, we can direct our own attention (or that of others) to significant features in the environment, formulate a plan, or articulate the steps to be taken in solving a problem.

7.2.2   Regulation, scaffolding and the Zone of Proximal Development

The mature, skilled individual is capable of autonomous functioning, that is of *self-regulation*. However, the child or the unskilled individual learns by carrying out tasks and activities under the guidance of other more skilled individuals (e.g. parents, teachers, etc.), initially through a process of *other-regulation*, typically mediated through language. That is, the child or the learner is inducted into a shared consciousness through collaborative talk, until eventually they take over (or *appropriate*) new knowledge or skills into their own individual consciousness; successful learning involves a shift from inter-mental activity to intra-mental activity. The process of supportive dialogue which directs the attention of the learner to key features of the environment, and which prompts them through successive steps of a problem, has come to be known as *scaffolding* (Wood *et al.* 1976).

The domain where learning can most productively take place is christened the *Zone of Proximal Development* (ZPD), i.e. the domain of knowledge or skill where the learner is not yet capable of independent functioning, but can achieve the desired outcome given relevant scaffolded help. The ZPD was defined by Vygotsky as: 'the difference between the child's developmental level as determined by independent problem solving and the higher level of potential development as determined through problem solving under adult guidance or in collaboration with more capable peers' (1978, p. 85). These ideas are illustrated in an example taken from general educational literature (Mercer 1996).

> *You have a square sheet of card measuring 15 cm by 15 cm and you want to use it to make an open cuboid container by cutting out the corners. What is the maximum capacity the container can have?*

EMILY: This box is bigger than what it should be 'cos if you get 15 by 15 you get 225, but if you times um 9 by 9 times 3 you still get 243 and I haven't got that much space in my box.

A: You have.

EMILY: But the 15 by ...

B: It can be, it can work, I think.

EMILY: But surely ...

B: You cut off corners.

EMILY: Yeh but that surely should make it *smaller*.

B: I think that is right.

EMILY: (*counting squares marked on the paper*) Hang on, 1, 2, 3, 4, 5 ...

C: You're not going to get 243.

EMILY: I shouldn't get 243 'cos if the piece of paper only had 225 then, um ...

C: Hang on, look ... 9 times 9 times how many was it up?

A: But don't you remember Emily it's got all this space in the middle.

EMILY: Yeh, but ...

A: It's got all that space in the middle.

EMILY: (*sounding exasperated*) No, it hasn't got anything to do with it. If my piece of paper had only 225 squares on it, I can't get more out of the same piece of paper.

A: You can because you're forgetting, things go *up* as well, not just the flat piece of paper like that.

EMILY: Oh yeh.

A: It's going up.

A: It's going up.

C: It's because, look, down here you've got 3 and it's going up.

A: You're going 3 up, it's getting more on it. Do you see it will be 243?

EMILY: Yeh.

C: It is right, it should be.

(Mercer 1996, pp. 34–5)

Here, Emily is a secondary school student who is struggling to make sense of a mathematical problem (which involves the relationship between area and volume). She is already proficient in the necessary arithmetical skills, so that the problem is in principle accessible to her (in Vygotskian terms, it lies within her personal ZPD). Her peers direct her attention to different aspects of the problem, illustrating the ideas of other-regulation and scaffolding.

Eventually the successive attempts of Emily's friends to direct her attention to the three-dimensional nature of the problem seem to be successful, as evidenced in her non-verbal reaction in Line 26, and her subsequent contributions. The claim is that a qualitative change in Emily's understanding has occurred, so that she could in future solve similar problems without help. In Vygotskian terms, Emily has *appropriated* the necessary concepts, and should be more capable of regulating her own performance on another similar occasion.

The metaphor of *scaffolding* has been developed in neo-Vygotskian discussions to capture the qualities of the type of other-regulation within the ZPD which is supposedly most facilitative of learning/appropriation of new concepts. According to Wood *et al.* (1976), scaffolded help has the following functions:

1 recruiting interest in the task;
2 simplifying the task;
3 maintaining pursuit of the goal;
4 marking critical features and discrepancies between what has been produced and the ideal solution;
5 controlling frustration during problem solving;
6 demonstrating an idealized version of the act to be performed.

As Donato puts it, 'scaffolded performance is a dialogically constituted interpsychological mechanism that promotes the novice's internalisation of knowledge co-constructed in shared activity' (1994, p. 41).

7.2.3   Microgenesis

The example just quoted illustrates in miniature the general principles of sociocultural learning theory. For Vygotsky, these principles apply on a range of different timescales. They apply to the learning which the human race has passed through over successive generations (*phylogenesis*), as well as to the learning which the individual human infant passes through in the course of its early development (*ontogenesis*). For the entire human race, as well as for the individual infant, learning is seen as first social, then individual. Consciousness and conceptual development are seen as first an inter-mental phenomenon, shared between individuals; later, the individual appropriates their own consciousness, which becomes an intra-mental phenomenon. For the human race, and also for the individual infant, language is the prime symbolic mediating tool for the development of consciousness.

Throughout their life, of course, human beings remain capable of learning; and the local learning process for more mature individuals acquiring new knowledge or skills is viewed as essentially the same. That is, new concepts continue to be acquired through social/interactional means, a process which can sometimes be traced visibly in the course of talk between expert and novice. This local, contextualized learning process is labelled *microgenesis*; it is central to sociocultural accounts of second language learning.

7.2.4   Private and inner speech

Young children are well known to engage in *private speech*, talk apparently to and for themselves, rather than for any external conversational partner. From the point of view of classic Piagetian theory of child development, this talk has been interpreted as evidence of children's *egocentrism,* or incapacity to view the world from another's point of view. However, private speech is interpreted very differently in sociocultural theory. Here, it is seen as evidence of the child's growing ability to regulate her own behaviour – when, for example, the child talks to herself through the painting of a picture, or solving a puzzle. For Vygotsky, private speech eventually becomes *inner speech*, a use of language to regulate internal thought, without any external articulation. Thus, for Vygotsky, private speech reflects an advance on the earliest uses of language, which are social and interpersonal. The fully autonomous individual has developed inner speech as a tool of thought, and normally feels no further need to articulate external private speech. However, when tackling a new task, even skilled adults may accompany and regulate their efforts with a private monologue.

7.2.5   Activity theory

The last important concept drawn from sociocultural theory which we need to consider is that of *activity theory*, developed by one of Vygotsky's successors, A. N. Leontiev (Lantolf and Appel 1994a, pp. 16–22; Leontiev 1981). Activity theory comprises a series of proposals for conceptualizing the social context within which individual learning takes place. The following account of the theory is offered by Donato and McCormick (1994).

> Activity is defined in terms of sociocultural settings in which collaborative interaction, intersubjectivity, and assisted performance occur ... In his analysis, Leontiev conceived activity as containing a subject, an object, actions, and operations. To illustrate these constituents of activity we use the classroom as an example. A student (a subject) is engaged in an activity, for example, learning a new language. An object, in the sense of a goal, is held by the student and motivates his or her activity, giving it a specific direction. In the case of our language learner, the object could range from full participation in a new culture to receiving a passing grade required for graduation.
>
> To achieve the objective, actions are taken by the student, and these actions are always goal-directed ... Different actions or strategies may be taken to achieve the same goal, such as guessing meaning from context, reading foreign language newspapers, or using a bilingual dictionary to improve reading comprehension ...

Finally, the operational level of activity is the way an action is carried out and depends on the conditions under which actions are executed. For example, how one attends to driving a car depends in large part on the context of the activity (e.g. weather conditions, purpose of trip, type of vehicle, etc). These operational aspects of actions can become routinized and automatic once the conscious goal is no longer attended to. Returning to our example of the language learner, if the goal of the learner was to become proficient in deriving meaning from context rather than from the bilingual dictionary, contextual guessing during reading becomes automatized once the learner becomes adept at this strategy ... The model of human activity depicted in activity theory is not static, however. Routinized operations (automatic strategies) can become conscious goal-directed actions if the conditions under which they are carried out change. In the case of our second language reader who has operationalised at the unconscious level the strategy of contextual guessing, it is quite conceivable that this strategy will be reactivated at the conscious level if the learner is confronted with a difficult passage beyond his or her strategic ability, i.e. if the conditions of strategy use change.

(1994, p. 455)

7.3   Applications of sociocultural theory to SLL

What are the particular lines of enquiry into second language learning which have been sparked off by the current climate of interest in sociocultural theory? In turn, we will consider a selection of L2 research studies which have appealed to a number of key Vygotskian ideas: private speech, activity theory, and the role of scaffolding in learning.

7.3.1   *Private speech and self-regulation in second language discourse*

Instances of private speech have been regularly noted in naturalistic studies of child L2 acquisition, as in other studies of child language. However, their significance has been variously interpreted. The following example is quoted by Hatch (1978), from a study by Itoh (1973) of a Japanese L1 child learning English as L2.

H:	House.
TAKAHIRO:	This house?
H:	House.
T:	House.
	To make the house.
	To make the house.
	To make the house.
	This?
	House.
	Garage.
	Garage house
	house

	big house
	Oh-no!
	broken.
H:	Too bad.
T:	Too bad.
H:	Try again.
T:	I get try.
	I get try.
H:	Good.

For Hatch, Takahiro's extended speech turn, accompanying a construction activity of some kind, is viewed somewhat negatively as 'not social speech at all but [only] language play' (p. 411). She goes on to argue defensively that the fact that it is merely 'language play' need not necessarily mean it is useless for language acquisition; but she does not analyse its positive functions any further. From a Vygotskian perspective, however, this extended spoken accompaniment to action provides evidence about the role of language in problem-solving and self-regulation. (It also provides evidence for the *appropriation* by the child of the new lexical item *house*, initially supplied by the supportive adult, but then quickly re-used by Takahiro in a range of syntactic frames.)

Later studies which explicitly bring Vygotskian conceptions of private speech to bear on language learner data have mostly worked with data elicited from older learners, in semi-controlled settings (see review by McCafferty 1994). In one of the first substantial attempts to apply any aspect of Vygotskian theory to second language learning, Frawley and Lantolf (1985) reported an empirical study of English L2 learners undertaking a narrative task, based on a picture sequence. They were critical of *schema theories* of narrative, which propose that stories are narrated in a deterministic manner, according to a previously internalized template (situation, actors, events, problems, resolutions, etc.); they also argued that *information processing models* of communication, which view communication primarily as the encoding and transmission of a predetermined message, could not account adequately for their data. (This is a common theme in sociocultural critiques of SLA research; see also Platt and Brooks 1994, pp. 498–9.)

The picture sequence used by Frawley and Lantolf comprised the following frames.

Frame 1: A boy walks along a road.
Frame 2: He sees an ice cream seller.
Frame 3: He buys a 50-cent ice cream cone.
Frame 4: He gives the cone to a small boy.
Frame 5: A man approaches the small boy.
Frame 6: The man takes the cone from the small boy. The small boy cries.

In re-telling this story, the English L2 learners produced accounts which were, as narratives, disjointed and incoherent. However, they incorporated into their accounts many utterances which involved direct reactions/descriptions of individual pictures (*I see a boy on the road*), or externalizations of the task itself (*You want me to say what they are doing? This is the problem now*, etc.). These metacomments were entirely absent from the fluent performances of a group of native speakers (*A little boy is walking down the street* ... etc.).

Frawley and Lantolf interpret the data as demonstrating the learners' need to 'impose order on the task by speaking and identifying the task' (p. 26). In Vygotskian terms, they argue that the learners are struggling to move beyond *object-regulation* (in this case, evidenced in direct reactions to the pictures, or descriptions of them) towards self-regulation and control over the task. Because they cannot take *self-regulation* for granted, their efforts to gain control are explicitly articulated throughout their performance.

Figure 7.1 shows a pair of narratives taken from a different study (McCafferty 1994, p. 426), which used a similar methodology.

McCafferty argues that many utterances incorporated within the narrative of the L2 subject are examples of private speech, which reflect object-regulation (*I see a man on ... in the picture*), other-regulation (here defined as any utterances which are dialogic in form, e.g. self-directed questions like *What do I see?*), and self-regulation (here defined as metacomments indicating that a subject has suddenly understood or mastered a source of difficulty, as here in Frame 6).

In this and other studies, McCafferty systematically contrasts the extent of private speech to be found in the narratives produced by learners at different levels of proficiency as well as by native speakers, demonstrating that there is a systematic relationship between the use of private speech to regulate task performance, and the degree of task difficulty. In a recent review, McCafferty (1994) argues that in producing L2 discourse, learners may expend just as much effort to self-regulate as to 'communicate', but the phenomenon has been comparatively neglected by researchers on L2 discourse; for example, we know little about the nature of private speech in which classroom learners may engage. In conclusion, he claims that 'a Vygotskian view of private speech affords a valuable window onto the intra-personal processes in which adult L2 learners engage in their efforts to self-regulate in the face of the very complex process of learning a second language' (1994, p. 434).

7.3.2   Activity theory and small group interaction

As we have seen earlier, Vygotskian theorists of SLL are generally critical of 'transmission' models of communication, in which ready-made messages are passed from speaker to hearer (e.g. Donato 1994, pp. 33–6; Platt and Brooks 1994, p. 498). Similarly, they are critical of input and interactional models of language learning in which 'negotiation of meaning' is central (see Chapter 6), which they view as failing to capture the prime characteristics of language use. According to Platt and Brooks, 'What we are suggesting is a more robust view that incorporates an understanding of talk or, more specifically, speech activity as cognitive activity that humans press into service in order to solve problems, regardless of its communicative intent' (p. 499).

The task in this study required subjects to narrate a series of six pictures concerning a hat seller who falls asleep under a tree only to wake up and find that a group of monkeys has taken his hats and is up in the tree above him. He eventually discerns that the monkeys imitate his actions and is able to retrieve the hats by throwing his own to the ground.

Low-intermediate L2 subject:

1) I see a man on ... in the picture. He's looking at some monkeys – the monkeys are in the tree. Monkeys are playing in the tree. There is a house next to the tree. There are some hats in baskets ... two baskets. Maybe the man is thinking about how happy are the monkeys? Maybe he's looking at the sky.

2) What do I see? There is another basket of hats. Now, the monkeys look at the man. The man is sleeping. Now, because the man is sleeping the monkeys are playing with the hats.

3) Suddenly, the man wakes up and looked at the monkeys. He surprised about the monkeys because the monkeys put on, on their, on their, on their heads the hats.

4) The man is angry. He wants to take his hats. The monkeys are happy, they are doing a sign, a sign of victory to the man ... 'we have the hats!' They have the hats.

5) Oh no! It's different! The monkeys are copying the signs of the man, and in this picture the man is thinking – I don't know about what. Maybe he's thinking about what he can – he do, and the monkeys, they take out, take off the hats and look at the man, and they are copying the same signs of the man.

6) Ah. Ok. Suddenly, the man had a ... has one idea – he, he thought, 'I'm going to fell down, fell down my hat so the monkeys are going to fell down, fall down they ... my hats too.' Ok. And the man fell down the hats and the monkeys copy to the man and do that too.

Adult native speaker

1) The man's watching the monkeys playing ... and the monkeys want to get all his hats – I guess.

2) And when he falls asleep the monkeys come down, get his hats, and put them on back in the tree.

3) When he wakes up, he realizes that the monkeys are wearing all of the hats that he wants to sell ... and he's pretty surprised.

4) He tries to get the monkeys to give him back his hats and gets mad at them, and the monkeys just imitate him.

5) Then, he starts thinking about the situation and the monkeys act like they're thinking about something too – imitating him.

6) In the end, he figures out that the monkeys will do what he does and so, ah, he throws down his hat and the monkeys imitate him ... so he gets his hats back and he's happy.

Fig. 7.1 Private speech in L2 narrative

Moreover, the tenets of activity theory (see above) lead researchers in this tradition to argue strongly for the distinctive nature of individual interactions as experienced by the participants, even where pre-set communicative tasks appear to be 'the same'. According to activity theory, the personal goals with which an individual approaches a particular task or problem may vary; thus, for example, a language learner may approach a conversational task under test conditions with a prime personal goal of achieving an accurate performance, even if the task designers intended it as a test of fluency. The entry levels of knowledge and skill which individuals bring to particular tasks will of course also vary, as well as being subject to change in the course of the task itself (in Vygotskian terms, the less expert participant can appropriate and internalize knowledge/skill which is collaboratively developed in the course of the interaction).

In support of these claims, Coughlan and Duff (1994) examined data gathered through an 'identical' picture description task in a variety of language learning settings, and argue that such features as subjects' willingness to stray off the point were highly context dependent (depending on how well they knew their interlocutor, how much time they believed was allocated to the task, the interlocutor's ongoing reactions, the sequence of tasks in which the picture description activity was embedded, etc.). Platt and Brooks (1994) recorded pairs and groups of students undertaking a variety of communicative problem-solving tasks in L2 classroom settings. They argue that student goals are critical in influencing the nature of the activities experienced. Their examples include:

1 students 'going through the motions' of English L2 task performance, rehearsing a problem which they appear already to understand (role playing the demonstration of an oscilloscope);
2 a student who engages in long stretches of private speech to regulate his own performance, as he addresses the 'same' oscilloscope demonstration task, apparently incapable of attending to his peers who try to redirect him;
3 students learning Swahili at beginner level who successfully carry out a map-based information exchange task, using a combination of paralinguistic means and single word paratactic constructions;
4 students making extensive use of L1 to define and redefine the ground rules for a jigsaw puzzle completion task, and to comment on task performance.

Platt and Brooks argue that these examples show students using their language resources (L1 and L2) both privately and collaboratively in order to solve the problems posed, i.e. primarily for regulatory purposes. In their view, the learning that has most obviously taken place has to do with task completion and problem-solving. However, the conventional rationale for inclusion of such tasks in the 'communicative' language learning curriculum – that language learning will result from the negotiation of comprehensible input – receives little support from their data: 'We do not presume to claim that

acquisition in the Chomskian sense is enabled (or impeded) in either setting'
(1994, p. 508).

Other researchers who have examined the socio-cognitive dimensions of
peer L2 interaction from a Vygotskian point of view include De Guerrero and
Villamil (1994). These authors looked at interactions during peer revision
activities, on an English L2 writing course. They analysed these interactions
in terms of the interplay between object-, other- and self-regulation, recording how participants moved flexibly between these cognitive stages, and arguing for resulting developmental benefits.

> In peer revision, the cognitive processes that are required for successful task
> completion are exercised in collaboration and then presumably internalized for
> eventual independent problem-solving. Students find themselves immersed in a
> situation where they not only have to exercise self-control over the task but also
> regulate and be regulated by the other. In other words, regulatory fluctuation
> probably always exists as no individual is at all times completely self-, other- or
> object-regulated. Peer revision is thus a potentially beneficial situation because
> it allows for interchangeability of roles and for continuous access to strategic
> forms of control in accordance with task demands ... At a certain stage of
> development, students need to be provided by others with strategic behaviour
> that they can later model and apply on their own. This is without doubt the
> ultimate goal of L2 writing instruction.
>
> (p. 493)

However, like Platt and Brooks, these writers do not explore or document
actual developments in L2 writing ability resulting from peer revision.

Finally, Donato and McCormick (1994) undertook a longitudinal study in
which they adopted the perspective of activity theory on the development of
learner strategies. They required a group of college students of French to document and reflect on their own growth and development in the spoken language over the course of one full semester, through the use of a
performance-based portfolio. Unlike learner diaries, the portfolio technique
required learners to produce evidence of their own ability to recognize and
use the language content introduced in class (e.g. audio recordings of their
spoken French performance), and to state why they thought particular portfolio items reflected advances in their L2 capability. No explicit strategy training was provided, yet the researchers argue that the portfolios provide genetic,
longitudinal evidence of growth in reported strategy use (*see* Figure 7.2 from
Donato and McCormick 1994, p. 460, for samples of increasing focus in the
strategies reported). This they attribute to a collective evolution in classroom
culture.

> The culture of this class consisted of a mediated, dialogic cycle of self-assess-
> ment, goal setting and strategy elaboration and restructuring. This process was
> brought about because students were purposefully socialized into constructing
> their own strategic learning through dialogue with self and teacher and con-
> nections to actual evidence of their growing abilities. From a sociocultural per-
> spective, the classroom culture can, therefore, be designed to move students
> beyond thoughtful consumption to reflective construction of language learning
> strategies.
>
> (p. 463)

Goal development

Unfocused (portfolio 1)	Focused (portfolio 2 or 3)
S1 I want to learn French.	I want to find a conversation partner.
S4 I want to learn and use new expressions.	I want to use more new expressions rather than the same vocabulary that I use each time in each situation.
S5 I want to improve my grammar.	I want to think of a specific situation in which I would use what we are learning.
S7 I want to speak more in class.	I want to identify conversational strategies when I hear them.
S9 I want to learn.	I want to try to find a conversation partner.

Strategy development

Unfocused (portfolio 2)	Focused (portfolio 3)
S2 I want to paraphrase more.	I tried to paraphrase 'Frequent Flyer Program'.
S3 I am going to carry a dictionary with me.	My friend and I practise speaking each day after class.
S4 I review verb tenses and expressions.	I use the portfolio itself to see progress and assess goals and achievement.
S5 I watch French films.	I review new expressions in each chapter, think of situations where I could use them and try to use them to myself.
S6 I use new expressions.	I speak French with C when we work together at the restaurant.
S7 I'll speak more.	Two times a week I call my friend on the phone and we have a French conversation.
S7 I'll learn more.	I'm keeping a vocabulary journal.
S8 I will speak more in class.	I take more risks in class. For example I used the word 'what' (previously discussed).
S9 I studied more.	When I hear you speak I write down words and phrases I don't know in my notebook.

Fig. 7.2 Developing focus in language learning strategies

7.3.3 Scaffolding and second language learning in the Zone of Proximal Development

We have just seen how learning strategy development can be accommodated within the framework of activity theory. But, how exactly does new language knowledge arise in the course of social interaction, and how is it internalized by the learner (or appropriated, to use Vygotskian terminology)?

Many naturalistic studies conducted by researchers working outside the Vygotskian tradition offer evidence which can be interpreted as showing the sharing and transfer of new L2 lexical and grammatical knowledge between speakers. We have already seen the child learner Takahiro appropriating and using the word *house*, offered to him by an adult carer (Hatch 1978, p. 410). Another of Hatch's examples, taken from Brunak *et al.* (1976), shows an adult learner eliciting and using an expression she needs (*last year*) from a co-operative interlocutor.

NS:	O that's a beautiful plant!
	I like that.
	Did you buy that?
RAFAELA:	Excuse me ...
	This is the ...
	October 24.
	The how you say ...
	The ... (writes '1974')
	year, ah?
NS:	1974. Last year.
R:	Ah! Last years.
NS:	One. (Correction of plural form)
R:	Last year.
	Last year a friend gave me it.

From an input/interaction perspective, such passages would be interpreted as instances of negotiation of meaning, conversational repair, etc., and would be seen as maximizing the relevance of the available input for the learner's acquisitional stage. From a Vygotskian perspective, it would presumably be argued more ambitiously that we are witnessing *microgenesis* in the learner's L2 system, through the appropriation of a new lexical item from the scaffolding talk of the native speaker.

However, those Vygotskian researchers who have addressed the issue of second language development most directly have typically done so in classroom rather than naturalistic settings. Several writers have looked at peer interaction in the performance of classroom activities with a focus on form (e.g. Donato 1994; Kowal and Swain 1994). For example, Donato cites a number of examples of adult English L1 learners of French working on English-to-French translation problems. These examples are taken from small group planning sessions which were the prelude to oral presentations, to take place in a later lesson. The example shows three learners collaborating to construct the past compound tense of the reflexive verb *se souvenir*, 'to remember'.

Protocol

A1	Speaker 1	... and then I'll say ... *tu as souvenu notre anniversaire de marriage* ... or should I say *mon anniversaire*?
A2	Speaker 2	*Tu as ...*
A3	Speaker 3	*Tu as ...*
A4	Speaker 1	*Tu as souvenu* ... 'you remembered?'
A5	Speaker 3	Yea, but isn't that reflexive? *Tu t'as ...*

A6   Speaker 1   Ah, *tu t'as souvenu.*
A7   Speaker 2   Oh, it's *tu es*
A7   Speaker 1   *Tu es*
A9   Speaker 3   *tu es, tu es, tu ...*
A10   Speaker 1   *T'es, tu t'es*
A11   Speaker 3   *tu t'es*
A12   Speaker 1   *Tu t'es souvenu.*

(Donato 1994, p. 44)

As Donato points out, no single member of the group possesses the ability to produce this complex form without help, yet through their successive individual contributions the verb form is collectively reshaped. Speaker 3 provides the reminder that the verb is reflexive, i.e. a supplementary pronoun must be inserted (line A5); Speaker 2 corrects the choice of auxiliary (line A7, *es* not *as*); and finally the first speaker can integrate these separate items of information so as to produce the correct form (line A12).

In support of the claim that linguistic development indeed follows from this type of collaborative interaction, Donato analysed the oral presentations which took place next day, and logged the extent to which forms worked on during the planning session were available for use. Thirty-two cases of scaffolded help had been identified during the planning sessions; 24 of the forms worked on collaboratively in this way were successfully re-used during the learners' individual oral presentations. Donato concludes that 'in this way, independent evidence is given that peer scaffolding results in linguistic development within the individual' (p. 52).

But are L2 forms which are the subject of scaffolded attention in form-focused talk really 'learned', i.e. appropriated into the learner's developing L2 system? The researchers in the Vygotskian tradition who pursue this issue furthest are Aljaafreh and Lantolf (1994). Their data comprise a group of longitudinal case studies of adult ESL learners receiving one-to-one feedback on weekly writing assignments. After the students had had a preliminary opportunity to re-read and locate errors in their own writing, the tutor and each student worked through the assignment together sentence by sentence. When errors were identified, the tutor aimed to scaffold the learner through the correction of the error in a contingent manner: 'the idea is to offer just enough assistance to encourage and guide the learner to participate in the activity and to assume increased responsibility for arriving at the appropriate performance' (p. 469).

The learners were tracked and audio-recorded through an eight-week cycle; the study focused on their developing capability (or microgenetic growth) on four grammatical points in written English (articles, tense marking, use of prepositions, and modal verbs). First, the researchers looked for an increase in accuracy in the use of these forms over time, as well as for the generalization of learning beyond the specific items which had received attention in tutorial discussion. Second, even where these errors continued to appear in students' writing, they looked for evidence of students' developing capacity to self-correct, and reducing dependency on other-regulation by the tutor.

Aljaafreh and Lantolf (1994, p. 471) developed a 'Regulatory Scale' to illustrate how the tutor's interventions could be ranged on a continuum from implicit to explicit correction; this scale is presented as Figure 7.3. Where students could be shown, over time, to require feedback which was moving closer to the 'Implicit' end of this scale, they were considered to be moving towards more independent and self-regulated performance, and this was consequently taken as positive evidence of learning.

The protocols presented in Figure 7.4 illustrate the type of data collected and discussed by Aljaafreh and Lantolf (1994, pp. 478–9). In Protocol L, we see the tutor and student F attempting to work out the correct tense markings for modal + main verb constructions. The tutor provides progressively more

---

Regulatory Scale—Implicit (strategic) to Explicit

---

0. Tutor asks the learner to read, find the errors, and correct them independently, prior to the tutorial.

1. Construction of a 'collaborative frame' prompted by the presence of the tutor as a potential dialogic partner.

2. Prompted or focused reading of the sentence that contains the error by the learner or the tutor.

3. Tutor indicates that something may be wrong in a segment (e.g., sentence, clause, line) – 'Is there anything wrong in this sentence?'

4. Tutor rejects unsuccessful attempts at recognizing the error.

5. Tutor narrows down the location of the error (e.g., tutor repeats or points to the specific segment which contains the error).

6. Tutor indicates the nature of the error, but does not identify the error (e.g., 'There is something wrong with the tense marking here').

7. Tutor identifies the error ('You can't use an auxiliary here').

8. Tutor rejects learner's unsuccessful attempts at correcting the error.

9. Tutor provides clues to help the learner arrive at the correct form (e.g., 'It is not really past but something that is still going on').

10. Tutor provides the correct form.

11. Tutor provides some explanation for use of the correct form.

12. Tutor provides examples of the correct pattern when other forms of help fail to produce an appropriate responsive action.

Fig. 7.3 Ranking error feedback on an implicit/explicit scale

(L) *F1*

1. T: Okay, 'to the ... [yeah] to the US. [Okay] In that moment I can't
2. ... lived in the house because I didn't have any furniture.'
3. Is that ... what what is wrong with that sentence, too?
4. What is wrong with the sentence we just read? ... 'In that
5. moment I can't lived in the house because I didn't have any
6. furniture' ... Do you see?
7. F: No
8. T: Okay ... ah there is something wrong with the verb with the
9. verb tense in this this sentence and the modal ... Do you know
10. modals?
11. F: Ah yes, I know
12. T: Okay, so what's what's wrong what's wrong here?
13. F: The tense of this live
14. T: Okay, what about the the ... is it just in this or in this, the
15. whole thing?
16. F: The whole this
17. T: Okay, how do you correct it? ... Okay, 'In that moment' ... What?
18. ... What is the past tense of can? what was
19. happening ... what ... the past, right? what was happening
20. ... what ... the event happened in the past right? so what
21. is the past tense of this verb can? ... Do you know?
22. F: No
23. T: Okay, ah could
24. F: Ah yes
25. T: Okay, 'I could not ...'
26. F: Live
27. T: Ah exactly, okay. So when you use this in the past then the second verb is the simple ...
28. F: yes
29. T: Form, okay ... aah 'in that moment I could not ...'
30. F: Live in the house

(M) *F1*

1. T: Okay, 'I called other friends who can't went do the party.' Okay,
2. what is wrong here?
3. F: To
4. T: 'Who can't went do the party because that night they worked at
5. the hospital.' Okay, from here 'I called other friends who
6. can't went do the party.' What's wrong in this?
7. F: To
8. T: Okay, what else? ... what about the verb and the tense? The
9. verb and the tense? ...
10. F: Could
11. T: Okay, here
12. F: Past tense
13. T: All right, okay, 'who [alright] could not.' Alright? And? ...
14. F: To
15. T: Here [points to the verb phrase], what's the right form?
16. F: I ... go
17. T: Go. Okay, 'could not go to [that's right] to the party ...'

(N) *F2*

1. T: Is there anything wrong here in this sentence? 'I took only Ani
2. because I couldn't took both' ... Do you see anything
3. wrong? ... Particularly here 'because I couldn't took both'
4. F: Or Maki?
5. T: What the verb verb ... something wrong with the verb ...
6. F: Ah, yes ...
7. T: That you used. Okay, where? Do you see it?
8. F: (Points to the verb)
9. T: Took? Okay
10. F: Take
11. T: Alright, take
12. F: (Laughs)

Fig. 7.4 Microgenesis in the language system

explicit feedback on the student's written error (cited in Lines 2/3), actually modelling the correct past tense form for modal auxiliary *can* in Line 23. Later in the same tutorial, the same problem is encountered again (Protocol M, Lines 1/2). Initially, the learner focuses on a different problem (she has written *do* for *to*, an error which she notices and corrects). However, once the tutor draws her attention to the incorrect verb pattern, she supplies successively the correct auxiliary past tense form *could*, and the untensed form of the main verb *go*. The researchers argue that this reduced need for other-regulation itself constitutes evidence for microgenetic development within the learner's Zone of Proximal Development.

Protocol N provides further performance data, this time from the tutorial which took place around the student's next assignment, one week later. The researchers claim that here again 'we see evidence of microgenesis both in production of the Modal + Verb construction and the extent of responsibility assumed by the learner for its production' (p. 479). The learner has independently produced the correct past tense form *could* in her written text. She has still marked the main verb incorrectly for tense, but interrupts the tutor to identify the error (Line 6), and offers the correct form *take* with very little hesitation (though her laughter and embarrassment indicate that self-regulation is still not automatized or complete). In later essays, this student's performance on this particular construction is error-free, and there is some evidence of generalization to other modals. For these researchers, such protocols clearly demonstrate the relevance of the Vygotskian constructs of regulation and microgenesis within the ZPD to language learning.

7.4   Evaluation

In comparison with most other theoretical perspectives on second language learning reviewed in this book, sociocultural theory is a relative newcomer to the field. What are its most original features, and how far have its claims been empirically established so far?

7.4.1   The scope and achievements of sociocultural research

Researchers working in a sociocultural framework are making an ambitious attempt to apply a general learning theory which has been very influential in other domains of social and educational research to the language learning problem. So far, a quite varied range of constructs (private speech, activity theory, scaffolding) has been appealed to, to address a variety of aspects of language learning (from the acquisition of lexis to the development of learning strategies). Studies to date have been relatively small in scale, and have generally employed interpretative research procedures. Thus in some studies, cross-sectional data are placed under qualitative scrutiny and searched for evidence of different levels and types of scaffolding and/or private speech. Following the 'genetic' method favoured by Vygotsky, other researchers gather longitudinal datasets, and search them for developmental sequences which supposedly indicate increasing self-regulation and control in the language learning process (e.g. Donato and McCormick 1994), and/or the appropriation of new language knowledge, as evidenced by the learners' increasingly independent use of the language items concerned (Aljaafreh and Lantolf 1994).

These research approaches are affected by some of the usual difficulties in interpreting naturalistic research. The students studied by Donato and McCormick conscientiously completed portfolios documenting their own progress, and seemed to develop increasingly sophisticated and focused learning strategies over time; but did the portfolio task play any causal role in improving their strategy use, or did it merely document it? The students studied by Aljaafreh and Lantolf improved the accuracy of their written English – but perhaps this would have happened anyhow, over time? In such studies, it is not yet clear that general causal relationships have been demonstrated.

7.4.2   *Sociocultural interpretations of language and communication*

Sociocultural theory views language as a 'tool for thought'. It is therefore critical of 'transmission' theories of communication, which are said to view language primarily as an instrument for the passage back and forth of predetermined messages and meanings. Dialogic communication is seen as central to the joint construction of knowledge (including knowledge of language forms), which is first developed inter-mentally, and then appropriated and internalized by the individual. Similarly, private speech, metastatement, etc. are valued positively as instruments for self-regulation, i.e. the development of autonomous control over new knowledge.

Beyond such general claims regarding the functions for which language may be used, however, sociocultural theorists of SLL do not offer any very thorough or detailed view of the nature of language as a formal system. What is the relative importance within the language system of words, or of grammar? Is language a creative, rule-governed system, or a patchwork of prefabricated chunks and routines, available in varying degrees for recombination? Up to now, sociocultural researchers in SLL have taken little interest in such general issues. In their empirical studies of language development within the ZPD, they have typically dealt in fragments of language, often isolated elements of morphology, the conventional focus of form-focused instruction, as we have seen in some of the transcripts quoted earlier (e.g. Donato 1994).

This limitation is recognized by researchers in the field (e.g. Aljaafreh and Lantolf 1994, p. 480); if this tradition is to move towards the mainstream in SLL research, it will need to locate itself more explicitly with respect to linguistic theory.

7.4.3   *The sociocultural view of (language) learning*

Like the cognitive perspectives reviewed in Chapter 4, sociocultural theorists assume that the same general learning mechanisms will apply to language, as apply to other forms of knowledge and skill. However, all learning is seen as first social, then individual; first inter-mental, then intra-mental. Also, learners are seen as active constructors of their own learning environment, which they shape through their choice of goals and operations. So, this tradition has a good deal to say of a theoretical kind about the *processes* of learning, and has invested considerable empirical effort in describing these.

What counts as 'learning' in this tradition, however, is not uncontroversial. Most of the Vygotskian studies which have looked specifically at language development have done so in the context of form-focused instruction. What is more, they have generally looked at oral discourse around the planning/review of written text. Donato (1994) argues that language items reviewed/co-constructed in this way have been 'learned', because they were re-used next day by individuals, in performing a (planned) oral presentation. Aljaafreh and Lantolf (1994) argue similarly that learning has taken place, on the grounds of increased accuracy in later written productions. But none of the studies published to date provide evidence of learners' spontaneous oral (re-)use of the scaffolded items, nor have they yet provided any long-term follow-up data.

Finally, the Vygotskian tradition as yet has very little to say on issues to do with rates and routes of learning. Do people who receive timely and effective scaffolding/means of mediation actually learn any faster than those who get less help? Does intervention in the ZPD merely scaffold people more rapidly along common routes of interlanguage development, or can these routes be bypassed/altered, by skilled co-construction? To date, the sociocultural SLL researchers have not addressed those language phenomena which could shed most light on these problems.

|8|

Sociolinguistic perspectives

At present, SLA could probably benefit from an enhanced sense of the empirical world's complex socio-cultural diversity.

(Rampton 1995a, p. 294)

8.1 Introduction

In this chapter we review aspects of the relationship between sociolinguistics and second language learning theory. In doing so, we undoubtedly move towards the margins of second language learning research. Up to now, as we have seen in earlier chapters, research and theorising about second language learning have concentrated mainly on modelling the development of language within the individual learner, in response to an environment defined fairly narrowly as a source of linguistic information. Throughout the recent history of second language learning studies, sociolinguistics issues have commonly been addressed as afterthoughts, and have not become the focus of sustained programmes of empirical research. Here we examine present trends, to see whether sociolinguistic ideas are becoming any more central to thinking about second language learning.

Sociolinguistics, or the *study of language in use*, is itself a diverse field, with multiple theoretical perspectives. This is clear from any of the current survey volumes (e.g. Coupland and Jaworski 1997; Holmes 1992; Hudson 1996; Romaine 1994). Here, we will necessarily be selective, identifying those strands within contemporary sociolinguistics which have had the most obvious influence on the field of second language learning.

We have just noted that mainstream sociolinguistics is primarily concerned with the study of language in use. Correspondingly, in second language learning studies, we find that one main strand of sociolinguistic influence is concerned with the description of L2 use. In the first part of this chapter, we will examine two approaches to the discovery of socially influenced patterns and structures in L2 use, one of them applying a qualitative methodology to the problem, the other applying a quantitative methodology. In the second part of the chapter, we will move to examine other strands in sociolinguistically influenced SLL research, which are more centrally concerned with explaining L2 learning/development. Successive main sections of the chapter will therefore deal with the following:

- the ethnography of L2 communication;
- variation in second language use;
- pidginization and acculturation;
- second language socialization.

8.2   Ethnography of L2 communication

8.2.1   Introduction

The *ethnography of communication* studies the social roles of language, in structuring the identities of individuals and the culture of entire communities and societies. In particular, linguistic anthropologists such as Hymes, Saville-Troike and others have studied the characteristics of *speech events* which have patterning and significance for members of a particular speech community (see e.g. Hymes 1972; Saville-Troike 1989). Examples of speech events with their own distinctive structures and routines in current urban society might be telephone conversations, service encounters (in shops, banks, etc.), classroom lessons, or job interviews. The ability to participate appropriately in relevant speech events is an important part of *communicative competence*, now generally accepted as the broad eventual target of L2 learning, as well as of L1 development.

The ethnography of L2 communication aims similarly to study contexts and events where participants are struggling to achieve communicative goals through the means of a second or other language. However, while the traditional ethnography of communication has typically studied relatively well-established and stable speech events, those studied by ethnographers of L2 communication have frequently been more fluid, transitory and changeable, reflecting the fact that roles and identities of participants may be much more problematic in cross-linguistic, cross-cultural encounters.

The ethnography of L2 communication has so far hardly scratched the surface of the myriad of settings in which L2s are put to practical use. However, in the work which has been done, we can draw a distinction between ethnographies of language use in L2 classrooms, and ethnographic studies of L2 use in other social settings (e.g. by migrant workers, in international business, or in multi-ethnic urban communities). A number of themes are prominent in ethnographic studies of L2 use, which are relatively neglected in other types of L2 research; and we will briefly exemplify these below, using selected examples of both classroom and non-classroom ethnographies. These themes are as follows:

- gatekeeping and power relations in L2 communication;
- mismatches and change in cultural expectations;
- speakers' identity and self-esteem;
- affect and emotion in L2 use.

8.2.2   Gatekeeping and power relations in L2 communication

How does the social position of the L2 learner affect opportunities for learning and the course of L2 development? Many classroom studies of L2 learning have noted the mismatch of *power relationships* between the teacher and students, with teachers typically seen as dominant figures who control the detail of L2 classroom discourse (Chaudron 1988, pp. 50–4). Some recent sociolinguistic studies have also drawn our attention to the problematic social relationships in which adult L2 learners can also find themselves. Adult immigrants, in particular, may regularly be subjected to discrimination and racial harassment. Yet they may depend for essential social goods and services on L2-medium interactions with representatives of the majority community, *gatekeepers* with whom they must negotiate successfully to obtain e.g. housing, jobs, or health care.

In Chapter 5 we have already encountered the European Science Foundation (ESF) project on adult migrants learning a range of L2s informally in a range of European settings. As we have seen, the main focus of the project was to analyse the learners' linguistic development over time, from a functional perspective. However, a subgroup within the ESF team also undertook more sociolinguistically orientated work, and concentrated in particular on examining adult migrants' encounters with a wide variety of gatekeepers (Bremer *et al.* 1993, 1996). These ESF sociolinguists focused on speech events such as job interviews, counselling/advice sessions, or service encounters (in shops, travel agencies, etc.), where the migrant workers were seeking some instrumental goal (to find work, to send a parcel, etc.). Sometimes the events studied were real, sometimes simulated, but in all cases they involved interaction with 'genuine' officials or service personnel, who controlled the desired outcomes. Thus these speech events involved a clear mismatch of power, with the TL speaker as the more powerful gatekeeper, the L2 speaker as the less powerful (potential) beneficiary of the encounter.

In their analysis, Bremer and her colleagues concentrate on how the participants in these unequal encounters succeeded (or failed) in developing and maintaining mutual understanding. For them, understanding is an interactive process, 'mutually constructed in the course of inferencing by all participants in an encounter' (Gumperz 1982, in Bremer *et al.* 1996, pp. 15–16).

A first example of the data collected and analysed by the ESF researchers in their work on gatekeeping encounters is taken from a meeting between a Moroccan informant (Abdelmalek), a learner of French as L2, and a French travel agent. This extract shows, first of all, how misunderstanding can arise from a mishearing of a single lexical element. (Abdelmalek mishears *par quoi* 'how', as *pourquoi* 'why', and proceeds to explain his reasons for needing to travel.) But second, it illustrates the additional communication problems arising from a mismatch in power relations, at least as perceived by Abdelmalek. It is not normally appropriate for a travel agent to enquire about a client's reasons for a trip, so why did Abdelmalek think that *pourquoi* 'why' was a reasonable interpretation of what he had heard? Bremer *et al.* suggest that Abdelmalek had already experienced many official encounters during his short stay in France, when he had been interrogated about his motives and his personal life; he assumed that a travel agent, too, had the right to ask such questions. But on this occasion the travel agent is merely puzzled, and starts to signal that the interaction has gone off the rails.

(1)   A: je partir a casablanca, maroc
             i am leaving for casablanca, morocco
       N: par quoi vous voulez partir ↑
             how do you wish to go ↑
       A: [se] beaucoup problèmes là-bas papa malade
             je partir tout de suite
             a lot of problems there father is ill
             i'm leaving right away
(5)   N: je comprends pas là qu'est ce que vous voulez
             où vous voulez aller ↑
             i dont understand that what do you want
             where do you want to go ↑
                    (Deulofeu and Taranger 1984, in Bremer *et al.* 1996, pp. 12–13)

Another example of the diverse ways in which unequal power relations can affect learners' participation in L2 speech events is offered by Losey (1995). Losey has conducted a classroom study, but she moves beyond a concern with teacher–student relations, to examine the classroom roles of different ethnic and gender groups. The study again involves adult minority informants, but the research setting is a North American adult literacy classroom. The students were a mix of monolingual (English L1) Anglo-Americans, and bilingual (Spanish L1) Mexican Americans. A first analysis showed that in teacher-led, English-medium whole-class discussions, the Anglo students dominated overwhelmingly. Closer study also showed a striking gender difference within the Mexican American group; the few Mexican American males participated at a similar rate to the Anglo students, while Mexican American women scarcely contributed at all to whole-class discussions, though they comprised almost half the class. In small group settings, however, whether with peers or with a tutor, these women talked freely, asking many work-related questions, and jointly solving problems. Losey attributes the women's silence in class to their powerless position as a 'double minority' (p. 655), in terms of both ethnicity and gender.

Together, these studies illustrate how unequal power relations can control both learners' overall opportunities and willingness to take part in L2 interaction, and also some of the consequences for their ongoing detailed decision-making, in interpreting what is said to them, and deciding how to respond.

8.2.3 Mismatches and change in cultural expectations

L2 speakers and their L1 interlocutors may bring with them very different expectations about the norms and routines which will prevail, in different kinds of speech event. Sociolinguists have taken an interest both in the problems of understanding and communication which may arise as a result, and also in the ways that speech events themselves may change, as new intercultural routines evolve.

The ESF researchers offer further examples which illustrate comprehension problems deriving from mismatches in such *cultural expectations*. A common problem in their data is shown, where the same L2 speaker Abdelmalek fails to recognize a hypothetical question, about wishes or preferences (what kind of work he would like to do), and reinterprets it as a factual question about his current work; the researchers argue that most migrant workers do not expect officials conducting a formal interview to take any interest in their personal hopes and plans. Similarly, they provide evidence of mismatches in job interviews, where officials expect candidates to 'sell' themselves, by volunteering information about their skills and qualifications, while migrants may expect only to answer direct questions. Even more striking is their example of a Turkish worker Ergun, asked by a housing officer whether his fiancée is pregnant; in this case the worker rejects the question as totally bizarre and incomprehensible, and a long misunderstanding ensues ('I am not yet married, how can I get a child?', p. 143).

N: hein + c'est bien ça + + bon eh hem +
hmm + all right then + + good
et maintenant quel type de + travail vous aimeriez faire là ↑
and now what kind of job would you like to do there ↑
A: comme le travail ↑
as a job ↑
N: hem
mm
A: ah parce que travail pas + le chômage
ah because don't work + unemployment
N: là + vous êtes au chômage + mais si vous avez un travail
there + you are unemployed + but if you have a job
quel type de travail vous cherchez/vous accepteriez ↑
what kind of job you are looking for/would you accept ↑
(...)

(Bremer *et al.* 1996, p. 57)

A striking example not only of mismatch but also of renegotiation of cultural norms in L2 use comes from Duff's ethnographic study of elite bilingual high schools in post-communist Hungary (Duff 1995, 1996). These high schools were licensed to use English as a medium of instruction in certain subjects (e.g. History), in parallel with the continuing use of Hungarian for the rest of the curriculum. Because of the high prestige of English, these schools could cream off the ablest students, and were relatively autonomous of Ministry control. They became centres of experimentation with new forms of classroom interaction and assessment, as part of a movement to reject traditional, 'tainted' educational practices.

Duff concentrates on the traditional oral assessment practice known as *felelés* (recitation), in which individual students had to recap orally on the content of a previous lesson, in an extended unscripted but formal presentation, and were graded for their performance. This practice continued in Hungarian-medium lessons in the dual-language schools, but was replaced by a variety of other oral assessment modes in the English-medium lessons (such as pre-prepared student 'lectures'). Duff documents the tensions and uncertainties which accompanied this change, as students and teachers struggled to establish new norms and routines both for oral classroom interaction and for assessment, and in some cases older practices reasserted themselves. Her analysis shows how these tensions were played out at a micro level in classroom interaction, as e.g. students openly criticized the English proficiency of their (Hungarian L1) subject teachers, or teachers mixed praise and criticism in a confused manner in response to obviously plagiarised 'lectures' (1996).

These examples show, on the one hand, that a degree of shared cultural knowledge is vital for L2 interaction to proceed co-operatively, but also that, in certain settings, L2 learners and their interlocutors may be pioneering new forms of speech event, in which old norms do not automatically apply, and are reconstructed in the course of interaction.

8.2.4   Speakers' social identity, face and self-esteem

The concept of *social identity* has been borrowed into SLL studies and applied linguistics from social psychology. The most notable theorist of social identity defined it as 'That part of an individual's self-concept which derives from his knowledge of his membership of a social group (or groups) together with the emotional significance attached to that membership' (Tajfel 1974, p. 69, quoted in Hansen and Liu 1997, pp. 567–8). Social identity, therefore, is the sense of 'belonging' to a particular social group, whether defined by ethnicity, by language, or any other means.

As originally proposed by Tajfel and others, the concept of social identity has come under criticism for being too static and too focused on the individual (though Tajfel himself is defended by McNamara 1997). The Canadian researcher Bonny Norton Pierce has aimed to develop a more comprehensive theory of social identity, one that 'integrates the language learner and the language learning context' (Pierce 1995, p. 12). For Pierce, social identity is not fixed, but dynamic; it is described as 'multiple, a site of struggle, and subject to change' over time (p. 20). Language, identity, and context mutually interact.

> I foreground the role of language as constitutive of and constituted by a language learner's social identity. It is through language that a person negotiates a sense of self within and across different sites at different points in time, and it is through language that a person gains access to – or is denied access to – powerful social networks that give learners the opportunity to speak.
>
> (p. 13)

Pierce conducted a longitudinal study of a small group of immigrant adult women, concentrating on changes in their social identity over time, and in particular, on their struggles to achieve the *right to speak* in L2 settings – or as Bourdieu puts it, 'the power to impose reception' (Bourdieu 1977, in Pierce 1995, p. 18). For example, Pierce describes how Martina, a Czech-speaking immigrant in her thirties, relied at first on her own children's support in undertaking a range of both public and domestic English-medium negotiations. But Martina viewed herself as the primary caregiver in the family, and struggled to resume these responsibilities herself (e.g. challenging the landlord by phone, in a disagreement over rental payments). Similarly, in the fastfood restaurant where she worked, she was bossed around initially by her teenage fellow workers; but soon she reasserted her status as an adult with authority over children, and claimed the 'right to speak' in this role.

> In restaurant was working a lot of children, but the children always thought that I am – I don't know – maybe some broom or something. They always said 'Go and clean the living room'. And I was washing the dishes and they didn't do nothing. They talked to each other and they thought that I had to do everything. And I said 'no'. The girl is only 12 years old. She is younger than my son. I said 'No, you are doing nothing, you can go and clean the tables or something'.
>
> (Pierce 1995, p. 23)

Pierce argues that as Martina's identity changed, from submissive immigrant to caregiver, so did her opportunities to speak and to learn English.

In their detailed analyses of ongoing L2 interactions, the ESF sociolinguists pay attention to the related social factors of *face* and *self-esteem*, and how they may be threatened or consolidated by attempts to negotiate understanding. They demonstrate clearly the grave threats to L2 speakers' self-esteem which can arise when misunderstandings are too frequent in interactional data. For example, they cite a Spanish L1 speaker Berta, now living in a French-speaking environment, attempting to get some shelves made to order in a woodworking shop (Bremer *et al.* 1996, p. 91). She fails to cope with the shop assistant's more technical enquiries, and eventually loses his attention to another customer – a highly face-threatening situation.

The researchers report a range of strategies employed by L2 speakers, in response to such threats. At one extreme, they found examples of *resistance*, i.e. more or less complete withdrawal from L2 interaction, and a reassertion of the speaker's L1 identity (e.g. by switching to monolingual L1 use); the minority speakers resorting to this strategy were most usually women. At the other extreme, they found speakers who worked hard during L2 interactions to assert a positive, native-speaker-like identity, by e.g. indicating explicitly that they had understood, or using excuse formulas when they had to inter-rupt to clarify meaning (p. 100). These were more usually men, though Berta herself is a striking example of a female learner who eventually discovered ways of asserting herself and taking more conversational control.

Many researchers in SLL have tried to explain differing degrees of learner success by appealing to relatively fixed and individual factors such as motiva-tion (see Section 1.5.2). Current research such as the examples cited here remind us that learners' attitudes and identity are dynamic, negotiable, socially contextualized, and subject to change, even within the framework of individual interactions.

8.2.5   *Affect and emotion in L2 use*

Krashen's *affective filter* is perhaps the best-known hypothesis in SLL theory, which tries to deal with the impact of attitudes and emotion on learning effectiveness (see Chapter 2). However, like the social psychological construct of motivation, the affective filter hypothesis can be criticized as insufficiently flexible and asocial.

For adult migrant learners such as Berta, the L2 is the only available com-municative option, in many difficult encounters with the powerful. Her emo-tional response to the L2 is inextricably entwined with the social context in which she has to use it. For example, Bremer *et al.* recorded a conversation with Berta in which she is retelling her experience in hospital, where she had gone to inquire after her child, hurt in an accident, late in the evening. She had located the relevant doctor, but he had sent her away, telling her only that she should come back tomorrow for more information. Her actual interac-tion with the doctor was not recorded, but Bremer *et al.* quote the conclusion of her narrative, with its vivid recollection of her strong feelings of anger, and how these feelings frustrated her L2–medium attempts to force the doctor to give her proper attention.

B: il me dit que je sorte tout de suite de/*del hospital* pasque bon je crois
     que c'est l'heure pasque + c'est la/la neuf + vingt ↑/vingt et un ↑ vingt et
     un heure je crois que c'est possible *por* ça
     he told me that i leave at once from/from the hospital because well i
     think it is the time because + it is nine + twenty ↑ twenty-one ↑ twenty-
     one i think it is possible that's why
N: oui mais c'est quend même pas normal
     yes but it is not really normally like that

B: oui c'est ça *lo que* jé dis pasque je suis très fâchée avec lui je le dis bon
    je n'/*yo/yo* voudrais que vous m'expliquiez qu'est-ce qui passe non non
    non il me dit
    yes it is what i said because i was very angry with him i told him well i
    don't/i
    i wish you would explain to me what happens no no no he told me

N: qu'est-ce que tu as fait alors ↑
    what did you do then ↑

B: bon je suis fâchée avel/avec lui *y* je le dis beaucoup de choses avec
    m/ + :et + je m'énervé beaucoup
    well i got angry with h/ with him and i told him a lot of things with m/
    and + i got very worked up

N: ah oui + je comprends ça oui + et tu es partie ↑
    yes + i understand it yes + and did you go ↑

B: alors oui il est parti pasque je n'avais le/avais le + que je suis fâchée je
    ou/je oubliais les mots en français *por por* dire + je ne/je ne trouvais
    + rien de mots *por* dire les choses que/que je le dis à lui *por* pasque
    n'est pas bon la manière qu'il me dit au revoir
    then yes he went because i did not have the/have the + that i was angry
    for/i forget the words in french to to say + i did not/did not find +
    nothing of words to say the things which/which I tell him because it is
    not good the manner he said goodbye to me
                                                        (Bremer *et al.* 1996, p. 94)

Affective strands in L2 learning have also been studied longitudinally by
means of diaries and other personal records kept by individual learners. A
recent example is the work done by Hilleson (1996), with students in the privileged environment of an international English-medium school in Singapore.
By this means he documented the students' reactions to their daily experiences in the school, both in terms of their academic classwork, and their
developing social relations with other students. In their early days at the
school, the students reported strong feelings of anxiety and frustration.

> I don't think people could get to know me. I looked a shallower person,
> narrower minded, less knowledge with less experiences. Of course, I couldn't
> talk about philosophy, I could talk about how's Japan or how's the weather. I
> sometimes felt sad I don't appear to them as I am. I was especially sad when
> people said 'Why are you so quiet, so unsociable!' In Japan I was noisier than
> other people. I tried to explain but they didn't believe it. That was sad.
>   (Japanese student Kato, quoted in Hilleson 1996, p. 255)

Like many other studies, these diary records show clear interactions between
affect and experience, however, with students growing in self-esteem and
security as their communicative abilities improve.

8.2.6 *Ethnography of L2 communication: conclusion*

If there is a single clear message from the ethnographic studies of L2
communication which we have reviewed here, it is that opportunities to use
(and therefore to learn) a second language are socially patterned, and often

not neutrally so, but in ways which increase the difficulty of the learning task. On the whole, the studies examined here have not made it their business to examine systematically the learning outcomes of the L2 communication patterns they describe. However, Bremer *et al.* do comment briefly on the interactional patterns which seem most likely to lead to an increase in learning opportunities.

> The data we have analysed show that the discourse of minority interactants who seem to be conscious of the learning issues and of the necessity to work on their ability to understand ... their majority partners involves:
>
> - the use of metalinguistic comments on understanding and non-understanding and attention to the linguistic issues;
> - initiative rather than dependency in their relationship to the majority partner in the interaction;
> - a sensitive management of issues of face;
> - an awareness of the issues in general.
>
> (1996, p. 105)

They note a gender bias in these opportunities: 'It is surely not by chance that so many of the women informants take the option of not indicating their problems with understanding and therefore progress less' (p. 104).

8.3   Variation in second language use

8.3.1   Introduction

Variability is an obvious feature of both child language and of learners' L2 interlanguage, which has been noted and discussed in many studies, and was briefly introduced in Section 1.4.4; Towell and Hawkins (1994) argue that it is one of the basic characteristics of interlanguage which learning theorists have to explain.

By variability, we refer to the fact that L2 learners commonly produce different versions of particular constructions, more or less close to the target language form, within a short timespan (even, perhaps, within succeeding utterances). In Chapter 2 we have already referred briefly to Schumann's case study of Alberto, an adult learner of English as L2 (1978a). Schumann reports an example of variability in Alberto's English interlanguage, where two alternative forms were in use to express negation. Alberto seemed to be a slow, almost fossilized learner, who

> showed considerably less development than any other subjects. He used both *no V* and *don't V* constructions throughout; however, *no V* was clearly the most dominant of the two and consistently achieved a higher frequency of use until the very last sample.
>
> (1978a, p. 20)

The point to note here is that although one pattern apparently dominated, two patterns were clearly in use simultaneously, by a single learner, over an extended period of time (the Alberto study ran over a period of 40 weeks). In Section 1.4.4 above, we have already cited other similar examples of variability for child L2 learners. (For a recent general review of empirical studies of variability in L2, see Ellis 1994, pp. 119–58.)

The phenomenon of variability has led to considerable debate in SLA literature, not least over the problems it creates for the notion of 'acquisition' itself. Is a target language form to be counted as 'acquired', on the first occasion when a learner is observed to use it without immediate prompting/ suppliance by an interlocutor? Or must we wait to accept that it has been fully 'acquired' until the learner is producing the form in 90 per cent or more of expected contexts? At different points in this book, we have encountered SLA theorists and researchers who have adopted such widely differing positions, as well as points in between (e.g. Huebner 1983, who brings a functionalist perspective to bear on the problem).

But apart from the need to take account of variability in trying to establish definitions of 'acquisition', we need also to explain why it is such a striking feature of L2 use. Different writers have linked variability in learners' L2 production to a wide variety of factors. Tarone (1988) groups these under four main types as follows.

1 *Variation according to linguistic context* (For example, Young has studied the extent to which Chinese L1 learners of English as L2 marked plural -*s* on English nouns: 1991. He found that several linguistic factors such as the position of the noun within the Noun Phrase, its syntactic function, and its phonological context, all affected the likelihood that these learners would produce the plural ending.)

2 *Variation according to psychological processing factors* (For example, systematic differences in performance have been found to exist, depending on the degree of planning involved in learners' L2 productions: e.g. Ellis 1987, Foster and Skehan 1996. Ellis has also proposed that variability may derive partly from processing constraints, i.e. the gradual acquisition of 'control' of the knowledge base: 1989.)

3 *Variation according to features of the social context (interlocutor, task or topic, social norms)* (In the 1991 study mentioned above, Young found that the identity of the interlocutor – Chinese or English – also influenced the likelihood that learners would mark/fail to mark English Nouns as plural.)

4 *Variation according to language function* (As we have seen in Section 5.3.2, Huebner has accounted for variability in the English interlanguage of his Hmong L1 subject Ge partly by demonstrating shifts in the functions for which Ge was using the (proto)copula form *isa*, and the article form *da*: Huebner 1983.)

Ellis (1994, p. 134) has proposed a similar typology of types of variability, shown here as Figure 8.1. One noticeable difference between this typology and Tarone's proposals is the inclusion of the category of *non-systematic variation*. Ellis has been willing to argue that some variation is random or unsystematic, on the basis of introspection into his own language use (1985b, p. 80). Others are sceptical about the validity of introspective data in studying this problem, and have argued that variation which seems 'unsystematic' may merely be variation for which the underlying system has not yet been discovered (Preston 1996a, 1996b; Schachter 1986). In general, researchers certainly aspire to 'explain' as much of the observed variability as possible.

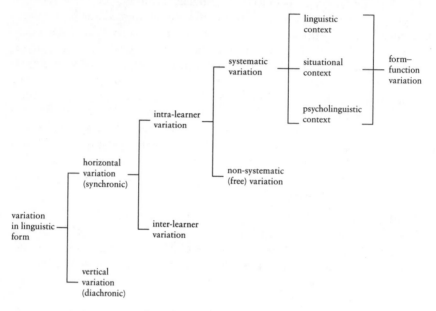

Fig. 8.1 A typology of variation in interlanguage

8.3.2 Quantifying learner variability

In trying to make sense of the variability phenomenon, one group of SLA researchers has turned to a quantitative approach to the description of variation in language use which was originally developed within mainstream sociolinguistics (see e.g. Bayley and Preston eds. 1996; Preston 1996b).

In the 1970s the sociolinguist William Labov pioneered this approach to studying patterns of variability in everyday speech. He concentrated on features in spoken language, often pronunciation features, where choices are possible which are endowed with positive or negative value by a given speech community. An example from contemporary spoken British English would be variation between the consonant [t] or glottal stop [?] to realize the /t/phoneme in words such as *better, Britain*, etc. The glottal stop variant is very common; yet it is typically described as 'lazy', 'sloppy' speech, etc., i.e. it has negative social value or prestige. Labov has proposed the term sociolinguistic *marker* for such items, whose use involves some value-laden choice.

Labov systematically recorded L1 speech samples from people representing different social groups, in a variety of situations. In a number of studies he and his followers have shown that the relative frequencies of use for more positively/negatively esteemed variants can be correlated with a range of factors such as the immediate linguistic context, the speaker's social class, and the formality/informality of the speech setting (for an overview, see e.g. Labov 1972).

Table 8.1 shows an example drawn from 1970s' quantitative research in the Labov tradition, discussed by Preston (1996b). This study investigated the simplification of word-final consonant clusters in English among African-American speakers from Detroit city (that is, the deletion of final [t] or [d] in these phonetic environments). The researchers recorded extended speech samples from their subjects, and analysed the percentage of final consonant clusters within which [t] or [d] deletion was found.

As Table 8.1 shows, in this study the percentage of observed occasions of deletion of final [t] and [d] could be linked both to the immediate linguistic context and to speakers' social class.

Researchers in this tradition moved to a greater level of statistical sophistication, with the development of a computer programme known as VARBRUL. (For an account of the development of VARBRUL, see Montgomery 1990; for an up-to-date guide to using current versions of the programme in second language research, see Young and Bayley 1996.) This programme is based on a statistical procedure known as logistic regression. VARBRUL draws on data such as that presented in Table 8.1, and calculates the statistical probability that speakers will produce one variant rather than another, in a range of given contexts. Probabilities are expressed in terms of weightings ranging from 1.00 to 0.00; a weighting of 0.50 or more means that a form is systematically more likely to be produced in a given environment, a

Table 8.1 t/d deletion in Detroit African-American speech

Environments	Social classes			
	Upper middle	Lower middle	Upper working	Lower working
Following vowel:				
-t/d is past morpheme (e.g., 'missed in')	0.07	0.13	0.24	0.34
-t/d is not past morpheme (e.g., 'mist in')	0.28	0.43	0.65	0.72
Following consonant:				
-t/d is past morpheme (e.g., 'missed by')	0.49	0.62	0.73	0.76
-t/d is not past morpheme (e.g., 'mist by')	0.79	0.87	0.94	0.97

Source: Wolfram and Fasold 1974, cited in Preston 1996b, p. 4

weighting of less than 0.50 means that this is less likely. One important feature of the VARBRUL programme is that it can handle simultaneously a number of different contextual factors which may influence learner production, and can also handle interactions between them.

Preston (1996b) has run the VARBRUL programme on hypothetical raw data based on the table presented earlier as Table 8.1. This VARBRUL analysis produced the pattern of probabilities for the different linguistic-context and social class factors shown in Table 8.2. (The term 'input probability' used in this table refers to the overall likelihood that the deletion rule will operate – note the specialized use of the term 'input' here!) In this hypothetical example we see that two linguistic factors, 'Following consonant' and 'Nonmorpheme' have probabilities higher than 0.50, and are therefore predictive of consonant deletion; the same applies for working-class membership (whether 'Upper' or 'Lower').

Preston and others have applied the VARBRUL tool to the study of variation in L2 use, and its relationship with a range of contextual factors. For example, a study by Bayley (1994), investigated variability in past tense marking by Chinese learners of English. This study looked at two groups of learners, of lower and higher English proficiency. Using the VARBRUL procedure, their L2 utterances were analysed to explore the possible influence of a linguistic factor, *perfectivity* (whether tenses were aspectually perfective or non-perfective), on past tense marking.

Table 8.3 shows part of the resulting analysis. Here, results are presented separately for the Lower English Proficiency (LEP) and Higher English Proficiency (HEP) groups of Chinese learner subjects. The overall 'input probability' for these two groups are very different, i.e. the LEP group is far less likely than the HEP group to mark English past tense forms morphologically. However, as far as the particular factor of perfectivity is concerned, the table shows almost identical probability values. This means that while

Table 8.2 VARBRUL results for t/d deletion by African American speakers from Detroit: hypothetical data inferred from Table 8.1

Result	Probability
Following vowel (V)	0.25
Following consonant (C)	0.75
Morpheme (M)	0.31
Nonmorpheme (N)	0.69
Upper middle class (UMC)	0.29
Lower middle class (LMC)	0.42
Upper working class (UWC)	0.60
Lower working class (LWC)	0.69
Input probability 0.60	

Source: Preston 1996b, p. 10

Table 8.3 Influence of perfectivity on past tense marking in Chinese learners of English

Verb type	Respondent Proficiency Level					
	Lower			Higher		
	P_i	%	N	P_i	%	N
Perfective	.67	42	856	.69	73	1406
Inperfective	.33	15	964	.31	38	1691
Input	.22	22	1820	.58	54	3097

Source: Bayley 1994, cited in Preston 1996b, p. 27

overall levels of past tense marking are very different across groups, the specific influence of the perfectivity factor does not change with learner proficiency level. (That is, in Preston's terms, the two groups of learners could be viewed as members of the 'same' speech community as far as this particular factor is concerned, 1996b, p. 27.)

On the other hand, Preston cites other factors from the same study by Bayley which pattern differently; thus for example, the LEP and HEP groups show very different probability profiles for past tense marking, when the influence of a different linguistic factor, the immediate phonetic environment, is examined (Preston 1996b, p. 28).

Empirical studies such as Bayley (1994), and others reported in Bayley and Preston (1996), confirm the view of Ellis and Tarone, that a wide variety of factors contribute to variability in L2 production. However, the variable L2 features studied in such work are not usually 'markers' in the Labov sense, that is, they do not typically carry social prestige or a social stigma. (An exception is Regan 1996, who studied variable deletion of the negative particle *ne* by L2 learners of French.) It is thus not very surprising that the main groups of factors which correlate most strongly with L2 variability seem to be linguistic rather than sociolinguistic in nature. However, studies such as Regan (1996) or Bayley (1996) confirm that sociolinguistic factors such as speech style or interlocutor also form an independent input into the selection of variable L2 forms.

8.3.3   Critiques of variability research

Within mainstream sociolinguistics, this quantitative approach to the study of language variation has been criticized on a number of grounds: e.g. for dealing with fragments of the language system only, and for a lack of theoretical motivation and of psycholinguistic plausibility (see e.g. Bickerton 1971; Romaine 1981). Labov's original proposal that the notion of linguistic competence must be expanded to include the concept of *variable rules* does not command general acceptance; critics have argued that it is psycholinguistically improbable that learners are continuously calculating probabilities and choosing between alternative forms in order to produce the 'right' mix of production data to fit such rules.

However, many sociolinguistic researchers continue to view VARBRUL and allied programmes as useful tools for 'assessing differential strengths of linguistic and social variables in determining linguistic behaviour' (Montgomery 1990, p. 113), regardless of the psycholinguistic status of variable rules. Preston accepts the criticism that variationist researchers have neglected to model the processes underlying variable performance, and proposes the metaphor of the gambler repeatedly tossing weighted coins, as a possible solution (e.g. 1996b, pp. 32–9). He argues that the speaker's underlying linguistic competence may include options or alternative realizations for particular forms. As utterances involving these forms are generated, weightings are attached to the different options, either by features of the underlying syntactic context, or by surface, articulatory features (such as the phonetic context). The eventual 'choice' made (i.e. whether the coin turns up heads or tails, to continue the metaphor) depends on the combined influence of the various weightings; it is not in any sense under the speaker's control. Preston's proposals may go some way to explaining variability in stable language systems, but they are not designed to tackle the related problem of how linguistic competence of this type might be acquired, as he recognizes (1996b, p. 34). (Connectionist models of language learning would seem to offer some possibilities here, but Preston does not make the link.)

Within SLA as well, various critics have questioned the adequacy of variation research on theoretical grounds (e.g. Gregg 1990; Wolfram 1991). Gregg argued essentially that variation is a performance phenomenon, and that there is no place for variable rules in the speaker's underlying competence. He also criticized Tarone (1988 etc.) and Ellis (1985a etc.), whom he views as the main proposers of a 'Variable Competence Hypothesis' in SLA, for their alleged failure to tackle the issue of acquisition.

> There is no explanation of the acquisition process, even of the comparatively few forms for which there is variability data available. Tarone, Ellis and others have given us a good deal of information about which forms are used when; which is to say that we have a good deal of description of variable use of certain forms. But description ... is not explanation. Such explanations as have been offered (see, for example, Tarone 1988: 60–110 for a review) are explanations of the choice of a given form in production; they do not explain how the forms themselves were originally acquired ... I am willing to entertain a proposed extension [to the UG explanation of acquisition] if only someone working within the variable competence model would put one forward.
>
> (1990, p. 379)

In their responses to Gregg's critique, Ellis (1990) and Tarone (1990) adopted somewhat different positions. For Tarone (1990), new forms first enter the learner's repertoire via collaborative discourse (as described by Hatch 1978); the learner is motivated to adopt these forms by a desire to accommodate to their interlocutor's speech (Beebe and Giles 1984). Ellis sums up as follows.

I have proposed that interlanguage growth is characterised by both free variation, when a new form is used together with an old form to perform a single
function, and systematic variation, when the new and old forms are assigned to
different functions. There is a constant flux between free and systematic
variation as new forms enter interlanguage. Elaboration and reorganization are
concurrent and necessary processes in interlanguage development.

(1990, p. 390)

Thus it seems that in response to Gregg's critique, both Tarone and Ellis
adopt essentially functionalist explanations for L2 variability, and its role in
L2 development. However, it is clear that the main strength of variationist
research in SLA so far has indeed been descriptive, clarifying the linguistic
contexts and functions for which variable forms are selected. Theoretical
claims about the role of variability in L2 development remain much more
speculative.

In particular, the quantitative tradition using VARBRUL methodology has
demonstrated the association of a range of factors in the immediate linguistic context with variable L2 performance. Interestingly, while this methodology was borrowed by L2 researchers from mainstream sociolinguistics, the
empirical findings of VARBRUL-based L2 research indicate quite strongly
that sociolinguistic factors are comparatively less important for L2 variation,
than more narrowly linguistic or functional contextual factors.

8.4   Pidginization and acculturation

8.4.1   *Schumann's proposals*

In the late 1970s, John Schumann made a number of theoretical proposals
about second language learning, linked to his case study of the adult L2
learner Alberto, which we have already referred to several times (Schumann
1978a, 1978b). He popularized the two linked concepts of *pidginization* and
acculturation, which served for a decade or more as some of the main representatives of sociolinguistic thinking in the field of second language acquisition, and which we have already mentioned briefly in Chapter 2 (see e.g.
discussions in McLaughlin 1987, Larsen-Freeman and Long 1991, Cook
1993).

The concept of pidiginization is inspired by the branch of sociolinguistics
which concerns itself with the study of *contact languages* (pidgins and creoles). Sebba (1997) provides a useful introduction to this field. Pidgin languages are contact varieties without native speakers, which arise in settings of
military or trade contact, slavery or plantation labour and summarizes (p. 69)
their main characteristics.

Pidgins:
- have no native speakers;
- are the result of contact between two or more languages;

- are not mutually intelligible with their source languages;
- usually draw most of their vocabulary from one language (the *lexifier*);
- have grammars which are *simplified* and *reduced* compared with the grammars of their input languages;
- tend to have simple phonological systems;
- tend to have analytic (*isolating*) or agglutinating morphology;
- tend to have *semantically transparent* relationships between words and meaning;
- have small vocabularies where words cover a wide semantic range.

Perhaps the best-studied modern example is Tok Pisin, one of several Pacific pidgins with English as *lexifier* (source language for most of the pidgin's vocabulary). Tok Pisin is widely spoken in Papua New Guinea, where it has fairly recently achieved the status of an official language.

Although they are without native speakers, and part of their origin in the lexifier language may be very obvious, pidgins have their own systematized grammar which must be acquired by their users. By comparison with other natural languages, however, the structure of pidgin languages appears simplified, in characteristic ways. According to Sebba, (1997, p. 39), the following cluster of features is usual in the grammar of pidgin languages:

- no definite or indefinite article;
- no copula *to be* (at least in present tense);
- tense, aspect, modality and negation marked externally to the verb – often by a content word like an adverb;
- no complex sentences (e.g. sentences involving relative clauses);
- no passive forms;
- very few or no inflections for number, case, tense, etc.;
- analytic constructions used to mark possessive, e.g. X of Y rather than Y's X.

All of these features may be found in other natural languages; however, the clustering of all or most of them is highly diagnostic of pidgins. Sebba believes that these features make pidgins highly learnable, especially when taken together with their semantic transparency, and limited vocabulary (1997, p. 54).

It is clear from the description just given that pidgins have some features in common with early stages of L2 learners' interlanguage systems, to which scholars such as Corder were drawing attention, at the time of Schumann's Alberto study. We know from many studies ranging from Schumann's own work, to the more recent work of the ESF project reviewed in Chapter 5, that the early interlanguages of untutored adults often lack verb inflections, for example. This kind of evidence led Schumann to claim by analogy that all (untutored) L2 learners begin by acquiring a pidgin-like variety: 'pidginization may be a universal first stage in second language acquisition' (1978a, p. 110). This must be so, he argued, because of universal cognitive constraints, which are responsible for the emergence of pidgins and other simplified codes: 'the code may reflect a regression to a set of universal primitive linguistic categories that were realised in early first language acquisition' (p. 112).

As far as Alberto himself was concerned, Schumann interpreted him as a learner who failed to move beyond the basic, pidginization stage, but fossilized at that point (i.e. his syntactic development came to a halt). This interpretation of Alberto's (lack of) development has actually been challenged recently, in a paper by Berdan (1996). Berdan used the VARBRUL procedure to re-analyse variability in Alberto's use of the forms *no* and *dont* as preverbal negative particles; using this more powerful statistical tool, he claimed that over time, Alberto could be shown to move (though very slowly) towards increased use of *dont*. This re-analysis challenges Schumann's claim that Alberto was a completely fossilized English L2 user; however, it does not affect the claim that he was strikingly behind the other learners in Schumann's study!

In order to account for Alberto's relative lack of development, Schumann turned to a range of measures drawn from social psychology: intelligence, age, social distance, psychological distance. He concluded that fossilization in Alberto's L2 English could best be attributed to a combination of social and psychological distance (i.e. lack of social integration with the target language community; lack of interest in using the target language for anything other than 'the communication of denotative referential information': p. 114).

Schumann ended by proposing the concept of *acculturation* as a way of accounting much more generally for the varying degrees of success achieved by (uninstructed adult) L2 learners. In his terms, whether learners moved beyond the initial, pidginization stage or not was dependent on the extent of social and psychological contact with the TL group: 'the degree to which a learner acculturates to the TL group will control the degree to which he acquires the second language' (Schumann 1986, p. 384). Among the social factors which Schumann suggested are likely to influence the learner's degree of acculturation are the power relations obtaining between the two language groups ('dominance'/'nondominance'); the 'integration strategy' of the L2 group (assimilation vs preservation); and high/low 'enclosure' (i.e. the extent to which work, churches, schools etc. are shared or not). Among the affective factors influencing acculturation are 'language/culture shock', motivation and 'ego-permeability' (degree of inhibition/disinhibition).

8.4.2 Critique of pidginization/acculturation theory

Schumann's proposals are important because they tried to provide an explanation for the widely recognized differential success of L2 learners, and not only to describe it. However, subsequent research has not offered consistent support for his proposals. As far as pidginization is concerned, Sebba's review of the origins and characteristics of true pidgin languages makes it clear that pidgins and early forms of learner interlanguage are not really the same, though they may have some common characteristics. The following problems arise with the 'early interlanguage = pidgin' proposal.

1 Pidgin languages such as Tok Pisin have their own systematic grammar, which has to be learned like any other L2 (even if this has characteristics which make it more easily learnable). That is, they are much more stable systems than (most) learner interlanguages, which are continually open to restructuring through contact with the target L2.
2 The list of syntactic features proposed by Sebba as characteristic of pidgins is not identical with the characteristics of early learner interlanguages.
3 The origins of pidgin languages are disputed among sociolinguists, and while universal processes of simplification, etc. are undoubtedly in play, they are not by any means the only factor involved in the development of a pidgin (Sebba 1997, pp. 70–98).
4 Other L2 researchers who have examined contemporary language contact situations in search of newly emerging pidgins have failed to produce convincing evidence that e.g. *Gastarbeiterdeutsch* (migrant worker L2 German) is stabilizing into a new pidgin (Hinnenkamp 1984, Blackshire-Belay 1993, quoted in Sebba 1997, p. 80).

As far as acculturation is concerned, it is possible to criticize some of Schumann's suggestions as either too static, or even circular. They depend on the assumption that characteristics such as learners' attitudes and motivation, or indeed their social relationships and degree of integration with the target language community, are fixed rather than evolving characteristics. Furthermore, when reviewing the impact of his own theoretical proposals in 1986, Schumann himself recognized that rather little empirical evidence could be found to support them, alongside a number of studies which offered counter-evidence. Altogether then, these proposals were a significant early attempt to address the neglected social side of language learning. In detail, they have not been supported by subsequent research. However, there are clear affinities between Schumann's proposals and several current strands of research; his proposals on pidginization can be linked to the ESF project's proposed 'basic learner variety', for example, and his acculturation hypothesis to work on L2 socialization (discussed below).

8.5   Second language socialization

8.5.1   *Introduction*

In this final section we turn to a further strand of sociolinguistic research which is centrally concerned with language learning and development: the study of *language socialization*. This work has its roots in anthropological linguistics (Foley 1997), and some key studies in this tradition are ethnographic studies of children learning to talk (and to read and write) their first language, in non-western, non-urban societies. Two of the most important studies are the work of Elinor Ochs in Western Samoa (e.g. Ochs 1988), and that of Bambi Schieffelin among the Kaluli people of Papua New Guinea (Schieffelin 1990). The work of Shirley Brice Heath on children's first language development among rural working-class communities in the SE United States can also be linked to this tradition (Heath 1983, 1986).

8.5.2   Developmental links between first language and culture

Researchers in the language socialization tradition believe that language and culture are not separable, but are acquired together, with each providing support for the development of the other.

> It is evident that acquisition of linguistic knowledge and acquisition of sociocultural knowledge are interdependent. A basic task of the language acquirer is to acquire tacit knowledge of principles relating linguistic forms not only to each other but also to referential and nonreferential meanings and functions ... Given that meanings and functions are to a large extent socioculturally organised, linguistic knowledge is embedded in sociocultural knowledge. On the other hand, understandings of the social organization of everyday life, cultural ideologies, moral values, beliefs, and structures of knowledge and interpretation are to a large extent acquired through the medium of language ... Children develop concepts of a socioculturally structured universe through their participation in language activities.
>
> (Ochs 1988, p. 14)

Drawing on their respective ethnographic studies, Ochs and Schieffelin (1984) compare child-rearing practices among the Kaluli, in Western Samoa, and among white, middle-class (WMC) Americans – all of which, of course, eventually lead to the successful development of competence in the relevant first language. They describe how in the WMC context, infants are viewed as conversational partners almost from birth, with caretakers interacting with them extensively one to one, and compensating for their conversational limitations by imputing meaning to their utterances, and engaging in clarification routines (e.g. by use of comprehension checks and recasts). In Samoa, by contrast, infants are not viewed as conversational partners at all for the first few months (though they are constantly in adult company, and are much cuddled and sung to). After this time, they are encouraged to get involved in multiparty, social interactions, e.g. being taught explicitly to call out the names of passers-by on the village road. Among the Kaluli, there is much direct teaching of interactional routines (*elema*); in both communities, children's unintelligible utterances are seldom clarified or recast. These differences are explained by reference to wider social structures which characterize the Pacific communities. For example, in the Samoan community described by

Ochs, individuals are strictly ranked, and higher-ranked persons do not have any particular responsibility to figure out the intended meanings of lower-ranked persons (such as small children); thus, extended comprehension checks and recasts of children's utterances would be inappropriate.

Ochs and Schieffelin (1984) thus provide some of the cross-cultural comparative data, which we noted earlier is rare in studies of L1 caretaker input (see Chapter 6). As well as examining the social context of language learning from a cross-cultural perspective, Ochs (1988) also examines selected linguistic aspects of interactions involving young L1 learners, and children's early productions. Here again, she finds interactions between linguistic development and socialization into particular roles and routines. For example, the first word produced by Samoan infants is generally claimed to be *tae* ('shit'), symbolic of the naughtiness and wildness expected of little children, and Ochs documented instances of infants' early vocalizations being interpreted in this way. Further examples have to do with register variation within Samoan, and three of these are summarized below.

1 The language offers a choice of first person pronouns, including the neutral form *a'u* ('I', 'me') and the form *ta ita* which is marked for affect, i.e. ('poor me'). In the early productions of the children studied by Ochs, the affect-marked form appeared several months before the neutral form (Ochs 1988, p. 186), linked to a speech act of 'begging' (usually for food); children generally 'are concerned with the rhetorical force of their utterances, and ... rhetorical strategies may account for certain acquisition patterns' (p. 188).

2 Samoan and Kaluli are both *ergative* languages (that is, the Subject of an intransitive verb and the Object of a transitive verb belong to the same ergative case, while the Subject of a transitive verb is nominative). However, Samoan-speaking children acquire the ergative case marker noticeably later than do Kaluli-speakers. Ochs explains this because of socially conditioned variability in adult usage. In Samoan, the ergative case marker 'is used more by men than by women and is more frequent in speech to nonfamily members than in speech among household intimates' (Ochs 1988, p. 102). Ochs suggests that the relative delay in acquisition of this form by Samoan children results from its absence from their caretakers' speech (normally, women around the household compound).

3 M. Platt has collaborated with Ochs in her study of Samoan children, and has examined *deictic* verbs in particular (1986). She has noted that children acquire the (semantically more complex) verb *give* earlier than the verb *come*. Again, this is attributed to characteristics of the social setting, where it is not appropriate for a low-ranking person (such as a child) to control the movements of a higher-ranking person (such as their carer). On the other hand, 'begging' (e.g. for food) is an accepted routine in which children may engage, and it is in this context that the verb *give* is useful.

8.5.3   Studies of second language socialization

Recently, some ethnographic studies of second language learning have also focused more explicitly on 'socialization through language and socialization to use language' (Ochs 1988, p. 14). Here we will examine just one example, which clearly illustrates this approach. This is a longitudinal study of young classroom learners of English as a Second Language, conducted by Jerri Willett in an elementary school with an international intake, linked to a prestigious university in the United States (Willett 1995).

In this study, the context for learning being studied is more restricted than those examined by L1 language socialization researchers such as Ochs and Heath (who tracked children mainly at home, but also followed them into the classroom and other public settings). However, Willett is equally concerned to place the observed interactions in a wider sociohistorical context, and pays considerable attention to the ideologies of teaching and learning which motivate the various actors in the classroom setting (teachers and students). Like Ochs, she links research methods drawn from ethnography (participant observation and interviewing) with Vygotskian sociocultural learning theory and with activity theory (see Chapter 7). She is interested in the contributions of social class and gender to the structuring of learners' experiences and opportunities to develop L2 competence. But Willett stresses that

> Language socialisation, however, is not a one-way process by which learners blindly appropriate static knowledge and skills. It occurs through the micropolitics of social interaction ... People not only construct shared understandings in the process of interaction, they also evaluate and contest those understandings as they struggle to further their individual agendas ... In the process of constructing shared understandings through negotiation, the social practices in which the interaction is embedded are altered and the relations, ideologies and identities are reshaped.
>
> (Willett 1995, p. 475)

In her study, Willett tracked a group of four 7-year-old ESL children through their first year of English-medium, mainstream schooling, in Grade 1 of the elementary school situated near a residential complex for international students. Willett herself acted as a teacher's assistant in their classroom throughout the year; as well as audio-recording the public talk of the classroom, some of the children's small group talk was recorded when children wore a radio-microphone. Only the girls agreed to wear the mike harness, however – a first sign that gender might be a significant issue in the study! Her 1995 report concentrates on their learning experiences and activities during a particular part of the daily classroom routine, phonics seatwork (i.e. individual work to practise literacy skills).

The three girls in the study – Yael, Ethan and Nahla – were from different ethnolinguistic backgrounds, though all were children of overseas students. However, they sat together throughout the year, and formed a close friendship group. Willett argues that all three succeeded in developing identities as 'good students', through co-operation and mutual support. Yael was outgoing and talkative, and acted as spokesperson for the group, e.g. when seeking adult help on a phonics task. Nahla and Etham were 'more attuned to written language' (p. 492), with Nahla a good reader, and Etham attentive to detail in whatever she was doing. By sharing these skills, all three could display competence in the phonics curriculum. As well as winning teachers' approval, their lasting friendship also lent them high status in the girls' subculture of the class, where being 'best friends' was valued.

The fourth child in the study was a Spanish L1 boy named Xavier. He was of Mexican American origin, and his father was a manual worker for the university. Willett claims that for such a child, ethnic and social class stereotyping may lead to lower expectations of academic success, and make it harder for him to gain the identity of 'good student' (p. 497). The boys' classroom subculture was more loosely grouped than the girls', with two competing groups; seating arrangements designed to keep boys apart meant that Xavier had no peers to consult on his phonics work.

> Xavier did not get help from his female seatmates because it went against classroom and playground norms. Moreover, he was not allowed to get out of his seat in order to get help from his bilingual friends – although, even if he could have sought help from them, he may not have gotten it as the boys typically competed with one another rather than helped one another. As a result Xavier had to rely on adults more frequently than Etham, Yael and Nahla to complete the high-status workbook tasks ... Consequently, he began to gain an identity as a needy child who could not work independently.
>
> (pp. 496–7)

Teacher and aides responded with differentiated, lower-status work (ESL workbooks, etc. in place of the mainstream tasks), which Xavier resented and resisted; for such 'solutions' made it difficult for Xavier to retain his status with the other boys.

Willett's study thus shows how 'the same' phonics curriculum, in a relatively privileged academic setting, could work very differently in the construction of different children's classroom identities. In particular she brings out the significance of gender in constraining the learning opportunities available to different individuals. She shows how children with somewhat different personalities and skills could co-operate to achieve school success.

But what about language learning? Willett claims that in the first few weeks and months, ESL children relied heavily on *prefabricated language chunks* picked up from adults and from fluent English-speaking peers, during routine events such as phonics seatwork. The first data extract given below comes from a mid-year recording of the three girls working on a phonics task; Willett shows that almost all utterances can be traced to regular classroom phrases used by L1 speakers (adults or children), or to the basal reader used with the class. Yet she argues that these appropriated chunks are being used 'to enact a socially significant event in order to construct identities as competent students (e.g. they can read, check progress, stay focused on the workbook ...), and construct collaborative relations with one another' (p. 490).

(January)

1	Yael:	What are you doing? What are you doing?
2	Etham:	'The lion let de ball get='
3	Nahla:	=Lookit here. Lookit. I know dis. I put dis. I dunno. Look it=
4	Etham:	=Look at dis. 'De lion let de mouse get—from—from='
5	Nahla:	'get from de lion'

. . .

11	Nahla:	Oh—uh—what are you doing? eh—do—do—do=
12	Yael:	=Where, where are you? You finish dis?
13	Nahla:	No I am not finish dis xix.
14	Etham:	Where are you?
15	Yael:	You here? Dis—is where I—finish.
16	Nahla:	Yeah

(Willett 1995, pp. 489–90)

Throughout the rest of the year, the girls' individual interactions with adults about phonics tasks remained routine, and showed continuing use of the same restricted repertoire of English phrases. However, 'the [continuing] limited language used by the children in adult/child transactions was imposed by their role as pupils rather than their language proficiency' (p. 492). In small group settings, their language use became adventurous and playful. A discussion between the girls towards the end of the school year (June), when they are struggling with some task instructions is shown below. Willett argues that by this time, 'the girls are using syntax to construct meaning rather than merely stringing prefabricated chunks together' (p. 494).

(June)

1	Yael:	Let's do the four [Question 4] one. Let's do the four one.
2	Nahla:	[Reads] 'Make Mr. Big's tracks go from the park.'
3	Yael:	Park, that's the park—track?
4	Nahla:	You don't know what's is track?
5	Yael:	That's the park.
6	Nahla:	Yeah, but we have to draw the tracks. How we draw the tracks?
7	Yael:	I know.
8	Nahla:	What?
9	Yael:	Do like this [she hesitates] . . . What is to draw de tracks?
10	Nahla:	The track is the—one follow you. I show you [draws animal tracks].
11	Yael:	No, is Mr. Big. What is a track?
12	Nahla:	I show you. The track is like dis [again draws animal tracks].
13	Yael:	That's a track?
14	Nahla:	Why you shut my book?
15	Yael:	Because I want to. Now let's do real work. Now.
16	Nahla:	I do a track. I show you track [she continues to draw animal tracks]
17	Yael:	What is dat?
18	Nahla:	Dis is a track.
19	Yael:	Dat is a track?
20	Nahla:	A track on a street [as opposed to a track in the snow from her basal reader].
21	Yael:	A track is dis? Where is the park? First you have to do a line to the park. Let's read it again.
22	Nahla:	OK. 'Make Mr. Big's track go from the car to the park.'

23 Yael: Yeah. A line you have to do.
24 Nahla: It does not say *line*. It says *track*.
25 Yael: Let's ask with her [to aide].

(Willett 1995, pp. 493–4)

This language growth accompanies the construction of identities as 'active and competent students' (e.g. they read directions, stay on task, provide explanations and definitions, solve problems, ask challenging questions, make arguments, seek help when needed) ... they use [the teacher's] ideology about the 'dignity and value of work'... as warrants for their own behaviour (e.g. Turn 15)' (p. 494).

Willett's study is one of the clearest attempts to apply a language social-ization perspective to L2 learning. Other examples can be quoted, e.g. the longitudinal study by E. Platt and Troudi (1997) of Mary, a 9-year-old Grebo-speaking Liberian girl during her first-ever year of schooling, in an American mainstream classroom. Researchers in this tradition challenge what they see as the mechanistic tradition of L2 interaction research, which we reviewed in Chapter 7. They believe that the difficulty experienced by 'mainstream' inter-actional research in finding consistent links between linguistic and pragmatic features of L2 interaction and L2 learning success have to do with premature and over-simplistic attempts at generalization within and across learner groups. Instead, researchers committed to a language socialization perspec-tive believe it is necessary to take account of interactions with the socio-cultural and sociohistorical context, and of activity theory, if we are to succeed in making meaningful connections between learners' L2 experiences and their language and cultural learning. However, as these sample studies show, L2 language socialization research has so far worked in limited contexts (primarily the classroom), with very small numbers of subjects. So far also, the accounts produced of L2 linguistic development within broader patterns of socialization and the construction of an L2 learner identity have been very sketchy (by comparison e.g. with the L1 language socialization work of Ochs and Schieffelin).

8.6   Evaluation: the scope and achievements of sociolinguistic enquiry

In this chapter we have introduced four different strands of sociolinguistic enquiry into L2 use and L2 development. One of these strands, the quantita-tive study of L2 variation, is very different from the others, focusing on the realizations of individual L2 morphemes. Despite its sociolinguistic origins, this line of enquiry seems to contribute most to our understanding of the psy-cholinguistics of L2 processing.

The remaining strands deal with L2 learning in a broad way, embedded in its social context. Indeed, L2 sociolinguists are arguably still mostly pre-occupied with the characterization of this context, and in particular, with providing longitudinal accounts of the social processes of L2 interaction. This work is typically qualitative and interpretative in nature, using the techniques of ethnography or of conversational analysis. It frequently involves case studies of individuals or groups of learners; in contrast to most other traditions, great attention is paid to the personal qualities of the learner, and their own social contribution to the learning context. On the other hand, it is rare to find in sociolinguistic work of this kind, any close attention being paid to the linguistic detail of the learning path being followed (i.e. to the learning *route*).

8.6.1 Sociolinguistic perspectives on interlanguage and interlanguage communication

One of the obvious strengths of the sociolinguistic tradition in SLA is the rich account offered of cross-cultural L2 communication. In Chapter 5, we noted that the functionalist tradition in SLA had paid relatively little attention to L2 interaction, despite being very interested in learners' naturalistic L2 output. The interactionist tradition reviewed in Chapter 6 does of course systematically analyse L2 interaction, but adopts a mainly quantitative approach, tallying the occurrence/non-occurrence of significant functions such as the negotation of meaning, recasts, etc. The ethnographers of L2 communication whose work we sampled in this chapter explore complete speech events in a much more holistic way. They take a multilevel view of conversational interaction; they are concerned with the relationships between linguistic and non-linguistic aspects of communication, rather than with the linguistic aspect *per se*, which is not seen as autonomous or pre-eminent.

In contrast to this holistic approach, the variationists discussed in Section 8.3 look at a range of low-level formal features in learner language, usually at variable realizations of a particular morpheme. They have demonstrated that such variability is patterned rather than random, and that it is generally linked to local features in the immediate linguistic context; in contrast to L1 variation studies, it seems that variability in L2 use is only weakly related to speech style and other social factors. Despite its sociolinguistic starting point, this particular research strand has rather little in common with other current L2 sociolinguistic work. But neither strand has much to say directly about 'core' linguistic issues, such as the nature of L2 grammar or the L2 lexicon.

8.6.2 Sociolinguistic perspectives on language learning and development

As far as language learning itself is concerned, it is clear that sociolinguists of L2 use have concentrated mainly on describing the context for language learning, and the speech events (from gatekeeping encounters to classroom lessons) through which it is presumed to take place. Like the Vygotskian sociocultural theorists discussed in Chapter 7, the L2 ethnographers studied here clearly believe that learning is a collaborative affair, and that language knowledge is socially constructed through interaction. However, they have paid less attention than the sociocultural theorists to the linguistic detail of expert/novice interaction, or to the 'microgenesis' of new language forms in the learner's L2 repertoire. There is no real parallel as yet in L2 'language socialization' studies to the detailed work of Ochs on linguistic development in L1 socialization (1988). Thus, while Ochs offers evidence to support the claim that the actual *route* of L1 development can be influenced by the nature and quality of interactions in which the child becomes engaged, this idea has not yet seriously been investigated for L2 development, from a 'socialization' perspective. Indeed, there are few or no examples in the ethnographic literature of detailed characterization of the route of learning being followed, which links this closely to an account of L2 use. (One exception is Tarone and Liu 1995; these researchers offer a small-scale study which begins to do this.)

On the other hand, current ethnographies of L2 communication and of L2 socialization offer a great deal of evidence about how the learning context, and the learner's evolving style of engagement with it, may affect the *rate* of L2 learning. The ESF project, with its longitudinal accounts of learners' involvement in L2 communication, is especially valuable here.

8.6.3　*Sociolinguistic accounts of the L2 learner*

Sociolinguists take an interest in a wide variety of L2 learners, from the youngest classroom learners to adult migrants. The L2 ethnographers that we have encountered take a more rounded view of the learner as a social being than was true for other perspectives we have surveyed. Thus, for example, dimensions such as gender and ethnicity are seen as potentially quite central for language learning success.

Most striking though, is the emphasis placed by contemporary ethnographic researchers such as Pierce and Willett on the dynamic and alterable nature of learners' identity and engagement with the task of L2 learning. Self-esteem, motivation, etc. are believed to be constructed and reconstructed in the course of L2 interaction, with significant consequences for the rate of learning and ultimate level of success. Alongside rich characterizations of the learning context, this is one of the most distinctive current themes offered by this particular perspective on L2 learning.

9

Conclusion

9.1   One theory or many?

Having come to the end of our survey of current trends in second language learning research, we are left with a reinforced impression of great diversity. Different research groups are pursuing theoretical agendas which centre on very different parts of the total language learning process; while many place the modelling of learner grammars at the heart of the enterprise, others focus on language processing, or on L2 interaction. Each research tradition has developed its cluster of specialized research procedures, ranging from the grammaticality judgement tests associated with UG-inspired research, to the naturalistic observation and recording practised by ethnographers and language socialization theorists. On the whole, grand synthesizing theories, which try to encompass all aspects of L2 learning in a single model, have not received general support. Rather than a process of theory reduction and consolidation, of the kind proposed by Beretta and others, we find that new theoretical perspectives (such as connectionism or sociocultural theory) have entered the field, without displacing established ones (such as Universal Grammar).

On the other hand, some attempts have been made at the principled linking of specific theories on a more modest scale, to account for different aspects of the L2 learning process; a clear example is that made by Towell and Hawkins to link UG theory with a theory of information processing.

9.2   Main achievements of recent SLL research

Drawing on the wealth of studies which have been carried out in the last ten years or so, what are the most significant changes which can be noted in SLL theorising in its many forms? From a linguistic perspective, the continuing application of Universal Grammar to the modelling of L2 competence has led to an increasingly sophisticated and complex range of proposals about the possible contents of that mysterious black box originally imported by Krashen into SLA research, the 'Language Acquisition Device'. One complication (arguably, a blurring of the original concept) is the growing view among some UG specialists that the innate language module may itself be modular, with different aspects of language knowledge being learned and stored relatively autonomously. The Universal Grammar approach has also been instrumental in providing sharper linguistic descriptions of learner language, and has helped to better document the linguistic route followed by L2 learners.

From a cognitive perspective, the main evolutionary developments have been the application of information processing models to domains complementary to the learning of grammar, e.g. the application of Anderson's ACT* model to the acquisition of learning strategies, or the development of fluency. As far as grammar learning itself is concerned, connectionist models offer a much more radical challenge to traditional linguistic thinking, given that they make do without the accepted paraphernalia of abstract rules and symbolic representations, and suggest that a network of much more primitive associationist links can underlie language learning and performance. However, the empirical evidence supporting these claims remains limited, and contentious in its interpretation.

Descriptively, recent work in the functionalist tradition has added substantially to our understanding of the course of L2 development, and especially the key role played by pragmatics and lexis in interlanguage communication, particularly in the early stages. Variationist studies also suggest that much L2 variability can be accounted for by evolving links between form and function.

But in terms of descriptive accounts, perhaps we have learned most from recent research about the contexts within which L2 learning takes place, and the kinds of interactions in which learners become engaged, and have also started seriously to investigate the links between interactional engagement and L2 learning itself. In their different ways, the interactionist, sociocultural, and sociolinguistic perspectives all address this issue. Together they have shown us how learners' engagement in L2 interaction is systematically influenced by power relations and other cultural factors. On the other hand, we have seen that these factors are not inalterably fixed, but can be renegotiated as learners build new identities. Both interactionist and sociocultural research, in their different ways, show how the ongoing character of L2 interaction can systematically affect the learning opportunities it makes available, and have started to demonstrate how learners actually use these opportunities.

However, a major limitation shared by these particular strands is that identified by Braidi (1995) in her commentary on the interactionist tradition in particular: the paucity of studies which track and document learners' linguistic development in detail over time, and link their evolving control of linguistic structure to a narrative account of their interactional experiences. As researchers in the sociocultural tradition have explicitly recognized, such links have so far been made on a limited scale, in respect of small 'patches' of language knowledge only. We have not yet seen the systematic linking over time of longitudinal accounts of interlanguage development like those provided by the functionalist strand, with evolving accounts of L2 negotiation, scaffolding, etc.

9.3   Future directions for SLL research

For the foreseeable future, it seems that L2 learning will be treated as a modular phenomenon, with different research programmes addressing different aspects. The influence of linguistics on the modelling of L2 competence is unlikely to diminish, so that we can expect to see continuing reflexes of evolving linguistic thinking in L2 research, as we have already seen in the application of successive versions of UG theory to the L2 problem. On the other hand, the application of general learning theories derived from cognitive psychology, neural science, etc. can also be expected to continue; the attempts to bring to bear on L2 learning such diverse general learning theories as connectionism, on the one hand, and Vygotskian sociocultural theory, on the other, are the main current examples, but others may follow.

While we believe these different research strands within SLA will retain their autonomy and individual impetus, however, we think that continuing attempts to cross-refer between them and examine relations between different learning 'modules' in a systematic way, a process already exemplified in e.g. the Towell and Hawkins work, will continue to prove a productive way of developing our understanding of the specific modular domains.

From a methodological point of view, one productive development within certain strands of L2 research is the greater use of computer-aided techniques for the analysis of L2 data. In the past, corpus-based studies of L2 development or L2 interaction have usually involved manual analysis of a very labour-intensive kind. Child language research has shown the potential of computer-aided analysis for the handling of corpus data, using software such as the CHILDES package (MacWhinney 1991). The development of electronic L2 corpora, plus work to devise appropriate tools for analysis, is making possible the more systematic linking of L2 grammar development with L2 interaction. They also facilitate much closer attention to L2 lexis and lexico-grammar, and to the role of prefabricated chunks and routines in L2 use and L2 learning. Advances in computer technology have also enabled the development of computer modelling of second language learning (e.g. the recent application of connectionism to the field of second language learning).

Such technical developments do not challenge the fundamental assumptions of second language learning research, which by and large have remained those of rationalist 'modern' science. In recent years, however, a number of critiques have developed of 'autonomous' applied linguistics and SLA, from more socially engaged perspectives (e.g. Pennycook 1994; Phillipson 1992); Rampton (1995b) charts what he sees as the rise of more 'ideological' forms of applied linguistics. We can find in contemporary theoretical discussions, proposals for more socially engaged forms of second language acquisition research, on the one hand (e.g. Block 1996), and for postmodern interpretations of L2 use and learning, on the other (reviewed by Brumfit 1997). Postmodernism offers a relativist critique of 'attempts to see human activity as part of a grand scheme, driven by notions of progressive improvement of any kind' (Brumfit 1997, p. 23). As far as language is concerned, it highlights problems of textuality, and the complex relationship between language and any sort of external reality; 'we are positioned by the requirements of the discourse we think we adopt, and our metaphors of adoption hide the fact that *it* adopts *us*' (Brumfit 1997, p. 25). The postmodern concept of intertextuality – the idea that all language use is a patchwork of borrowings from previous users – has been claimed to be of central importance for L2 learning (Hall 1995).

So far, however, the critical and postmodern commentary on SLA has not dislodged its central modernist assumptions. It will be for the future to tell how much impact it eventually makes on programmes of L2 empirical enquiry; this evolution will evidently be linked to wider ongoing debates in the social sciences.

9.4 Second language learning research and language education

We noted in Chapter 2 that theorising about L2 learning has its historic roots in reform movements connected to the practical business of language teaching. (Howatt shows that this has been true since Renaissance times at least: 1984, pp. 12–72.) In the last quarter century, however, as we have clearly seen, it has become a much more autonomous field of enquiry, with an independent, 'scientific' rationale. But what kind of connections should this now relatively independent research field maintain, with its language teaching origins? From time to time, it has been argued that the 'scientific' findings of SLA should guide the practices of classroom teachers; the recommendations which flowed from Krashen's Input Hypothesis, in the form of the 'Natural Approach' to language pedagogy, are an obvious example (Krashen and Terrell 1983). Another example which we encountered briefly earlier is the Teachability Hypothesis advanced by Pienemann, who suggests that new L2 items might most effectively be taught in sequences which imitate empirically documented developmental sequences.

Ellis (1997) reviews a number of well-known difficulties with such a top-down, rationalist approach to linking research-derived theory and classroom practice. The findings of SLA research are not sufficiently secure, clear and uncontested, across broad enough domains, to provide straightforward prescriptive guidance for the teacher (nor, perhaps, will they ever be so). They are not generally presented and disseminated in ways accessible and meaningful to teachers; the agenda of SLA research does not necessarily centre on the issues which teachers are most conscious of as problematic. But most importantly, teaching is an art as well as a science, and irreducibly so, because of the constantly varying nature of the classroom as a learning community. There can be no 'one best method', however much research evidence supports it, which applies at all times and in all situations, with every type of learner. Instead, teachers 'read' and interpret the changing dynamics of the learning context from moment to moment, and take what seem to them to be appropriate contingent actions, in the light of largely implicit, proceduralized pedagogic knowledge. This has been built up over time very largely from their own previous experience, and usually derives only to a much more limited extent from study or from organized training.

However, present SLA research offers a rich variety of concepts and descriptive accounts, which can help teachers interpret and make better sense of their own classroom experiences, and significantly broaden the range of pedagogic choices open to them. For example, SLL research has produced descriptive accounts of the course of interlanguage development, which show that learners follow relatively invariant routes of learning, but that such routes are not linear, including phases of restructuring and apparent regression. Such accounts have helped teachers to understand patterns of learner error and its inevitability, and more generally, to accept the indirect nature of the relationship between what is taught and what is learned. Similarly, in the recent literature, discussions about the role of recasts and negative evidence in learning (reviewed in Chapter 6), about scaffolding and microgenesis (Chapter 7), or about language socialization (Chapter 8) have great potential to stimulate teacher reflections on the discourse choices available to them, when enacting their own role as L2 guide and interlocutor.

Of course, the subfield of research on 'instructed SLA' (Spada 1997) plays a special role in addressing concerns somewhat closer to those of the classroom teacher, and may offer opportunities for more direct involvement of teachers as research partners. But even 'instructed SLA' research is not identical with problem-solving and development in language pedagogy, and does not ensure a shared agenda between teachers and researchers. There is a continuing need for dialogue between the 'practical theories' of classroom educators, and the more decontextualized and abstract ideas deriving from programmes of research. Researchers thus have a continuing responsibility to make their findings and their interpretations of them as intelligible as possible to a wider professional audience, with other preoccupations. We hope that this book contributes usefully to this dialogue.

Bibliography

Aarts, J. 1991: Intuition-based and observation-based grammars. In Aijmer, K. and Altenberg, B. (eds), *English corpus linguistics*. Harlow: Longman, 44–62.

Adams, M. 1978: Methodology for examining second language acquisition. In Hatch, E. M. (ed.), *Second language acquisition*. Rowley, MA: Newbury House, 278–96.

Adiv, E. 1984: Language learning strategies: the relationship between L1 operating principles and language transfer in L2 development. In Andersen, R. (ed.), *Second languages: a cross-linguistic perspective*. Rowley, MA: Newbury House, 125–42.

Aitchison, J. 1989: *The articulate mammal*. London: Unwin Hyman.

Aljaafreh, A. and Lantolf, J. P. 1994: Negative feedback as regulation and second language learning in the Zone of Proximal Development. *Modern Language Journal* 78, 465–83.

Andersen, R. (ed.) 1983: *Pidginisation and creolisation as language acquisition*. Rowley, MA.: Newbury House.

—— 1984: *Second languages: a cross-linguistic perspective*. Rowley, MA: Newbury House.

—— 1990: Models, processes, principles and strategies: second language acquisition inside and outside of the classroom. In Van Patten, B. and Lee, J. (eds), *Second language acquisition – foreign language learning*. Clevedon: Multilingual Matters, 45–68.

Andersen, R. and Shirai, Y. 1994: Discourse motivations for some cognitive acquisition principles. *Studies in Second Language Acquisition* 16, 133–56.

—— 1996: The primacy of aspect in first and second language acquisition: the pidgin–creole connection. In Ritchie, W. and Bhatia, T. (eds), *Handbook of second language acquisition*. San Diego: Academic Press, 527–708.

Anderson, J. 1980: *Cognitive psychology and its implications*. New York: Freeman.

—— 1983: *The architecture of cognition*. Cambridge, MA: Harvard University Press.

—— 1985: *Cognitive psychology and its implications*, 2nd edn. New York: Freeman.

—— 1993: *Rules of the mind*. Hillsdale, NJ: Erlbaum.

—— 1995: *Learning and memory*. New York: John Wiley.

Anderson, J. and Fincham, J. 1994: Acquisition of procedural skill from examples. *Journal of Experimental Psychology: Learning, Memory and Cognition* 20, 1322–40.

Bailey, N., Madden, C. and Krashen, S. 1974: Is there a 'natural sequence' in adult second language learning? *Language Learning* 24, 235–43.

Bayley, R. 1994: Interlanguage variation and the quantitative paradigm: past tense marking in Chinese-English. In Tarone, E., Gass, S. M. and Cohen, A. (eds), *Research methodology in second language acquisition*. Hillsdale, NJ: Lawrence Erlbaum, 157–81.

—— 1996: Competing constraints on variation in the speech of adult Chinese learners of English. In Bayley, R. and Preston, D. R. (eds), *Second language acquisition and linguistic variation*. Amsterdam: John Benjamins, 97–120.

Bayley, R. and Preston, D. R. (eds) 1996: *Second language acquisition and linguistic variation*. Amsterdam: John Benjamins.

Beebe, L. M. and Giles, H. 1984: Speech accommodation theories: a discussion in terms of second language acquisition. *International Journal of the Sociology of Language* 46, 5–32.

Bellugi, U., Van Hoek, K., Lillo-Martin, D. and O'Grady, L. 1993: The acquisition of syntax in young deaf signers. In Bishop, D. and Mogford, K. (eds), *Language development in exceptional circumstances*. Hove: Lawrence Erlbaum Associates, 132–50.

Berdan, R. 1996: Disentangling language acquisition from language variation. In Bayley, R. and Preston, D. R.(eds), *Second language acquisition and linguistic variation*. Amsterdam: John Benjamins, 203–44.

Beretta, A. (ed.) 1993: Theory construction in SLA. Special issue of *Applied Linguistics*, 14, 221–4.

Berko, J. 1958: The child's learning of English morphology. *Word* 14, 150–77.

Bialystok, E. 1990: *Communication strategies: a psychological analysis of second-language use*. Oxford: Basil Blackwell.

—— 1991: Metalinguistic dimensions of bilingual language proficiency. In Bialystok, E. (ed.), *Language processing in bilingual children*. Cambridge: Cambridge University Press, 113–40.

Bialystok, E. and Kellerman, E. 1987: Communication strategies in the classroom. In Das, B. (ed.), *Communication and learning in the classroom community*. Singapore: SEAMEO Regional Language Centre, 160–75.

Bickerton, D. 1971: Inherent variability and variable rules. *Foundations of Language* 7, 457–92.

Bishop, D. and Mogford, K. (eds) 1993: *Language development in exceptional circumstances*. Hove: Lawrence Erlbaum Associates.

Bley-Vroman, R. 1989: What is the logical problem of foreign language learning? In Gass, S. and Schachter, J. (eds), *Linguistic perspectives on second language acquisition*, Cambridge: Cambridge University Press, 41–68.

Block, D. 1996: Not so fast: some thoughts on theory culling, relativism, accepted findings and the heart and soul of SLA. *Applied Linguistics* 17, 63–83.

Bloomfield, L. 1933: *Language*. New York: Holt, Rinehart and Winston.

Bohannon, J. N., Macwhinney, B. and Snow, C. 1990: No negative evidence revisited: beyond learnability or who has to prove what to whom. *Developmental Psychology* 26, 221–6.

Bohannon, J. N., Padgett, R. J., Nelson, K. E. and Mark, M. 1996: Useful evidence on negative evidence. *Developmental Psychology* 32, 551–5.

Braidi, S. M. 1995: Reconsidering the role of interaction and input in second language acquisition. *Language Learning* 45, 141–75.

Braine, M. D. S. 1971: The acquisition of language in infant and child. In Reed, C. E. (ed.), *The learning of language*. New York: Appleton-Century-Crofts, 7–95.

Bremer, K., Broeder, P., Roberts, C., Simonot, M. and Vasseur, M-T. 1993: Ways of achieving understanding. In Perdue, C. (ed.), *Adult language acquisition: cross-linguistic perspectives*. Volume 2: *The Results*. Cambridge: Cambridge University Press, 153–95.

Bremer, K., Roberts, C., Vasseur, M.-T., Simonot, M. and Broeder, P. 1996: *Achieving understanding: discourse in intercultural encounters*. Harlow: Longman.

Brown, R. 1973: *A first language: the early stages*. Cambridge, MA: Harvard University Press.

Brumfit, C. J. 1997: Theoretical practice: applied linguistics as pure and practical science. *AILA Review* 12, 18–30.

Brumfit, C. J. and Johnson, K. (eds) 1979: *The communicative approach to language teaching*. Oxford: Oxford University Press.

Brumfit, C. J. and Mitchell, R. 1990: The language classroom as a focus for research. In Brumfit, C. J. and Mitchell, R. (eds), *Research in the language classroom*. ELT Documents 133. Modern English Publications/The British Council, 3–15.

Bruner, J. 1985: Vygotsky: a historical and conceptual perspective. In Wertsch, J. (ed.), *Culture, communication and cognition: Vygotskian perspectives*. Cambridge: Cambridge University Press, 21–34.

Budwig, N. 1995: *A developmental–functionalist approach to child language*. Mahwah, NJ: Lawrence Erlbaum Associates.

Butterworth, B. and Harris, M. 1994: *Principles of developmental psychology*. Hove: Lawrence Erlbaum.

Butterworth, G. and Hatch, E. 1978: A Spanish-speaking adolescent's acquisition of English syntax. In Hatch, E. (ed.), *Second language acquisition*. Rowley, MA: Newbury House, 231–45.

Caplan, D. 1987: *Neurolinguistics and linguistic aphasiology: an introduction*. Cambridge: Cambridge University Press.

—— 1992: *Language: structure, processing, and disorders*. Cambridge, MA: MIT Press.

Carroll, S. 1995: The hidden danger of computer modelling: remarks on Sokolik and Smith's connectionist learning model of French gender. *Second Language Research* 11, 193–205.

Cazden, C. 1972: *Child language and education*. New York: Holt, Rinehart and Winston.

Cazden, C. B., Cancino, H., Rosansky, E. and Schumann, J. 1975: *Second language acquisition sequences in children, adolescents and adults: final report*. Washington, DC: National Institute of Education.

Chaudron, C. 1985: Intake: on models and methods for discovering learners' processing of input. *Studies in Second Language Acquisition* 7, 11–14.

—— 1988: *Second language classrooms: research on teaching and learning*. Cambridge: Cambridge University Press.

Chomsky, N. 1957: *Syntactic structures*. The Hague: Mouton.

—— 1959: Review of B. F. Skinner, *Verbal behavior*. *Language* 35, 26–58.

—— 1965: *Aspects of the theory of syntax*. Cambridge, MA: MIT Press.

—— 1968: *Language and mind*. New York: Harcourt Brace Jovanovich.

—— 1975: *Reflections on language*. New York: Pantheon.

—— 1981: *Lectures on government and binding*. Dordrecht: Foris.

—— 1986a: *Knowledge of language, its nature, origin, and use*. New York: Praeger.

—— 1986b: *Barriers*. Cambridge, MA: MIT Press.

—— 1987: Transformational grammar: past, present, and future. In *Studies in English language and literature*. Kyoto: Kyoto University, 33–80.

—— 1988: *Language and problems of knowledge: the Managua lectures*. Cambridge, MA: MIT Press.

—— 1995: *The minimalist program*. Cambridge, MA: MIT Press.

Clahsen, H. 1982: *Spracherwerb in der Kindheit: eine Untersuchung zur Entwicklung der Syntax bei Kleinkindern*. Tübingen: Gunter Narr Verlag.

—— 1984: The acquisition of German word order: a test case for cognitive approaches to L2 development. In Andersen, R. (ed.), *Second languages: a cross-linguistic perspective*. Rowley, MA: Newbury House, 219–42.

Clahsen, H. and Muysken, P. 1986: The availability of universal grammar to adult and child learners – a study of the acquisition of German word order. *Second Language Research* 2, 93–119.

Clark, E. 1985: The acquisition of Romance, with special reference to French. In Slobin, D. (ed.), *The crosslinguistic study of language acquisition*. Hillsdale: Lawrence Erlbaum Associates, 687–782.

Cook, V. 1993: *Linguistics and second language acquisition*. Basingstoke: Macmillan Press.

—— 1997: *Inside language*. London: Edward Arnold.

Cook, V. and Newson, M. 1996: *Chomsky's Universal Grammar: an introduction.* Oxford: Blackwell.

Corder, S. P. 1967: The significance of learners' errors. *International Review of Applied Linguistics* 5, 161–9.

Coughlan, P. and Duff, P. A. 1994: Same task, different activities: analysis of an SLA task from an Activity Theory perspective. In Lantolf, J. P. and Appel, G. (eds), *Vygotskian approaches to second language research.* Norwood, NJ: Ablex Publishing Corporation, 173–94.

Coupland, N. and Jaworski, A. 1997: *Sociolinguistics: a reader and coursebook.* Basingstoke: Macmillan.

Crystal, D. 1987: *The Cambridge encyclopedia of language.* Cambridge: Cambridge University Press.

—— 1991: *A dictionary of linguistics and phonetics.* Oxford: Blackwell.

Dechert, H. 1983: How a story is done in a second language. In Færch, C. and Kasper, G. (eds), *Strategies in interlanguage communication.* London: Longman, 175–95.

De Graaff, R. 1997: The eXperanto experiment: effects of explicit instruction on second language acquisition. *Studies in Second Language Acquisition* 19, 249–276.

De Groot, A. 1992: Determinants of word translation. *Journal of Experimental Psychology: Learning, Memory and Cognition* 18, 1000–18.

De Guerrero, M. C. M. and Villamil, O. S. 1994: Social-cognitive dimensions of interaction in L2 peer revision. *Modern Language Journal* 78, 484–96.

Dekeyser, R. 1993: The effect of error correction on L2 grammar knowledge and oral proficiency. *Modern Language Journal* 77, 501–14.

—— 1997: Beyond explicit rule learning: automatizing second language morphosyntax. *Studies in Second Language Acquisition* 19, 195–221.

De Villiers, P. A. and De Villiers, J. G. 1973: A cross-sectional study of the development of grammatical morphemes in child speech. *Journal of Psycholinguistic Research* 1, 299–310.

Deutsch, W. and Budwig, N. 1983: Form and function in the development of possessives. *Papers and Reports on Child Language Development* 22, 36–42.

Dietrich, R., Klein, W. and Noyau, C. 1995: *The acquisition of temporality in a second language.* Amsterdam: John Benjamins.

Dittmar, N. 1984: Semantic features of pidginised learners of German. In Andersen, R. (ed.), *Second languages: a cross-linguistic perspective.* Rowley, MA: Newbury House, 243–70.

—— 1993: Proto-semantics and emergent grammars. In Dittmar, N. and Reich, A. (eds), *Modality in language acquisition.* Berlin: Walter de Gruyter, 213–33.

Dittmar, N. and Reich, A. 1993: *Modality in language acquisition.* Berlin: Walter de Gruyter.

Donato, R. 1994: Collective scaffolding in second language learning. In Lantolf, J. P. and Appel, G. (eds), *Vygotskian approaches to second language research.* Norwood, NJ: Ablex Publishing Corporation, 33–56.

Donato, R. and McCormick, D. 1994: A sociocultural perspective on language learning strategies: the role of mediation. *Modern Language Journal* 78, 453–64.

Duff, P. A. 1995: An ethnography of communication in immersion classrooms in Hungary. *TESOL Quarterly* 29, 505–37.

—— 1996: Different languages, different practices: socialization of discourse competence in dual-language school classrooms in Hungary. In Bailey, K. M. and Nunan, D. (eds), *Voices from the language classroom*. Cambridge: Cambridge University Press, 407–33.

Dulay, H. and Burt, M. 1973: Should we teach children syntax? *Language Learning* 24, 245–58.

—— 1974a: You can't learn without goofing: an analysis of children's second language errors. In Richards, J. (ed.), *Error analysis*. London: Longman, 95–123.

—— 1974b: Errors and strategies in child second language acquisition. *TESOL Quarterly* 8, 129–36.

—— 1974c: Natural sequences in child second language acquisition. *Language Learning* 24, 37–53.

—— 1975: Creative construction in second language learning and teaching. In Burt, M. and Dulay, H. (eds), *New directions in second language learning, teaching, and bilingual education*. Washington, DC: TESOL, 21–32.

Dulay, H., Burt, M. and Krashen, S. 1982: *Language two*. New York: Oxford University Press.

Edwards, D. and Mercer, N. 1987: *Common knowledge: the development of understanding in the classroom*. London: Methuen.

Ellis, N. 1996a: Sequencing in SLA: phonological memory, chunking and points of order. *Studies in Second Language Acquisition* 18, 91–126.

—— 1996b: Analyzing language sequence in the sequence of language acquisition: some comments on Major and Ioup. *Studies in Second Language Acquisition* 18, 361–8.

Ellis, N. and Schmidt, R., 1997: Morphology and longer distance dependencies: laboratory research illuminating the A in SLA. *Studies in Second Language Acquisition* 19, 145–171.

Ellis, R. 1985a: Sources of variability in interlanguage. *Applied Linguistics* 6, 118–31.

—— 1985b: *Understanding second language acquisition*. Oxford: Oxford University Press.

—— 1987: Interlanguage variability in narrative discourse: style-shifting in the use of the past tense. *Studies in Second Language Acquisition* 9, 1–20.

—— 1989: Sources of intra-learner variability in language use and their relationship to second language acquisition. In Gass, S., Madden, C., Preston, D. and Selinker, L. (eds), *Variation in second language acquisition*. Volume II: *psycholinguistic issues*. Clevedon: Multilingual Matters, 22–45.

—— 1990: A response to Gregg. *Applied Linguistics* 11, 384–91.

—— 1994: *The study of second language acquisition*. Oxford: Oxford University Press.

—— 1997: *SLA research and language teaching*. Oxford: Oxford University Press.

Elman, J., Bates, E., Johnson, M., Karmiloff-Smith, A., Parisi, D. and Plunkett, K. 1996: *Rethinking innateness: a connectionist perspective on development*. Cambridge, MA: MIT Press.

Færch, C. and Kasper, G. (eds) 1983a: *Strategies in interlanguage communication*. London: Longman.

—— 1983b: Plans and strategies in foreign language communication. In Færch, C. and Kasper, G. (eds), *Strategies in interlanguage communication*. London: Longman, 20–60.

Farrar, M. J. 1992: Negative evidence and grammatical morpheme acquisition. *Developmental Psychology* 28, 90–98.

Felix, S. 1978: Some differences between first and second language acquisition. In Waterson, N. and Snow, C. (eds), *The development of communication*. New York: Wiley and Sons, 469–79.

Ferguson, C. and Slobin, D. (eds) 1973: *Studies of child language development* New York: Holt, Rinehart and Winston.

Flynn, S. 1983: *A study of the effects of principal branching direction in second language acquisition: the generalization of a parameter of Universal Grammar from first to second language acquisition*. Doctoral dissertation, Cornell University, Ithaca, New York.

—— 1984: A universal in L2 acquisition based on a PBD typology. In Eckman, F., Bell, L. and Nelson, D. (eds), *Universals of second language acquisition*. Rowley, MA: Newbury House, 75–87.

—— 1987: *A parameter-setting model of L2 acquisition: experimental studies in anaphora*. Dordrecht: Reidel.

—— 1996: A parameter-setting approach to second language acquisition. In Ritchie, W. and Bhatia, T. (eds), *Handbook of second language acquisition*. San Diego: Academic Press, 121–58.

Fodor, J. A. 1983: *The modularity of mind*. Cambridge, MA: MIT Press.

Foley, W. A. 1997: *Anthropological linguistics: an introduction*. Oxford: Blackwell.

Foster, P. and Skehan, P. 1996: The influence of planning and task type on second language performance. *Studies in Second Language Acquisition* 18, 299–323.

Foster, S. 1990: *The communicative competence of young children*. Harlow: Longman.

Frawley, W. and Lantolf, J. 1985: Second language discourse: a Vygotskian perspective. *Applied Linguistics* 6, 19–44.

Fries, C. 1945: *Teaching and learning English as a foreign language*. Ann Arbor: University of Michigan Press.

Gallaway, C. and Richards, B. J. (eds) 1994: *Input and interaction in language acquisition*. Cambridge: Cambridge University Press.

Gardner, R. C. 1985: *Social psychology and second language learning: the role of attitudes and motivation*. London: Edward Arnold.

Gardner, R. C. and Macintyre, P. D. 1992: A student's contributions to second language learning. Part I: cognitive variables. *Language teaching* 25, 211–20.

—— 1993: A student's contributions to second language learning. Part II: affective variables. *Language teaching* 26, 1–11.

Gass, S. M. 1996: Second language acquisition and linguistic theory: the role of language transfer. In Ritchie, W. C. and Bhatia, T. K. (eds), *Handbook of second language acquisition*. San Diego: Academic Press, 317–45.

Gass, S. and Selinker, L. 1994: *Second language acquisition: an introductory course*. New Jersey: Lawrence Erlbaum.

Gass, S. M. and Varonis, E. M. 1994: Input, interaction and second language production. *Studies in Second Language Acquisition* 16, 283–302.

Gasser, M. 1990: Connectionism and universals of second language acquisition. *Studies in Second Language Acquisition* 12, 179–99.

Gee, J. and Savasir, I. 1985: On the use of 'will' and 'gonna': towards a description of activity-types for child language. *Discourse Processes* 8, 143–75.

Gerhardt, J. 1990: The relation of language to context in children's speech: the role of HAFTA statements in structuring 3-year-olds' discourse. *Papers in Pragmatics* 4, 1–57.

Givón, T. 1979: From discourse to syntax: grammar as a processing strategy. In Givón, T. (ed.) *Syntax and semantics* Volume 12. New York: Academic Press, 81–112.

—— 1985: Function, structure and language acquisition. In Slobin, D. (ed.) *The cross-linguistic study of language acquisition*. Hillsdale, NJ: Lawrence Erlbaum, 1005–27.

Gopnik, M. and Crago, M. B. 1991: Familial aggregation of a developmental language disorder. *Cognition* 39, 1–50.

Green, P. S. and Hecht, K. 1992: Implicit and explicit grammar: an empirical study. *Applied Linguistics* 13, 168–84.

Gregg, K. 1984: Krashen's monitor and Occam's razor. *Applied Linguistics* 5, 79–100.

—— 1990: The Variable Competence Model of second language acquisition and why it isn't. *Applied Linguistics* 11, 364–83.

Grondin, N. and White, L. 1996: Functional categories in child L2 acquisition of French. *Language Acquisition* 5, 1–34.

Hall, J. K. 1995: (Re)creating our worlds with words: a sociohistorical perspective of face-to-face interaction. *Applied Linguistics* 16, 206–32.

Hamers, J. and Blanc, M. 1989: *Bilinguality and bilingualism*. Cambridge: Cambridge University Press.

Hansen, J. G. and Liu, J. 1997: Social identity and language: theoretical and methodological issues. *TESOL Quarterly* 31, 567–76.

Harley, B. and Hart, D. 1997: Language aptitude and second language proficiency in classroom learners of different starting ages. *Studies in Second Language Acquisition* 19, 379–400.

Harley, T. 1995: *The psychology of language: from data to theory.* Hove: Erlbaum (UK) Taylor and Francis.

Harris, M. and Coltheart, M. 1986: *Language processing in children and adults: an introduction.* London: Routledge.

Hatch, E. M. 1978: Discourse analysis and second language acquisition. In Hatch, E. M. (ed.) *Second language acquisition: a book of readings.* Rowley, MA: Newbury House, 401–35.

Hawkins, R. and Chan, Y. 1997: The partial availability of Universal Grammar in second language acquisition: the 'failed functional features hypothesis'. *Second Language Research* 13, 187–226.

Heath, S. B. 1983: *Ways with words.* Cambridge: Cambridge University Press.

—— 1986: What no bedtime story means: narrative skills at home and school. In Schieffelin, B. B. and Ochs, E. (eds), *Language socialisation across cultures.* Cambridge: Cambridge University Press, 97–124.

Hernandez-Chavez, E. 1972: Early code separation in the second language speech of Spanish-speaking children. Paper presented at the Stanford Child Language Research Forum, Stanford, Stanford University.

Hilleson, M. 1996: 'I want to talk with them, but I don't want them to hear': an introspective study of second language anxiety in an English-medium school. In Bailey, K. M. and Nuna, D. (eds), *Voices from the language classroom.* Cambridge: Cambridge University Press, 248–75.

Hoekstra, T. and Schwartz, B. 1994: *Language acquisition studies in generative grammar.* Amsterdam: John Benjamins.

Holmes, J. 1992: *An introduction to sociolinguistics.* Harlow: Longman.

Houck, N., Robertson, J. and Krashen, S. 1978: On the domain of the conscious grammar: morpheme orders for corrected and uncorrected ESL student transcripts. *TESOL Quarterly* 12, 335–9.

Howatt, A. P. R. 1984: *A history of English language teaching.* Oxford: Oxford University Press.

—— 1988: From structural to communicative. *Annual Review of Applied Linguistics* 8, 14–29.

Hudson, R. 1996: *Sociolinguistics*, 2nd edn. Cambridge: Cambridge University Press.

Huebner, T. 1983: *The acquisition of English.* Ann Arbor: Karoma.

Hulstijn, J. 1997: Second language acquisition research in the laboratory: possibilities and limitations. *Studies in Second Language Acquisition* 19, 131–43.

Hulstijn, J. and Hulstijn, W. 1984: Grammatical errors as a function of processing constraints and explicit knowledge. *Language Learning* 34, 23–43.

Hymes, D. 1972: Models of the interaction of language and social life. In Gumperz, J. and Hymes, D. (eds), *Directions in sociolinguistics: the ethnography of communication.* New York: Holt, Rinehart and Winston, 35–71.

Johnson, J. and Newport, E. 1989: Critical period effects in second language learning: the influence of maturational state on the acquisition of ESL. *Cognitive Psychology* 21, 60–99.

Johnson, K. 1996: *Language teaching and skill learning.* Oxford: Blackwell.

Juffs, A. and Harrington, M. 1995: Parsing effects in second language sentence processing: subject and object asymmetries in *wh*-extraction. *Studies in Second Language Acquisition* 17, 483–516.

Karmiloff-Smith, A. 1979: *A functional approach to child language.* Cambridge: Cambridge University Press.

—— 1986a: From meta-processes to conscious access: evidence from children's metalinguistic and repair data. *Cognition* 23, 95–147.

—— 1986b: Stage/structure versus phase/process in modelling linguistic and cognitive development. In Levin, I. (ed.), *Stage and structure: reopening the debate.* Norwood, NJ: Ablex, 164–90.

—— 1987: Function and process in comparing language and cognition. In Hickmann, M. (ed.), *Social and functional approaches to language and thought.* London: Academic Press, 185–202.

—— 1992: *Beyond modularity.* Cambridge, MA: MIT Press.

Kasper, G. (ed.) 1996: The development of pragmatic competence. Special issue of *Studies in Second Language Acquisition,* 18, 2.

Kasper, G. and Kellerman, E. (eds) 1997: *Communication strategies: psycholinguistic and sociolinguistic perspectives.* London: Longman.

Kellerman, E. 1991: Compensatory strategies in second language research: a critique, a revision, and some (non-)implications for the classroom. In Phillipson, R., Kellerman, E., Selinker, L., Sharwood Smith, M. and Swain, M. (eds), *Foreign/second language pedagogy research.* Clevedon: Multilingual Matters, 142–61.

Kellerman, E., Ammerlaan, A., Bongaerts, T. and Poulisse, N. 1990: System and hierarchy in L2 compensatory strategies. In Scarcella, R., Andersen, E. and Krashen, S. (eds), *Developing communicative competence in a second language.* New York: Newbury House, 163–78.

Kellerman, E. and Bialystok, E. 1997: On psychological plausibility in the study of communication strategies. In Kasper, G. and Kellerman, E. (eds), *Communication strategies: psycholinguistic and sociolinguistic perspectives.* London: Longman, 31–48.

Klein, W., Dietrich, R. and Noyau, C. 1993: The acquisition of temporality. In Perdue, C. (ed.), *Adult language acquisition: cross-linguistic perspectives.* Volume 2: *The results.* Cambridge: Cambridge University Press, 73–118.

Klein, W. and Perdue, C. 1992: *Utterance structure: developing grammars again.* Amsterdam: John Benjamins.

Klima, E. and Bellugi, V. 1966: Syntactic regularities in the speech of children. In Lyons, J. and Wales, R. (eds), *Psycholinguistic papers.* Edinburgh: Edinburgh University Press, 183–219.

Kowal, M. and Swain, M. 1994: Using collaborative language production tasks to promote students' language awareness. *Language Awareness* 3, 73–93.

Krashen, S. 1977a: The monitor model of adult second language performance. In Burt, M., Dulay, H. and Finocchiaro, M. (eds), *Viewpoints on English as a second language*. New York: Regents, 152–61.

—— 1977b: Some issues relating to the monitor model. In Brown, H., Yorio, C. and Crymes, R. (eds), *Teaching and learning English as a second language: some trends in research and practice*. Washington, DC: TESOL, 144–48.

—— 1978: Individual variation in the use of the monitor. In Ritchie, W. (ed.) *Second language acquisition research: issues and implications*. New York: Academic Press, 175–83.

—— 1981: *Second language acquisition and second language learning*. Oxford: Pergamon.

—— 1982: *Principles and practice in second language acquisition*. Oxford: Pergamon.

—— 1983: Newmark's ignorance hypothesis and current second language acquisition theory. In Gass, S. and Selinker, L. (eds), *Language transfer in language learning*. Rowley, MA: Newbury House, 135–53.

—— 1985: *The input hypothesis: issues and implications*. Harlow: Longman.

Krashen, S. and Scarcella, R. 1978: On routines and patterns in second language acquisition and performance. *Language Learning* 28, 283–300.

Krashen, S. and Terrell, T. 1983: *The natural approach: language acquisition in the classroom*. Hayward, CA: Alemany Press.

Labov, W. 1972: *Sociolinguistic patterns*. Philadelphia: University of Pennsylvania Press.

Lado, R. 1957: *Linguistics across cultures*. Ann Arbor: University of Michigan Press.

—— 1964: *Language teaching: a scientific approach*. New York: McGraw-Hill.

Lakshmanan, U. 1993: The boy for the cookie – some evidence for the non-violation of the case filter in child second language acquisition. *Language Acquisition* 3, 55–91.

—— 1995: Child second language acquisition of syntax. *Studies in Second Language Acquisition* 17, 301–29.

Lakshmanan, U. and Selinker, L. 1994: The status of CP and the tensed complementizer *that* in developing L2 grammars of English. *Second Language Research* 10, 25–48.

Lange, D. 1979: Negation in natürlichen Englisch-Deutschen Zweitsprachenerwerb: eine Fallstudie. *International Review of Applied Linguistics* 17, 331–48.

Lantolf, J. P. 1994a: Introduction to the Special Issue. *Modern Language Journal* 78, 418–20.

—— (ed.) 1994b: Sociocultural theory and second language learning: Special issue, *Modern Language Journal* 78, 4.

—— 1996: Second language acquisition theory building? In Blue, G. and Mitchell, R. (eds), *Language and education*. Clevedon: BAAL/Multilingual Matters, 16–27.

Lantolf, J. P. and Appel, G. 1994a: Theoretical framework: an introduction to Vygotskian perspectives on second language research. In Lantolf, J. P. and Appel, G. (eds), *Vygotskian approaches to second language research*. Norwood, NJ: Ablex Publishing Corporation, 1–32.

—— (eds) 1994b: *Vygotskian approaches to second language research*. Norwood, NJ: Ablex Publishing Corporation.

Larsen-Freeman, D. and Long, M. H. 1991: *An introduction to second language acquisition research*. Harlow: Longman.

Lee, D. 1992: *Universal grammar, learnability, and the acquisition of English reflexive binding by L1 Korean speakers*. Doctoral dissertation, University of Southern California, Los Angeles.

Lenneberg, E. 1967: *Biological foundations of language*. New York: Wiley.

Leontiev, A. N. 1981: *Problems of the development of mind*. Moscow: Progress Publishers.

Levelt, W. 1989: *Speaking: from intention to articulation*. Cambridge, MA: MIT Press.

Lieven, E. V. M. 1994: Crosslinguistic and crosscultural aspects of language addressed to children. In Gallaway, C. and Richards, B. (eds), *Input and interaction in language acquisition*. Cambridge: Cambridge University Press, 56–73.

Lightbown, P. and Spada, N. 1993: *How languages are learned*. Oxford: Oxford University Press.

Long, M. H. 1980: *Input, interaction and second language acquisition*. Doctoral dissertation, University of California, Los Angeles.

—— 1981: Input, interaction and second language acquisition. In Winitz, H. (ed.), *Native language and foreign language acquisition*. *Annals of the New York Academy of Sciences* 379, 259–278.

—— 1983a: Native speaker/non native speaker conversation and the negotiation of comprehensible input. *Applied Linguistics* 4, 126–41.

—— 1983b: Linguistic and conversational adjustments to non-native speakers. *Studies in Second Language Acquisition* 5, 177–93.

—— 1985: Input and second language acquisition theory. In Gass, S. M. and Madden, C. G. (eds), *Input in second language acquisition*. Rowley, MA: Newbury House, 377–93.

—— 1990a: The least a second language acquisition theory needs to explain. *TESOL Quarterly* 24, 649–66.

—— 1990b: Maturational constraints on language development. *Studies in Second Language Acquisition* 12, 251–85.

—— 1993: Assessment strategies for SLA theories. *Applied Linguistics* 14, 225–49.

—— 1996: The role of the linguistic environment in second language acquisition. In Ritchie, W. C. and Bhatia, T. K. (eds), *Handbook of second language acquisition*. San Diego: Academic Press, 413–68.

Loschky, L. 1994: Comprehensible input and second language acquisition: what is the relationship? *Studies in Second Language Acquisition* **16**, 303–23.

Losey, K. M. 1995: Gender and ethnicity as factors in the development of verbal skills in bilingual Mexican American women. *TESOL Quarterly* **29**, 635–61.

Lust, B., Hermon, G. and Kornfilt, J. 1994: *Syntactic theory and first language acquisition: cross-linguistic perspectives* (2 volumes). Hillsdale: Lawrence Erlbaum.

Lyster, R. and Ranta, E. 1997: Corrective feedback and learner uptake: negotiation of form in communicative classrooms. *Studies in Second Language Acquisition* **19**, 37–61.

MacWhinney, B. 1989: Competition and connectionism. In MacWhinney, B. and Bates, E. (eds), *The crosslinguistic study of sentence processing.* Cambridge: Cambridge University Press, 422–57.

—— 1991: *The CHILDES project: tools for analyzing talk.* Hillsdale, NJ: Erlbaum.

MacWhinney, B. and Anderson, J. 1986: The acquisition of grammar, In Gopnik, I. and Gopnik, M. (eds), *From models to modules.* Norwood, NJ: Ablex, 3–23.

MacWhinney, B. and Bates, E. (eds) 1989: *The crosslinguistic study of sentence processing.* Cambridge: Cambridge University Press.

MacWhinney, B. and Chang, F. 1995: Connectionism and language learning. In Nelson, C. A. (ed.), *Basic and applied perspectives on learning, cognition and development. The Minnesota Symposia on Child Psychology,* Volume 28. Mahwah, NJ: Lawrence Erlbaum Associates, 33–57.

MacWhinney, B. and Leinbach, J. 1991: Implementations are not conceptualizations: revising the verb learning model. *Cognition* **29**, 198–256.

Martohardjono, G. and Gair, J. W. 1993: Apparent UG inaccessibility in second language acquisition: misapplied principles or principled misapplications? In Eckman, F. (ed.), *Confluence: linguistics, L2 acquisition and speech pathology,* Amsterdam: John Benjamins, 79–103.

McCafferty, S. 1992: The use of private speech by adult second language learners: a cross-cultural study. *Modern Language Journal* **76**, 179–89.

—— 1994: Adult second language learners' use of private speech: a review of studies. *Modern Language Journal* **78**, 421–36.

McClelland, J. and Rumelhart, D. (eds) 1986: *Parallel Distributed Processing: explorations in the microstructure of cognition:* Volume 1: *Foundations.* Volume 2: *Psychological and biological models.* Cambridge, MA: MIT Press.

McLaughlin, B. 1987: *Theories of second language learning.* London: Edward Arnold.

—— 1990: Restructuring. *Applied Linguistics* **11**, 113–128.

McLaughlin, B. and Heredia, J. L. C. 1996: Information-processing approaches to research on second language acquisition and use. In Ritchie, W. C. and Bhatia, T. K. (eds), *Handbook of second language acquisition.* San Diego: Academic Press, 213–28.

McNamara, T. 1997: What do we mean by social identity? Competing frameworks, competing discourses. *TESOL Quarterly* 31, 561–7.

Meara, P. 1996a: The classical research in L2 acquisition. In Anderman, G. M. and Rogers, M. A. (eds), *Words, words, words: the translator and the language learner*. Clevedon: Multilingual Matters, 27–40.

—— 1996b: The dimensions of lexical competence. In Brown, G., Malmkjaer, K. and Williams, J. (eds), *Performance and competence in second language acquisition*. Cambridge: Cambridge University Press, 35–53.

Meisel, J. 1997: The acquisition of the syntax of negation in French and German: contrasting first and second language development. *Second Language Research* 13, 227–63.

Meisel, J., Clahsen, H. and Pienemann, M. 1981: On determining developmental stages in natural second language acquisition. *Studies in Second Language Acquisition* 3, 109–35.

Mellow, J. D., Reeder, K. and Forster, E. 1996: Using time-series research designs to investigate the effects on instruction on SLA. *Studies in Second Language Acquisition* 18, 325–50.

Mercer, N. 1995: *The guided construction of knowledge*. Clevedon: Multilingual Matters.

—— 1996: Language and the guided construction of knowledge. In Blue, G. and Mitchell, R. (eds), *Language in education*. Clevedon: BAAL/ Multilingual Matters, 28–40.

Milon, J. P. 1974: The development of negation in English by a second language learner. *TESOL Quarterly* 8, 137–43.

Montgomery, M. 1990: Introduction to variable rule analysis. *Journal of English Linguistics* 22, 111–8.

Morgan, J. L., Bonamo, K. M. and Tavis, L. L. 1995: Negative evidence on negative evidence. *Developmental Psychology* 31, 180–97.

Myles, F. 1995: Interaction between linguistic theory and language processing in SLA. *Second Language Research* 11, 235–266.

Myles, F., Hooper, J. and Mitchell, R. (forthcoming 1998): Rote or rule? Exploring the role of formulaic language in classroom foreign language learning. To appear in *Language Learning* 48.

Myles, F., Mitchell, R. and Hooper, J. (forthcoming 1999): Interrogative chunks in French L2: A basis for creative construction? To appear in *Studies in Second Language Acquisition*.

Nation, P. 1990: *Teaching and learning vocabulary*. New York: Newbury House.

Ochs, E. 1986: Introduction: In Schieffelin, B. B. and Ochs, E. (eds), *Language socialisation across cultures*. Cambridge: Cambridge University Press, 1–13.

—— 1988: *Culture and language development: language acquisition and language socialisation in a Samoan village*. Cambridge: Cambridge University Press.

Ochs, E. and Schieffelin, B. B. 1984: Language acquisition and socialisation: three developmental stories and their implications. In Shweder, R. and LeVine, R. (eds), *Culture theory: essays on mind, self and emotion*. Cambridge: Cambridge University Press, 276–320.

Oliver, R. 1995: Negative feedback in child NS-NNS conversation. *Studies in Second Language Acquisition* 17, 459–81.

O'Malley, J. and Chamot, A. 1990: *Learning strategies in second language acquisition*. Cambridge: Cambridge University Press.

Pennycook, A. 1994: *The cultural politics of English as an international language*. Harlow: Longman.

Perdue, C. (ed.) 1993a: *Adult language acquisition: cross-linguistic perspectives*. Volume 1: *Field Methods*. Cambridge: Cambridge University Press.

—— (ed.) 1993b: *Adult language acquisition: cross-linguistic perspectives*. Volume 2: *The Results*. Cambridge: Cambridge University Press.

Perdue, C. and Klein, W. 1993: Concluding remarks. In Perdue, C. (ed.), *Adult language acquisition: cross-linguistic perspectives*. Volume 2: *The Results*. Cambridge: Cambridge University Press, 253–72.

Peters, A. M. and Boggs, S. T. 1986: Interactional routines as cultural influences upon language acquisition. In Schieffelin, B. B. and Ochs, E. (eds), *Language socialisation across cultures*. Cambridge: Cambridge University Press, 80–96.

Phillipson, R. 1992: *Linguistic imperialism*. Oxford: Oxford University Press.

Piaget, J. 1970: *Genetic epistemology*. Columbia, OH: Columbia University Press.

Piaget, J. and Inhelder, B. 1966: *The psychology of the child*. Trans. H. Weaver. New York: Basic Books, 1969.

Piatelli-Palmarini, M. (ed.) 1980: *Language and learning: the debate between Jean Piaget and Noam Chomsky*. London: Routledge and Kegan Paul.

Pica, T. 1994: Research on negotiation: what does it reveal about second-language learning conditions, processes and outcomes? *Language Learning* 44, 493–527.

Pica, T., Young, R. and Doughty, C. 1987: The impact of interaction on comprehension. *TESOL Quarterly* 21, 737–58.

Pienemann, M. 1981: *Der Zweitspracherwerb ausländischer Arbeitskinder*. Bonn: Bouvier.

—— 1987: Determining the influence of instruction on L2 speech processing. *Australian Review of Applied Linguistics* 10, 83–113.

—— 1989: Is language teachable? Psycholinguistic experiments and hypotheses. *Applied Linguistics* 10, 52–79.

—— 1992a: Psycholinguistic processes in language acquisition. Paper presented at the 1992 EUROSLA Conference in Jyväskylä, Finland.

—— 1992b: Psycholinguistic mechanisms in second language acquisition. Unpublished manuscript.

Pierce, B. N. 1995: Social identity, investment, and language learning. *TESOL Quarterly* 29, 9–31.

Pine, J. M. 1994: The language of primary caregivers. In Gallaway, C. and Richards, B. R. (eds), *Input and interaction in language acquisition.* Cambridge: Cambridge University Press, 15–37.

Pinker, S. 1989: *Learnability and cognition.* Cambridge, MA: MIT Press.

—— 1991: Rules of language. *Science* 253, 530–5.

—— 1994: *The Language Instinct.* London: Penguin Books.

Pinker, S. and Prince, A. 1988: On language and connectionism: analysis of a parallel distributed processing model of language acquisition. *Cognition* 28, 73–193.

Platt, E. and Brooks, F. B. 1994: The 'acquisition-rich environment' revisited. *Modern Language Journal* 78, 497–511.

Platt, E. and Troudi, S. 1997: Mary and her teachers: a Grebo-speaking child's place in the mainstream classroom. *Modern Language Journal* 81, 28–49.

Platt, M. 1986: Social norms and lexical acquisition: a study of deictic verbs in Samoan child language. In Ochs, E. and Schieffelin, B. B. (eds), *Language socialization across cultures.* Cambridge: Cambridge University Press, 127–52.

Plunkett, K. and Marchman, V. 1991: U-shaped learning and frequency effects in a multi-layered perception: implications for child language acquisition. *Cognition* 38, 43–102.

Poulisse, N. 1993: A theoretical account of lexical communication strategies. In Schreuder, R. and Weltens, B. (eds), *The bilingual lexicon.* Amsterdam: John Benjamins, 157–89.

—— 1997: Compensatory strategies and the principles of clarity and economy. In Kasper, G. and Kellerman, E. (eds), *Communication strategies: psycholinguistic and sociolinguistic perspectives.* London: Longman, 49–64.

Preston, D. 1989: *Sociolinguistics and second language acquisition.* Oxford: Blackwell.

—— 1996a: Variationist linguistics and second language acquisition. In Ritchie, W. C. and Bhatia, T. K. (eds), *Handbook of second language acquisition.* San Diego: Academic Press, 229–65.

—— 1996b: Variationist perspectives on second language acquisition. In Bayley, R. and Preston, D. R. (eds), *Second language acquisition and linguistic variation.* Amsterdam: John Benjamins, 1–45.

Radford, A. 1990: *Syntactic theory and the acquisition of English syntax.* Oxford: Basil Blackwell.

—— 1997: *Syntax: a minimalist introduction.* Cambridge: Cambridge University Press.

Rampton, B. 1995a: *Crossing: language and ethnicity among adolescents.* Harlow: Longman.

—— 1995b: Politics and change in research in applied linguistics. *Applied Linguistics* 16, 233–56.

—— 1997: A sociolinguistic perspective on L2 communication strategies. In Kasper, G. and Kellerman, E. (eds), *Communication strategies: psycholinguistic and sociolinguistic perspectives.* London: Longman, 279–303.

Raupach, M. 1987: Procedural learning in advanced learners of a foreign language. In Coleman, J. and Towell, R. (eds), *The advanced language learner*. London: AFLS/SUFLRA/CILT, 123–55.

Ravem, R. 1968: Language acquisition in a second language environment. *International Review of Applied Linguistics* 6, 175–85.

Regan, V. 1996: Variation in French interlanguage: a longitudinal study of sociolinguistic competence. In Bayley, R. and Preston, D. R. (eds), *Second language acquisition and linguistic variation*. Amsterdam: John Benjamins, 177–201.

Richards, B. J. 1994: Child-directed speech and influences on language acquisition: methodology and interpretation. In Gallaway, C. and Richards, B. J. (eds), *Input and interaction in language acquisition*. Cambridge: Cambridge University Press, 74–106.

Richards, B. J. and Gallaway, C. 1994: Conclusions and directions. In Gallaway, C. and Richards, B. J. (eds), *Input and interaction in language acquisition*. Cambridge: Cambridge University Press, 253–69.

Richards, J. (ed.) 1974: *Error analysis: perspectives on second language learning*. London: Longman.

Ritchie, W. C. and Bhatia, T K. 1996a: Second language acquisition: introduction, foundations and overview. In Ritchie, W. C. and Bhatia, T. K. (eds), *Handbook of second language acquisition*. San Diego: Academic Press, 1–46.

—— 1996b: *Handbook of second language acquisition*. San Diego: Academic Press.

Rivers, W. M. 1964: *The psychologist and the foreign-language teacher*. Chicago: University of Chicago Press.

—— 1968: *Teaching foreign-language skills*. Chicago: University of Chicago Press.

—— 1994: Comprehension and production: the interactive duo. In Barasch, R. M. and James, V. (eds), *Beyond the monitor model*. Boston, MA: Heinle and Heinle, 71–95.

Robinson, P. 1997: Individual differences and the fundamental similarity of implicit and explicit adult second language learning. *Language Learning* 47, 45–99.

Rogoff, B. 1990: *Apprenticeship in thinking*. Cambridge: Cambridge University Press.

Romaine, S. 1981: The status of variable rules in linguistic theory. *Journal of Linguistics* 17, 93–119.

—— 1988: *Pidgin and creole languages*. Harlow: Longman.

—— 1994: *Language in society: an introduction to sociolinguistics*. Oxford: Oxford University Press.

—— 1995: *Bilingualism*. 2nd edn, Oxford: Blackwell.

Rumelhart, D. and McClelland, J. 1986: On learning the past tense of English verbs. In McClelland, J. and Rumelhart, D. (eds), *Parallel Distributed Processing: explorations in the microstructure of cognition*.

Volume 2: *Psychological and biological models*. Cambridge, MA: MIT Press, 216–71.

Sabouraud, O. 1995: *Le langage et ses maux*. Paris: Editions Odile Jacob.

Saleemi, A. 1992: *Universal Grammar and language learnability*. Cambridge: Cambridge University Press.

Salkie, R. 1990: *The Chomsky update: linguistics and politics*. London: Routledge.

Sato, C. 1990: *The syntax of conversation in interlanguage development*. Tübingen: Gunter Narr Verlag.

Saville-Troike, M. 1989: *The ethnography of communication: an introduction*. 2nd edn, Oxford: Basil Blackwell.

Schachter, J. 1986: In search of systematicity in interlanguage production. *Studies in Second Language Acquisition* 8, 119–34.

—— 1990: On the issue of completeness in second language acquisition. *Second Language Research* 6, 93–104.

—— 1996: Maturation and the issue of Universal Grammar in second language acquisition. In Ritchie, W. and Bhatia, T. (eds), *Handbook of second language acquisition*. San Diego: Academic Press, 159–193.

Schieffelin, B. B. 1985: The acquisition of Kaluli. In Slobin, D. I. (ed.), *The crosslinguistic study of language acquisition*, Volume 1. Hillsdale, NJ: Lawrence Erlbaum, 525–95.

—— 1990: *The give and take of everyday life: language socialisation of Kaluli children*. Cambridge: Cambridge University Press.

Schlyter, S. 1986: Surextension et sous-extension dans l'acquisition des verbes de mouvement/déplacement. In Giacomi, A. and Véronique, D. (eds), *Acquisition d'une langue étrangère*. Aix-en-Provence: Université de Provence, 475–91.

Schmidt, R. 1990: The role of consciousness in second language learning. *Applied Linguistics* 11, 129–58.

—— 1992: Psychological mechanisms underlying second language fluency. *Studies in Second Language Acquisition* 14, 357–85.

—— 1994: Deconstructing consciousness in search of useful definitions for applied linguistics. *AILA Review* 11, 11–26.

Schmidt, R. and Frota, S. 1986: Developing basic conversational ability in a second language: a case study of an adult learner of Portuguese. In Day, R. R. (ed.), *Talking to learn: conversation in second language acquisition*. Rowley, MA: Newbury House, 237–322.

Schumann, J. 1978a: *The pidginisation process: a model for second language acquisition*. Rowley, MA: Newbury House.

—— 1978b: the acculturation model for second language acquisition. In Gingras, R. (ed.), *Second language acquisition and foreign language teaching*. Arlington, VA: Center for Applied Linguistics, 27–50.

—— 1978c: Social and psychological factors in second language acquisition. In Richards, J. (ed.), *Error analysis: perspectives on second language learning*. London: Longman.

——— 1986: Research on the acculturation model for second language acquisition. *Journal of Multilingual and Multicultural Development* 7, 379–92.

Schwartz, B. 1993: On explicit and negative evidence affecting and affecting competence and 'linguistic behavior'. *Studies in Second Language Acquisition* 15, 147–63.

Schwartz, B. and Sprouse, R. 1994: Word order and nominative case in nonnative language acquisition: a longitudinal study of (L1 Turkish) German interlanguage. In Hoekstra, T. and Schwartz, B. (eds), *Language acquisition studies in generative grammar: papers in honor of Kenneth Wexler for the GLOW 1991 Workshops*. Amsterdam: John Benjamins, 317–68.

Sebba, M. 1997: *Contact languages: pidgins and creoles*. Basingstoke: Macmillan Press.

Selinker, L. 1972: Interlanguage. *International Review of Applied Linguistics* 10, 209–31.

——— 1992: *Rediscovering interlanguage*. London: Longman.

Sharwood Smith, M. 1981: Consciousness-raising and the second language learner. *Applied Linguistics* 2, 159–68.

——— 1993: Input enhancement in instructed SLA: theoretical bases. *Studies in Second Language Acquisition* 15, 165–79.

——— 1994: *Second language learning: theoretical foundations*. Harlow: Longman.

Shiffrin, R. M. and Schneider, W. 1977: Controlled and automatic human information processing. II: perceptual learning, automatic, attending, and a general theory. *Psychological Review* 84, 127–190.

Sinclair, J. 1991: *Corpus, concordance, collocation*. Oxford: Oxford University Press.

Singleton, D. 1995: A critical look at the critical period hypothesis in second language acquisition research. In Singleton, D. and Lengyel, Z. (eds), *The age factor in second language acquisition*. Clevedon: Multilingual Matters, 1–29.

Skehan, P. 1989: *Individual differences in foreign language learning*. London: Edward Arnold.

Skinner, B. F. 1957: *Verbal behavior*. New York: Appleton-Century-Crofts.

Slobin, D. 1970: Universals of grammatical development in children. In Flores d'Arcais, G. and Levelt, W. (eds), *Advances in psycholinguistics*. Amsterdam: North-Holland Publishing.

——— 1973: Cognitive prerequisites for the development of grammar. In Ferguson, C. and Slobin, D. (eds), *Studies of child language development*. New York: Holt, Rinehart and Winston, 175–208.

——— 1979: *Psycholinguistics*. 2nd edn, Glenview, Ill.: Scott, Foresman and Company.

——— 1985a: Crosslinguistic evidence for the Language-Making Capacity. In Slobin, D. (ed.), *The crosslinguistic study of language acquisition*, Volume 2. Hillsdale, NJ: Lawrence Erlbaum Associates, 1159–249.

Slobin, D. (ed.) 1985b: *The crosslinguistic study of language acquisition* (2 volumes). Hillsdale, New Jersey: Lawrence Erlbaum Associates.

Smith, N. V. and Tsmipli, I.-M. 1995: *The mind of a savant: language learning and modularity*. Oxford: Blackwell.

Snow, C. E. 1994: Beginning from baby talk: twenty years of research on input and interaction. In Gallaway, C. and Richards, B. R. (eds), *Input and interaction in language acquisition*. Cambridge: Cambridge University Press, 3–12.

Sokolik, M. E. 1990: Learning without rules: PDP and a resolution of the adult language learning paradox. *TESOL Quarterly* 24, 685–96.

Sokolik, M. E. and Smith, M. 1992: Assignment of gender to French nouns in primary and secondary language: a connectionist model. *Second Language Research* 8, 39–58.

Sokolov, J. L. and Snow, C. E. 1994: The changing role of negative evidence in theories of language development'. In Gallaway, C. and Richards, B. R. (eds), *Input and interaction in language acquisition*. Cambridge: Cambridge University Press, 38–55.

Sorace, A. 1996: The use of acceptability judgements in second language acquisition research. In Ritchie, W. and Bhatia, T. (eds), *Handbook of second language acquisition*. San Diego: Academic Press, 375–409.

Spada, N. 1997: Form-focussed instruction and second language acquisition: a review of classroom and laboratory research. *Language Teaching* 30, 73–87.

Spada, N. and Lightbown, P. 1993: Instruction and the development of questions in L2 classrooms. *Studies in Second Language Acquisition* 15, 205–24.

Spolsky, B. 1989: *Conditions for second language learning*. Oxford: Oxford University Press.

Steinberg, D. 1993: *An introduction to psycholinguistics*. London: Longman.

Stubbs, M. 1996: *Text and corpus analysis*. Oxford: Blackwell.

Swain, M. 1985: Communicative competence: some roles of comprehensible input and comprehensible output in its development. In Gass, S. M. and Madden, C. G. (eds), *Input in second language acquisition*. Rowley, MA: Newbury House, 235–53.

Swain, M. and Lapkin, S. 1995: Problems in output and the cognitive processes they generate: a step towards second language learning. *Applied Linguistics* 16, 371–91.

Tarone, E. 1977: Conscious communication strategies in interlanguage. In Brown, H., Yorio, C. and Crymes, R. (eds), *On TESOL '77*. Washington, DC: TESOL, 194–203.

—— 1983: Some thoughts on the notion of 'communication strategy'. In Færch, C. and Kasper, G. (eds), *Strategies in interlanguage communication*. London: Longman, 61-74.

—— 1984: Teaching strategic competence in the foreign language classroom. In Savignon, S. and Berns, M. (eds), *Initiatives in communicative language teaching*. Reading, MA: Addison Wesley, 127–36.

—— 1988: *Variation in interlanguage*. London: Edward Arnold.

—— 1990: On variation in interlanguage: a response to Gregg. *Applied Linguistics* 11, 392–400.

Tarone, E. and Liu, G.-Q. 1995: Situational context, variation and second language acquisition theory. In Cook, G. and Seidlhofer, B. (eds), *Principle and practice in applied linguistics*. Oxford: Oxford University Press, 107–24.

Thomas, M. 1991: *Universal Grammar and knowledge of reflexives in a second language*. Doctoral dissertation, Harvard University, Cambridge, MA.

Thorndike, E. 1932: *The fundamentals of learning*. New York: Columbia Teachers College.

Towell, R. and Hawkins, R. 1994: *Approaches to second language acquisition*. Clevedon: Multilingual Matters.

Towell, R., Hawkins, R. and Bazergui, N. 1996: The development of fluency in advanced learners of French. *Applied Linguistics* 17, 84–115.

Trahey, M. 1996: Positive evidence in second language acquisition: some long-term effects. *Second Language Research* 12, 111–39.

Trahey, M. and White, L. 1993: Positive evidence and preemption in the second language classroom. *Studies in Second Language Acquisition* 15, 181–204.

Tran-Chi-Chau. 1975: Error analysis, contrastive analysis and students' perception: a study of difficulty in second language learning. *International Review of Applied Linguistics* 13, 119–43.

Tsimpli, I.-M. 1991: Functional categories and maturation: the prefunctional stage of language acquisition. *UCL Working Papers in Linguistics* 3, 128–48.

Vainikka, A. and Young-Scholten, M. 1994: Direct access to X' theory: evidence from Korean and Turkish adults learning German. In Hoekstra, T. and Schwartz, B. (eds), *Language acquisition studies in generative grammar: papers in honor of Kenneth Wexler from the GLOW 1991 Workshops*. Amsterdam: John Benjamins, 265–316.

Valian, V. 1990: Null subjects: a problem for parameter-setting models of language acquisition. *Cognition* 35, 105–22.

Van Lier, L. 1994: Forks and hope: pursuing understanding in different ways. *Applied Linguistics* 15, 328–46.

Véronique, D. 1986: L'apprentissage du français par des travailleurs marocains et les processus de pidginisation et de créolisation. In Giacomi, A. and Véronique, D. (eds), *Acquisition d'une langue étrangère*. Aix-en-Provence: Université de Provence, 559–84.

Vygotsky, L. S. 1962: *Thought and language*. Cambridge, MA: MIT Press.

—— 1978: *Mind in society: the development of higher psychological processes*. Cambridge, MA: Harvard University Press.

Wagner, and Firth, 1997: Communication strategies at work. In Kasper, G. and Kellerman, E. (eds), *Communication strategies: psycholinguistic and sociolinguistic perspectives*. London: Longman, 323–44.

Wardhaugh, R. 1986: *An introduction to sociolinguistics*. Oxford: Blackwell.

Watson, J. 1924: *Behaviorism*. New York: Norton.

Weinert, R. 1995: The role of formulaic language in second language acquisition: a review. *Applied Linguistics* 16, 180–205.

Wertsch, J. V. 1985: *Vygotsky and the social formation of mind*. Cambridge, MA: Harvard University Press.

Wexler, K. and Culicover, P. W. 1980: *Formal principles of language acquisition*. Cambridge, MA: MIT Press.

White, L. 1989: *Universal Grammar and second language acquisition*. Amsterdam: John Benjamins.

—— 1991: Adverb placement in second language acquisition: some effects of positive and negative evidence in the classroom. *Second Language Research* 7, 133–61.

—— 1992: Subjacency violations and empty categories in L2 acquisition. In Goodluck, H. and Rochemont, M. (eds), *Island constraints*. Dordrecht: Kluwer, 445–64.

—— 1996: Universal Grammar and second language acquisition: current trends and new directions. In Ritchie, W. and Bhatia, T. (eds), *Handbook of second language acquisition*. San Diego: Academic Press, 85–120.

White, L., Travis, L. and MacLachlan, A. 1992: The acquisition of *wh*-question formation by Malagasy learners of English: evidence for Universal Grammar. *Canadian Journal of Linguistics* 37, 341–68.

Willett, J. 1995: Becoming first graders in an L2: an ethnographic study of L2 socialisation. *TESOL Quarterly* 29, 473–503.

Wode, H. 1978: Developmental sequences in naturalistic L2 acquisition. In Hatch, E. (ed.), *Second language acquisition*. Rowley, MA: Newbury House, 101–17.

—— 1981: *Learning a second language*. Tübingen: Gunter Narr Verlag.

Wolfe Quintero, K. 1992: Learnability and the acquisition of extraction in relative clauses and *wh*-questions. *Studies in Second Language Acquisition* 14, 39–70.

Wolfram, W. 1991: Interlanguage variation: a review article. *Applied Linguistics* 12, 102–6.

Wood, D., Bruner, J. and Ross, G. 1976: The role of tutoring in problem solving. *Journal of Child Psychology and Psychiatry* 17, 89–100.

Young, R. 1991: *Variation in interlanguage morphology*. NY: Peter Lang.

Young, R. and Bayley, R. 1996: VARBRUL analysis for second language acquisition research. In Bayley, R. and Preston, D. R. (eds), *Second language acquisition and linguistic variation*. Amsterdam: John Benjamins, 253–306.

Yule, and Tarone, E. 1990: Eliciting the performance of strategic competence. In Scarcella, R., Andersen, E. and Krashen, S. (eds), *Developing communicative competence in a second language*. New York: Newbury House, 179–94.

—— 1997: Investigating communication strategies in L2 reference: pros and cons. In Kasper, G. and Kellerman, E. (eds), *Communication strategies:*

psycholinguistic and sociolinguistic perspectives. London: Longman, 17–30.

Zobl, H. 1980: The formal and developmental selectivity of L1 influence on L2 acquisition. *Language Learning* 30, 43–57.

—— 1995: Converging evidence for the 'acquisition-learning' distinction. *Applied Linguistics* 16, 35–56.

Author index

Subject index